MW00770131

YOU UNDERSTAND AMERICAN?

*The Collected Verse of Gennaro Angiulo and
Some Friends of Ours*

By Howie Carr

Howie Carr

Frandel, LLC

TABLE OF CONTENTS

ACKNOWLEDGMENTS

As always, assembling a book like this requires the efforts of many people, and I would like to thank some of those involved in producing *You Understand American?*

First of all, again, thanks to my wife Kathy, also known as the mailroom manager. And to my staff at my radio network who were involved in various facets of the book's production, especially Cloe Amaral, my assistant who was in charge of all the photographs. Also thanks to my daughter Charlotte's friend, Trey Taylor, who worked on cleaning up some of the old surveillance photos of Jerry Angiulo's associates.

Jennifer Welsch, who once again put the book together for me, did her usual outstanding job in short order.

Thanks also to the *Boston Herald,* for generously allowing me to use many of the news photos in their archives, including the one on the cover of Angiulo under arrest by the FBI in 1983.

Most of the photos are public mugshots. Several other photos on pages xviii, 119 and 120, are from the Massachusetts State Police's surveillance of Whitey Bulger's garage on Lancaster Street in the West End.

Three photos were purchased from Getty Images and were originally taken by photographers for *The Boston Globe.*

On page x, Francesco Angiulo, center, is escorted from Boston PD Area A station after his arrest, by FBI agent John "Zip" Connolly, left, pointing, September 20, 1983. (Photo by Ted Dully.)

On page 6, Gennaro Angiulo after his acquittal on first-degree murder charges in state court, January 17, 1968. (Photo by Philip Preston.)

On page 46, Jason Angiulo and Johnny Cincotti watch as jurors in the Angiulo trial visit the Dog House at 98 Prince Street. (Photo by Wendy Maeda.)

Note On Sources

Almost all the material here comes from the FBI bugs of 98 Prince Street and 51 North Margin Street in early 1981. The first poem on page 2 was recorded on a law enforcement bug at Jay's Lounge on Tremont Street in the 1960s.

A few of the works are taken from either Jerry Angiulo's court appearances or other evidence presented in court (such as his insults to the Coast Guardsman in Quincy in 1972). Other parts re-create his interactions with Boston reporters over the years, as recorded in daily newspaper accounts. One of Larry's poems comes from a post-conviction interview he gave to his local North Shore newspaper.

I have also included a few random observations by Frank Salemme to Congressional staffers in 2003 and by Angelo "Sonny" Mercurio to a judge in 1997, in addition to the reported statements of one Joey DiFronzo, deceased. Finally, you will read (in prose) two explanatory FBI reports by convicted Mob hitman Stevie Flemmi as recorded by his fellow convicted organized-crime hitman, John "Zip" Connolly, who had a second job as an FBI agent.

INTRODUCTION

Nobody who ever ran into Gennaro J. Angiulo forgot it.

Jerry Angiulo, the longtime Mafia boss of Boston, didn't speak with you. He spoke at you—in fact, more likely than not, he screamed at you. Loudly. And often obscenely—way beyond profane, as you will see if you continue reading.

And this is probably the moment to warn the reader that if you are offended by graphic language, this is not the book for you.

Parental discretion advised—strong language.

It didn't matter if you were one of his underworld associates, a cop, a prosecutor or a reporter, Jerry Angiulo yelled, hollered, ranted and raved. In his calmer moments, he merely harangued, or declaimed.

I knew a guy who did thirty days with Angiulo in a Massachusetts county jail back in the 1970s. The Boss had unleashed an XXX-rated tirade on a young Coast Guardsman who'd had the temerity to cite him for unsafe boating in a narrow "No Wake" channel heading into Marina Bay in Quincy.

Angiulo's fellow jailbird, a small-time local politician who'd been caught with his hand in the cookie jar, beamed with pride as he told me what Jerry had said to him:

"Kid, you do time like a million bucks!"

It was obviously one of the proudest moments of the guy's life. People always remembered their interactions, or should I say their run-ins, with Jerry, even secondhand dressing-downs. I know I do.

As a columnist for the Boston *Herald,* I sporadically covered his federal racketeering trial back in 1985–86. After I'd written my column, I wouldn't return to the courtroom until days later, when I needed another column.

Jerry never appreciated my droll efforts, so on the mornings my columns would appear, he'd scan the press gallery in court looking for me. When he couldn't find me, he'd start yelling at one of my fellow reporters from the *Herald.*

"You tell Carr to come see me when he sobers up!"

Or, "Tell Carr to lay off that Irish milk!"

Word would get back to me, quickly. In Boston, whatever your line of work, it always did. When Jerry Angiulo bellowed, people listened. Until he was finally taken off the board, they often trembled. By the time he was yelling at me, I could chuckle, because he wasn't going anywhere except back to the Charles Street Jail after his trial ended for the day.

In his day, Jerry Angiulo cut a wide swath across Boston, and not just in In Town. Back in the eighties, local TV newscasts were huge, important. The stations' news anchors were major celebrities.

The two most prominent newsreaders in Boston were a husband-and-wife team, Chet Curtis and Natalie Jacobson. They worked at Channel 5, the top-rated ABC affiliate. Like a lot of males in Boston, Jerry developed a serious crush on Natalie. She was the anchor Madonna of Boston.

Jerry always cut a dapper figure, but Saturday nights were stepping-out time. He'd get all dressed up and stroll down to one of the neighborhood's fine-dining spots.

One Saturday night he was holding court at Polcari's, on Causeway Street, where Filippo is now.

Chet and Natalie came in, with a well-heeled out-of-town honcho, maybe from a major advertising agency, or perhaps a potential buyer of the then locally owned outlet.

Jerry spotted Natalie and his face lit up. He immediately sent over a round of drinks to her table. When the cocktails arrived, Chet and Natalie looked over to Angiulo and nodded their thanks.

Naturally, Jerry took that as an invitation to come over. Practically drooling over Natalie, he loomed over their table, directing his bon mots toward her and her second-banana husband, totally ignoring the out-of-town big shot.

Finally, the stranger had had enough. He was apparently not accustomed to not being the one fawned over.

"Excuse me," he said to Jerry Angiulo, "but who are you?"

Jerry, all sixty-seven inches of him, slowly turned to confront the man, to respond to this lèse-majesté.

"Who . . . am . . . I?" he said slowly, staring at the man. "Who . . . am . . . I?"

He paused for effect.

"My name is Gennaro Angiulo," he said, matter-of-factly.

The rich guy from out of town was smoking a cigarette. He blew some smoke toward Angiulo.

"And what do you do?" he asked Jerry.

"What . . . do . . . I . . . do?" Angiulo repeated. He glanced over at Chet and Nat, smiled a sly grin, then turned back to the other guy.

"What do I do?" he said again, then paused for effect before continuing. "I run organized crime in this town."

The out-of-towner's jaw dropped. He looked over at his hosts, the reigning royal couple of Boston media. They nodded at him in affirmation. Gennaro Angiulo was indeed what he said he was.

Those were the days.

Power? Money? Status? You name it, Jerry Angiulo had it. The Boston Police Department (BPD) and other local cops were in his back pocket. As the Red Sox were headed to the World Series in the Impossible Dream season of 1967, Jerry was locked up in the Charles Street Jail awaiting trial on murder charges.

His guards all suddenly had tickets to Fenway Park for the final games in the Sox' pennant run, and then for the World Series.

When Jerry's mother died in 1975, traffic for her funeral was directed by a deputy superintendent of the BPD. The convoy of seventeen flower cars full of floral tributes was led to the cemetery in Malden by a BPD police cruiser and three motorcycle cops.

How many cops did Jerry have on his pad? After the FBI bugs were pulled out of the Dog House in April 1981, more than forty Boston police officers were quietly transferred or retired.

Money? Following the removal of the bugs, the feds raided 98 Prince Street and confiscated $700,000 in cash and negotiable securities. Months earlier, Jerry had purchased his new sixty-eight-foot yacht, the modestly named *St. Gennaro*, for $300,000.

Cash.

This book re-creates, in verse form, Jerry's now almost-forgotten reign as the Boss, when he ran the In Town rackets and so much more from his late mother's home at 98 Prince Street.

It was called the Dog House because his sainted mother used to sell hot dogs out of her little grocery store there, as she and her husband raised their six sons in the teeming North End slums during the Depression.

A few blocks away his lieutenant, Ilario M. A. Zannino—Larry Baione—was likewise presiding over his own criminal fiefdom at 51 North Margin Street. It was across the street from Regina's Pizza. Larry's club later became the home of a doggie day-care center known as The Dogfather.

In early 1981, the local Boston FBI office got a court order to bug both Mafia clubhouses.

The antics of Jerry and Larry at the two locations were recorded and then transcribed by their own personal Boswells—Boston FBI agents, as many as six of whom may have been taking payoffs from Jerry's rivals in the Boston underworld.

The irony, which was obviously not public knowledge at the time, is thick.

To understand just how compromised the FBI investigation was, look at this photograph of the arrest of Jerry's brother, Frankie the Cad, in September 1983.

The FBI agent on the left is John "Zip" Connolly. In 2007, Connolly would be convicted in state court in Miami of second-degree murder in a 1982 mob hit—a year before he so publicly handcuffed Frankie the Cad, who was never convicted of a single crime of violence.

Connolly was being paid so much money by non-Mafia gangsters Whitey Bulger and Stevie Flemmi that sometimes he didn't even bother to cash his FBI paychecks for months at a time, as a secretary would later testify at his federal racketeering trial in Boston. (She found them in the bottom drawer of his desk.)

And remember, Connolly was only one of six FBI agents that Bulger and Flemmi were paying off, in return for being kept out of the indictments and in some cases, actually receiving audio copies of the feds' tapes.

No wonder Jerry was so angry about being arrested by the G-men, even if he couldn't yet grasp just how utterly corrupt the Boston office of the FBI had become.

You Understand American? is not another tome about the bloody, cocaine-fueled reign of Whitey Bulger and Stevie Flemmi, which began in earnest after the Angiulo-Baione crew was taken down by these FBI recordings.

If you want to learn more about the Bulgers and their bloody reign, you can check out some of my earlier books. (There's a bibliography in the back.)

The Mafia headquarters were bugged for months in early 1981, but it took more than two years for the feds to transcribe the tapes. The wiseguys were arrested in 1983 and their trials began in federal court in 1985, first of Angiulo and his brothers, and then of Larry Baione in 1986.

At trial, the Boston media seemed more interested in slobbering over the exploits of the aw-shucks G-men rather than recounting the mobsters' zany rants and drunken escapades. Of course, no one understood then just how thoroughly the local FBI office had been corrupted by Bulger and Flemmi.

Every day, before playing the tapes at the old courthouse in Post Office Square, the feds would hand out transcripts to the jury, as well as to reporters. All you had to do was listen and follow along with the transcriptions.

The gangsters' harangues were dutifully reported, but often downplayed, buried deep inside the newspapers in short sidebar xii · You Understand American?

stories. Perhaps it was the endless stream of obscenities and gratu-
itous slurring of just about everybody who wasn't a Friend of Ours.
But more than that, many of the reporters seemed genuinely mesmer-
ized by the "hero" FBI agents.

The post-trial books were more of the same—worshipfully detail-
ing the derring-do of the local Dudley Do-Rights, who turned out to
be anything but.

Sometimes the reporters even alibied for the feds when Jerry
Angiulo would scream at them in court. Angiulo particularly de-
tested Jeremiah O'Sullivan, the sanctimonious head of the Organized
Crime Task Force, whom he denied as "Father Flanagan," after Bing
Crosby's priest character in *Going My Way*.

Repeatedly, as you will see, Angiulo would loudly hint in court-
room outbursts that O'Sullivan, in his youth, had worked for In Town
as a numbers runner, either in Brighton, Allston, or Watertown, de-
pending on the day.

The first time Angiulo said it in court, at his initial bail hearing, the
Globe claimed that Angiulo was referring to a raid the feds had made
on a Watertown bookie with a car dealership. That wasn't true. Angiulo
always mentioned a "pool hall."

O'Sullivan never directly responded to the charges before his
death in 2009 at age sixty-six. A decade earlier, he had suffered a
series of heart attacks and strokes years after being called as a witness
at a federal hearing into FBI-DOJ corruption to protect Jerry's non-
Mafia rivals.

Until recently, I hadn't thought about the Dog House tapes for
years. I was sporadically working on a stalled showbiz project—stop
me if you've heard this one before.

I'd been looking for some true-life dialogue to use as comic relief
between all the gangland hits when I remembered some of Jerry's per-
orations: "You think I need tough guys? I need intelligent tough guys!"

I retrieved my yellowing stacks of transcripts from the trial and
soon realized I might be onto something here.

Remember Phil Rizzuto, the great New York Yankees infielder
who became an even greater radio color man? A couple of fans tran-
scribed Rizzuto's rambling non sequiturs from the Yankees' broadcasts
and converted them into free verse.

Their book was entitled *O Holy Cow!* It was hilarious.

I figured Jerry's thoughts would translate into verse at least as well as Scooter's. Because like Rizzuto, a fellow World War II Navy veteran, Jerry had what every successful poet must have—a unique voice.

In a short essay on F. Scott Fitzgerald's *The Great Gatsby,* critic Lionel Trilling defined that essential quality that all poets, in fact all writers, share:

"What underlies all success in poetry, what is even more important than the shape of the poem or its wit or its metaphor, is the poet's voice."

Gennaro "the Voice" Angiulo. He was a raconteur of the rackets, an impresario of invective, a virtuoso of venom. He certainly had what Trilling described as the voice.

"It either gives us confidence in what is being said or it tells us we do not need to listen."

When you listen to Jerry's heated orders to his wayward college boy son Jason—"That's a fuckin' order 'cause you're a fuckin' idiot!"—how can you not have complete confidence in such a voice?

Jerry could speak with such authority because he was an expert on everything. You could just ask him.

No, wait, you didn't need to ask Jerry, because he would tell you. In no uncertain terms, either.

Some kinds of illegal activity, Jerry did in fact understand better than anyone—gambling, for instance.

And cops—he'd seen enough of them planting evidence on guys, usually guns, usually during traffic stops. He knew why no wiseguy should ever talk to a cop out on the street. (Because in court, when tapes or bugs are being introduced into evidence, the law could testify that they knew your voice from those brief conversations outside the Dog House or some low dive in the Combat Zone.)

But Jerry also fancied himself an expert on subjects about which he had absolutely no experience—like murders. On occasion, after a few imported brandies, he'd admit that he and his brothers weren't really "tough guys."

Still, as you listen to Jerry's detailed instructions to Richie Gambale on how to whack Walter LaFreniere, you might get the impression that Jerry was a charter member of Murder Inc.

Who hasn't had a boss or two like that—a vice president of sales who's never made a cold call, a union business agent who's never been on the factory floor or driven a truck, a judge who's never tried a case, an editor who's never left the newsroom to cover a story.

Jerry ordered up plenty of mayhem, but he never actually got his hands dirty. That was a big difference between him and most of the wiseguys he dealt with, both inside and outside the Mafia.

Larry Baione is the other dominant voice in what might be called The Dog House School of Poetry. He knew how to "crack" a guy, to use his preferred synonym for *kill*. He even built a crematorium at his family's farm in Franklin, for his own personal use.

Larry Baione knew how to make guys do the Houdini. Many of his victims were never found. He's the one who insisted on blowing up Joe Barboza's lawyer—to make an example of him. No wonder he kind of appreciated Whitey Bulger—they were two peas in a pod. Serial killers.

Larry is a cruder presence here—not for Baione, Jerry's esoteric legal musings on what constitutes, say, an "unconscious stool pigeon." Larry couldn't be bothered with how to answer trick gotcha questions from the grand jury. He never saw a problem a machine gun couldn't solve.

Larry was what other wiseguys always called "capable." As in, *capable* of killing somebody, anybody, and getting away with it. A lot of wiseguys had their particular skills, running card games, arson, stealing artwork, hijacking trucks, hot-wiring cars, etc.

But only certain parties were *capable*, and Baione was among the most capable.

Throughout, Baione presents as a man of action: "I want to kill Harvey Cohen very shortly."

Baione the Bard is no Angiulo. Artistically, Larry is to Jerry what the Dave Clark Five were to the Beatles, what Jan and Dean were to the Beach Boys. Still, as Larry himself might describe his hard-boiled oeuvre, "Don't underrate it!"

Larry Baione truly believed in "This Thing." That's why he always deferred to Jerry. He was a sucker for all the Mafia mumbo jumbo—the burning Mass cards, the kissing, the profuse flattery, the oaths in Italian, etc.

But rank had its privileges for Larry as well. As the top-kick sergeant for This Thing in Boston, Larry brooked no shit from any of his enlisted men, because they hadn't earned "the stripes."

For a quarter century, with the strong-armed assistance of Larry Baione, Jerry Angiulo remained atop the Boston rackets. After service in the Navy during World War II, he became a numbers runner for the entrenched Mustache Petes who'd run crime in his native North End since Prohibition.

In 1950, Sen. Estes Kefauver announced that his Rackets Committee would be holding an upcoming round of televised hearings in Boston. Most of the old-timers decided to retire back to the Old Country.

Jerry stepped into the breach and was soon the dominant bookmaker in the North End—In Town.

The Kefauver hearings in Boston never happened. But Joe Lombardo and the rest of the old-timers had found retirement to their liking. They ceded In Town to Angiulo and the rest of his Greatest Generation . . . of gangsters.

Only one problem: Jerry and his brothers didn't have the same kind of muscle at their disposal as other local wiseguys, including the non-Italian crews. The Angiulos were susceptible to being shaken down, until finally Jerry decided to make a visit to Providence to visit Raymond L. S. Patriarca, the godfather of the New England Mafia.

Jerry took with him a bag of cash—$50,000 or $100,000, depending on the story.

Whatever the exact amount, that was all it took. Angiulo now ran In Town for the Patriarca Crime Family. His muscle would be Larry Baione, a brutal South End street thug two years younger than Jerry. Together, they worked with or bought out or ran off or killed whomever crossed their crooked path.

Pragmatism was all. They paid off cops, bribed jurors, supported underworld cohorts who got locked up, got their people out of town ahead of the indictments, and kept them in cash while they were on the lam.

They didn't give a fuck, to use their favorite word.

Jerry and Larry were also, as you are about to discover, comic stylists of a sort.

Like many great comedians, both surrounded themselves with entourages of second bananas—Angiulo with his brothers, son, and nephews, Larry with the dim-bulb likes of Ralphie "Chong" Lamattina and Johnny Cincotti.

You'll meet them all here.

Jerry was fond of saying, "Our specialty is accounting," and indeed it was. He'd worked his way up in the daily numbers game, a lucrative racket in those pre-lottery days. In addition, In Town provided "protection." They also handled sports betting, mostly horses and to a lesser degree dogs.

Damon Runyon once famously wrote that all horse players die broke. What he meant was that anyone who bets inevitably ends up on the short end of the ledger sheet. Perforce, anyone who runs an illegal betting operation eventually becomes a loan shark.

By 1980, the new state lottery was rapidly supplanting the illegal daily numbers, which had long been called "nigger pool." Shylocking had become the major cash cow of the Angiulo crime empire.

Loan-sharking is what so many of the tapes concern—deadbeat gamblers, up to and including Larry Baione, who later admitted to a reporter that he would bet on an ant race if nothing else were available (see page 164).

Despite all his bluster, Angiulo was prone to panic as well as rage. In 1968 he stood trial for murder for the first time—charged with arranging the killing of a small-time ex-boxer who'd been holding up his protected card games.

As the jury filed back into the courtroom with its verdict, his three thug codefendants stood stoically.

But, the *Globe* noted on the front page the next day, Angiulo "seemed to sag, his hands clutching the dock rail . . . Several times he fought back tears by closing his eyes. He bit his lips and swallowed continuously."

They were all acquitted. A juror had been paid off. The verdict was in the bag, but Jerry was still visibly panicking.

The major witness against the four men was Joe Barboza, a former mob hitman who'd become the first mobster recruited by the FBI into the Witness Protection Program. He wasn't directly involved in the murder. However, one of Angiulo's codefendants, Bernie Zinna, a thirty-four-year-old hood from Revere, had filled Barboza in on what had happened.

Zinna had been identified as one of the stickup men of the Mafia-protected card games. Barboza said he and Jerry's other two codefendants were given an offer he couldn't refuse—either kill the ex-boxer who'd fingered the games, or be "cracked" themselves.

When Barboza asked him why he'd done something so foolhardy as sticking up Angiulo's games, Zinna said he'd only made $1,500 the year before working for In Town.

"They give us crusts of bread and keep the heavy stuff," Zinna was quoted as saying by Barboza.

Barboza asked Zinna why he would agree to kill his friend.

"You know the Office," Zinna said. "How could we get all of them? It was them or us."

A year later, after his acquittal, Zinna survived an assassination attempt in Revere. He didn't survive the second attempt. He was shot four times in the head and left dead in his car.

Seven years later, Joe Barboza himself was cracked, in San Francisco. You'll be reading about that hit soon enough.

When the FBI installed the bugs at the Dog House in early 1981, Jerry had just flown to Florida to spend the winter on his brand-new yacht.

Taking possession of the *St. Gennaro*, Jerry's younger son said at his funeral in 2009, "was the proudest day of his life."

At the age of sixty-one, the former Navy chief boatswain's mate was lounging in Florida, "jerkin' off," as he would put it on the tapes. But it was not a tranquil time in the Boston underworld.

The Winter Hill Gang, the other major force in Boston organized crime, was in turmoil after its top leadership had been decimated in a race-fixing scandal so big that it even made the cover of *Sports Illustrated*.

Jerry had cautioned "the Hill" not to do business with Fat Tony Ciulla, the mastermind of the nationwide scam. Jerry had almost had Ciulla clipped years earlier for "past-posting" races on him at Suffolk Downs. Fat Tony's mother had interceded with Jerry to spare his worthless hide.

Angiulo had wisely warned the Hill that Fat Tony was no good (as had Fat Tony's brother-in-law). As soon as he was charged by the feds, Ciulla flipped and took them all down.

But the arrests of the gang bosses from Somerville were bad news for In Town as well. Not only could the Hill "straighten a thing out," as Larry pointed out, but they also owed Jerry a quarter of a million bucks from their earlier failed sports-betting enterprises.

By early 1981, Jerry's friend Howie Winter was under arrest and Johnny Martorano was about to flee. The two new bosses of the Winter Hill Gang—unindicted coconspirators in the race-fixing case—were Whitey Bulger and Stevie Flemmi.

Jerry didn't really trust them, and his instincts proved correct. They'd been kept out of the race-fixing indictment because they were FBI "informants," and because they were bribing multiple G-men with cash, wine, and tips about their underworld rivals, Italian and Irish both.

During the bugging of the Dog House, Bulger and Flemmi were getting their own real-time copies of the tapes from the agents they'd paid off.

Despite being mentioned multiple times on the Dog House bugs, neither Bulger nor Flemmi were indicted. In 2013, at Bulger's racketeering trial, Flemmi named six Boston FBI agents who had been paid off with cash by the non-Mafia gangsters. Only one ever went to prison—John "Zip" Connolly, for racketeering and second-degree murder in Florida. Zip's boss accepted thousands of dollars in cash and cases of wine as bribes, and was soon promoted to director of the FBI training academy in Quantico, Virginia.

None of the six FBI agents named in court as taking payoffs from Bulger and Flemmi ever lost their pensions, not even convicted hitman Connolly.

Shortly after the bugs were installed, Jerry Angiulo found himself dealing with an even more intractable problem. A different federal grand jury was snooping around one of his illegal high-stakes card games. His son Jason had lent $2,000 to the son-in-law of one of Jerry's wiseguy associates, who ran a strip joint in the Combat Zone.

Jerry's attempts to get that situation under control make up much of *You Understand American?* Interestingly, the grand jury seemed to have had little interest in Jason Angiulo until after the bugs were installed at the Dog House.

After eavesdropping for a while on the mundane daily debt-collection business of the Angiulo organization, the feds realized that without Jerry, they didn't have much more than a routine gambling case. And Jerry had no plans to return to Boston until spring.

Somebody decided that the quickest way to get Gennaro off the *St. Gennaro* and back to Boston was to subpoena his son, as well as his favorite associate, Skinny Kazonis.

It was a smart play, much too crafty for the corrupt, lazy clock-punchers in the local FBI to have thought up. Who came up with the idea? Stevie Flemmi would be my first guess, Whitey second.

Soon after Jerry returned, a street kid in the North End stumbled upon a camera that had been posted on Prince Street outside the Dog House. That should have been the tip-off. Once upon a time Jerry would have instantly vacated the entire neighborhood. But, as he later mourned, he had "fallen asleep."

Instead, he and the boys just kept idly speculating as to where the G-men had placed the bug. It's all in Chapter 13.

Altogether, the G-men recorded about 850 hours of conversations. Only 150 or so hours have ever been made public. The rest ended up on the cutting-room floor. A lot of very important people in Boston were no doubt relieved, chief among them Whitey and Stevie.

Still, despite whatever has been lost to history, the surviving tapes provide an entertaining look back at organized crime in the twentieth century.

And the impresario is Jerry Angiulo, in all his profane bluster.

In the early 1970s, a Watertown car dealer was recorded on a State Police bug asking one of his bookmaking customers if he ever stopped by Angiulo's headquarters.

"Nah," the guy said, "too much yelling."

Even in durance vile, Jerry never mellowed. In 1992, he was brought back to Boston for one of his final appeals. By then he'd been incarcerated for nine years. He was seventy-three years old, but he was the same old Jerry.

"Gennaro Angiulo," the judge wrote in denying the appeal, "treated the oral hearing as a vacation from prison, an opportunity to meet and greet supporters. Choosing to represent himself, his argument consisted of nothing but puerile ranting."

Jerry was finally released from prison in September 2007. He was eighty-eight years old, his kidneys failing, and he would be dead within two years.

After his departure from the scene, one knucklehead crew of mobsters after another vainly tried to fill Jerry's imported calfskin Ferragamo loafers.

Raymond Patriarca's son, Junior, also known as "Rubber Lips," took over the entire family. In 1989 he presided over the first Mafia initiation ever recorded by the FBI. It was such a humiliation that the national LCN Commission renamed the Patriarca Crime Family the New England Crime Family.

Before that embarrassing recorded initiation began in Medford, J.R. Russo was reminiscing to a younger thug, Vinnie "the Animal" Ferrara, about earlier Mafia induction ceremonies back during Dog House days.

"I wanna make a bigger speech," J.R. Russo explained. "That's traditional. Jerry used to make big speeches in other, in other directions, but not that."

Speeches in other directions. That was one way of putting it.

"We always did that ourselves," J.R. continued. "He never—'cause Jerry never knew how to give a ceremony."

But Vinnie Ferrara seemed unclear about who this guy Jerry was. "Who's that?" he inquired.

"Jerry Angiulo!" J.R. Russo yelled.

Tempus fugit. Just six years after being lugged by the FBI at Francesco's, Jerry was already fading in memory, even to his own wiseguys from In Town.

But once upon a time, Jerry Angiulo was the Boss, the Voice. You understand American?

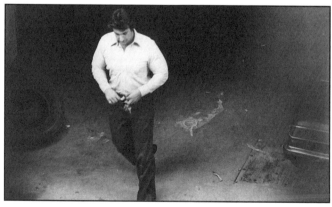

Vinnie Ferrara: How could you forget Jerry?

Dramatis Personae

Gennaro J. "Jerry" Angiulo: the Boss

Ilario M.A. "Larry Baione" Zannino: the Caporegime

Francesco "Frankie the Cad" Angiulo: Brother, bookkeeper. (Nickname from his love of Cadillacs)

Donato "Smiley," "Danny" Angiulo: Brother, hitman

Nicole "Nicky" Angiulo: Brother, consigliere

Michele "Mikey" Angiulo: Brother, go-fer

Jason Brion Angiulo: Son

Jimmy "Jones" Angiulo: Nephew

Johnny Orlandella: Nephew

William J. "Skinny" Kazonis: Associate

Baione Regime

Ralphie "Chong" Lamattina: Soldier (nickname from his allegedly Asian-looking eyes)

Johnny Cincotti: Soldier

J.R. Russo: Soldier

Nikola "Nicky" Giso: Soldier

Freddie "Cement Head" Simone: Soldier

Domenic Isabella: Soldier

Carmen Tortora: Associate

The Law

Jeremiah "Father Flanagan" O'Sullivan: Federal prosecutor, New England Organized Crime Strike Force.

Edward Quinn: FBI agent

Joseph Jordan: Boston police commissioner

Winter Hill Gang
(Offstage)

Howie Winter: Boss, Jerry's friend, in jail

Johnny Martorano: Boss, soon to go on the lam

James "Whitey" Bulger: Serial killer, FBI informant

Stevie Flemmi: Serial killer, FBI informant

WELCOME TO THE DOG HOUSE

Folk wisdom on a plaque hanging on the wall of 98 Prince Street next to Gennaro Angiulo's framed honorable discharge from the U.S. Navy in 1945 as a chief boatswain's mate. Words transcribed by the press pool during the jury's visit to the Dog House, October 1985.

The Boss

When the Lord made man, all the parts of the body argued over who would be the boss.

The brain explained that since he controlled all the parts of the body, he should be the boss.

The stomach countered that since he digested all the food, he should be the boss.

The eyes said that without them, man would be helpless, so they should be the boss.

The legs said that because man couldn't move without them, they should be the boss.

Then the asshole applied for the job.

The other parts of the body laughed so hard that the asshole became mad and closed up.

After a few days, the brain went foggy, the legs got wobbly, the stomach got ill.

The eyes got crossed and unable to see.

They all conceded and made the asshole boss.

Moral of the story: You don't have to be a brain to be the boss.

Just an asshole . . .

CHAPTER 1

SELECTED VERSE OF
GENNARO ANGIULO

Them Heebie-Jeebies

I'll fuckin' wager you
Anybody that deals in junk
Will tell the fuckin'
Motherfuckin' fed
Any fuckin' thing he wants.

The problem is,
This kid goes to the can
And he ain't got
No pills,
No marijuana.

He ain't got nothing.
He starts to get
Them heebie-jeebies.

On the Unexpected Passing of an Old Associate

He can't be
Fuckin' dead!
He owes me
Fourteen thousand bucks.

Atlantic City Memories

You go to the same joint,
Atlantic City.
They give you a fuckin' suite.
They wine you,
They dine you,
They put oil up your ass.

I went to Atlantic City.
The sheriffs were waiting
In the airport.

"Mister Angiulo?"

"Yeah?"

"Just turn around
And get on the next plane
And get the fuck outta here."

On Irish Cops

It takes a special guy
To be a cop
To begin with.
He's disturbed up here . . .

That's why all Irishmen
Are cops.
They love it.

Alone they're a piece of shit.
When they put on the uniform
And they get a little power,
They start destroying
Everything.

Would Jason Angiulo Stand Up for His Dear Old Dad?

It's a hell
Of a fuckin' theory,
Ain't it?

You wouldn't be
The first son
That turned in
His father.

Take my word on it.
That I can bet you on.

And on the other hand,
You must remember
There are a lot
Of guys in Leavenworth
And a lot of guys
In Lewisburg
That protected their sons.

They went,
"He had
Nothing to do with it.
It was me!"

(The poet raises his voice to declaim with passion:)

There'll be no such
Fuckin' thing here!
We will be men
Or mice!

On Running a Las Vegas "Charity Night"

Nobody would do
Like I do things.
I would walk up that club
If I was Spucky,
I'd break his fucking jaw.
That's number one.

And then I'd tell him
Another thing.
If you ever run
A Vegas night
In this joint,
I'll kill you
And your motherfucking
Generation.

Now, screw!

When a guy asks you
About running
A Vegas night,
What the fuck
Are you telling him
You got fifty percent coming?

It's for charity
You fuckin' asshole!

The Road Not Taken

Shoulda stayed single.
I was single,
I'd be fucking long gone.

That's the one thing
We got going for us.
No one can hide from us.
But we can hide
From everybody.
Like, if you ever wanted
That's the one thing
We got going for us.
And plenty of money.
You know that.

You know,
When you're on the lam
You need a lot
Of fuckin' money.

Contemplations After a Not-Guilty Verdict in a Murder Trial, 1968

I never really knew
Why I fought in World War II
Until today.

I found out why today
In that courtroom,
From what happened
In that courtroom.

I don't want to say anything now.
I just want to see
My seventy-three-year-old mother.
This thing has been bothering her.
I haven't seen her in six months.

I won and I'll be right home, Ma!

I am innocent.
I felt all along
This would be the outcome.

Jerry Angiulo after his acquittal, 1968.

"We Got a Louse"

How the fuck
Can we allow
Twenty-two fuckin' guys
To get caught
With one fuckin' telephone?

Every motherfuckin' stop!
They didn't miss a fuckin' one,
Did they?

That's a very
Interesting question.

We got a louse
In the middle of us.
You understand American?

CHAPTER 2

SELECTED VERSE OF
LARRY BAIONE

How to Clip a Guy

If you're clipping people,
I always say,
Make sure if you're clipping people
You clip the people around him first.
But get them together!
'Cause everybody's got a friend, Jerry.

He could be
The biggest motherfucker
In the world.

But someone, someone likes the guy.
That's the guy that sneaks you.
You don't even know it.

Ode to J.R. Russo, Who Slew Joe Barboza in San Francisco

A very brilliant guy
Who stepped right out
With the fuckin' carbine.

Him and me discussed everything.
Then he had to leave.
He made snap decisions.

There, he couldn't get in touch
With nobody.
And then he accomplished
The whole fuckin' pot,
Didn't he?
Am I right?

J.R. used to tell me,
I wish I could go
On the lam.

He got his fuckin' wish.
He's fuckin' everybody,
Enjoyin' himself.

J.R. Russo designed his own clothes—including his hats.

Bilingual Larry

Do you understand, Ralph?
Dominic fatte
A cazzo e me!

That means,
Mind your own
Fuckin' business!

Instructions to a Lawyer to Investigate the Statute of Limitations in California

Don't make any mistakes.
Me and some certain people
Are waiting patiently
Because we're involved
With something
You know nothing about.
But the results
Could be devastating.

Pensees on Two Underworld Associates

Shorty McDuff?
Don't mention Mel Golden.
Don't talk Mel Golden or Shorty.
They're two assholes.

Shorty McDuff is the biggest fuckin' . . .
Weren't we talking about . . .
A weasel of a cocksucker?

This Thing

This Thing
Comes first.
Johnny, This Thing
We got here
Is beautiful.
You understand?

This Thing
Is so beautiful
That if someone
Slapped Debbie
In the mouth tonight,
Your girl,
We would kill.

Don't underrate it.

Will the Kid Stand Up?

Very important
What kind of a kid
He is, is he?
Do you think
He'll do
The eighteen months?

Let's not go into
That legality,
'Cause when they
Close that cell door,
I've been there,
For ten years.

You understand?

I'm a fucking man.
I didn't like it at all.
I almost went over the gate
Four fucking times.

Bow Tie

Favorite,
I seen the favorite
The other night,
Dennis, with the little . . .

That little bow tie,
Did you see him?
When I went over to the game,
He had a little bow tie on.
You know these black bow ties?
How much does he pay the kid?

On a Barbooth Game

I am sending for Vinnie
And his partner,
Fat Vinnie.

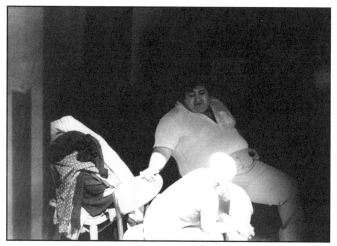

Fat Vinnie awaiting the call at Whitey Bulger's garage.

CHAPTER 3

THE JERRY AND LARRY SHOW

Illegal Here, Illegal There—
A Disquisition on RICO

ANGIULO:
They don't prove
That a legitimate business
Was infiltrated,
We're off the hook.
We can do any fucking thing
We want.
They can stick RICO.

BAIONE:
Illegal.

ANGIULO:
I wouldn't be
In a legitimate business
For all the fuckin' money
In the world to begin with.

Who the fuck
Are we talking about?

The laws say that whoever
Infiltrates legitimate businesses
In interstate commerce
Shall be susceptible to this.

BAIONE:
That's right.

ANGIULO:
Our argument is,
We're illegitimate business.

BAIONE:
We're a shylock.

ANGIULO:
We're a shylock.

BAIONE:
Yeah.

ANGIULO:
We're a fuckin' bookmaker.

BAIONE:
Bookmaker.

ANGIULO:
We're selling marijuana.

BAIONE:
We're not infiltrating.

ANGIULO:
We're, we're, we're
Illegal here,
Illegal there!
Arsonists!
We're every fucking thing!

BAIONE:
Pimps!

ANGIULO:
So what?

BAIONE:
Prostitutes!

ANGIULO:
The law does not cover us.
Is that right?
Well, I hope the fuck . . .

BAIONE:
That's the argument.
We're not infiltrating
Legitimate business.

Larry and Jerry on the Possibility of Execution in California for the Barboza Hit

BAIONE:
Gas chamber!

ANGIULO:
The who chamber?

BAIONE:
Gas.

ANGIULO:
Where?

BAIONE:
And they got two chairs, Jerry.
We can hold hands
Together.

ANGIULO:
Oh, oh, oh, oh
Never, never!

BAIONE:
They've got two
Double chairs.
No shit.
I won't go
Any other
Fuckin' way.

ANGIULO:
We'll, we'll go separate.
We'll toss the fuckin' coin.

BAIONE:
I love him.
I love him.

ANGIULO:
Just my luck!

BAIONE:
I love him.
And I want him
With me!

ANGIULO:
Fuck that shit!
Toss the coin.
Sorry, Larry.
You go first.
Just your luck!

BAIONE:
Is that what
You're gonna say?
You shoulda been
A lawyer!

ANGIULO:
Here comes
The phone ringing.
You're walking out.

BAIONE:
Reprieve!

ANGIULO:
Too late!

On the Greed of Murdered Philadelphia Mobster Tony Bananas

BAIONE:
He was the kind of guy
Would walk up to you
With a shotgun,
Hit you right in front
Of your house.

ANGIULO:
What was his purpose?

BAIONE:
Who the fuck knows?
Who knows?

ANGIULO:
I mean,
We talkin' money here?
How much fuckin' money
They got there?

BAIONE:
Multimillionaire,
Tony Bananas.

ANGIULO:
I don't understand it.

BAIONE:
More fuckin' money than—

ANGIULO:
What's the purpose?

BAIONE:
Power.
They need power.
Jerry, they get crazy.

A Heated Debate on the Reliability of Skinny Kazonis' Reports

ANGIULO:
What's the difference?

BAIONE:
Lot of fuckin' difference.
That's the way you got it back
From Mr. Fuckin' Skinny.
Go ahead.

ANGIULO:
Don't ever say
"Fuckin' Skinny."
Skinny works for us.

BAIONE:
Yeah, but he's
A fuckin' liar.

ANGIULO:
Skinny will do . . .
He's not a liar!
Hold, hold Larry!

BAIONE:
Well,
He's a fabricator.

ANGIULO:
Wait a minute.
Well, don't call him
A fuckin' liar.

BAIONE:
He's a fabricator.

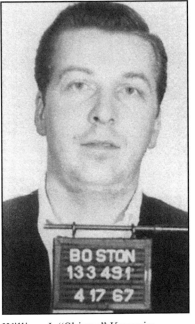

William J. "Skinny" Kazonis: Jerry's favorite.

ANGIULO:
Now you're goin'
A little too far here.

BAIONE:
Well, he's a fabricator.

ANGIULO:
If you wanna stop
This conversation,
Just start that.
Okay?

BAIONE:
It's up to you
To stop it, Jerry.

ANGIULO:
I'll stop it—

BAIONE:
But he's a fabricator—

ANGIULO:
Well, that's the way
It is.

BAIONE:
He's brought stories
Back here
And they weren't so, Jerry.
He added to it.

ANGIULO:
How you tell it
And how he tells it
Are two different people.
How I tell it is different too,
You know?

BAIONE:
That's right.

ANGIULO:
Good boy.
I'm tellin' it a tough way too.
You're thinkin' about the way
I'm tellin' it too, now.

BAIONE:
Right.
I don't believe
It was told that way.

Handling a Guy that Mouths Off to a Friend of Ours

A dialogue among LARRY BAIONE, GENNARO ANGIULO and RALPHIE CHONG

BAIONE:
Why is it when,
When Howie Rubin says
To Johnny:

"Johnny,
You suckin' cunt tonight, today?"

ANGUILO:
Even if he did suck it,
You gotta hit him!

BAIONE:
I said, "Johnny,
Call Howie Rubin in.
This is an order."

And you ask him,
"Who the fuck is he think he is,
He's talking about suckin' cunt?"

And then bat him
In the fuckin' mouth.

RALPHIE CHONG:
I seen a guy fly out the room!

(Postscript: Why was Howie Rubin even hanging out with these wise-guys? The answer is that, according to Stevie Flemmi, he was relaying information from the U.S. attorney's office back to Prince Street. Flemmi told FBI agent/mob hitman Zip Connolly that he was afraid Howie Rubin was going to get him killed. From Flemmi's FBI file:)

FBI File

BS 183A-84
JC/sct
1.

On 8/8/83, BS 955-TE expressed extreme concern for maintaining the confidentiality of his relationship with the FBI and stated that there are "leaks" coming from the United States Attorney's office. Source advised that he would not be fearful of Jerry O'Sullivan of the Strike Force as he trusts him but stated that Jerry Angiulo and Larry Zannino are being tipped off to details of the federal investigation on the mafia, i.e., approximate dates of indictments and number of people to be indicted. Source advised that the leaks are coming from two sources. Howie Rubin's girlfriend who works for the U.S. Attorney's office and Mark Wolf, the Assistant U.S. Attorney.

Source advised that Wolf is very close to an unknown Jewish male who is married to the sister of Bruce Swerling. Bruce Swerling is the son of the late Bert Swerling, who was an ex-fire adjuster in Roxbury. Bert Swerling "did business" on various arsons in Roxbury with the old Roxbury mob.

This unknown male who is close to Mark Wolf is also close to Howie Rubin and everything that Wolf tells this unknown Jewish male is relayed automatically to Howie Rubin, who then runs to "Prince Street" to provide Jerry Angiulo and Larry Zannino with the information. In the case of Howie Rubin's girlfriend, she simply passes on to Rubin any and all information that she is privy to and this information is in turn relayed to Prince Street.

THE ABOVE INFORMATION IS SINGULAR IN NATURE AND ... ...
BE DISSEMINATED OUTSIDE THE BUREAU WITHOUT FIRST CON ...
ING THE WRITER.

(Post-postscript: Mark Wolf, the assistant U.S. attorney who was also an "unconscious stool pigeon," as Jerry would say, later became a federal judge in Boston.)

The Meaning of Money, Especially When You're in the Can
By LARRY BAIONE, as prompted by GENNARO ANGIULO

ANGIULO:
Larry, when you were born
Broke like all of us were,
You know, money becomes
Very important.

LARRY BAIONE:
Not Larry Baione.
Never did when I was broke
And never did when I had
Fuckin' money.

When I come home,
I made up my mind,
I wouldn't give a guy
A fuckin' buck.

Larry Baione when he was broke
and in prison.

I'd like to know
How many five hundreds and G notes
I gave away.

And I shouldn't give
A fuckin' buck
To nobody.
Honest to God,
I mean that.

CHAPTER 4

A PORTRAIT OF THE ARTISTS AS
YOUNG MEN

High School Yearbooks and
Early Mug Shots

JENNARO J. ANGIULO, "Jerry"
*One touch of nature makes the whole
world kin.*
Ambition: Criminal lawyer
Suffolk Law School

Gennaro Angiulo, with first name misspelled, in Boston
English High School yearbook, 1937.

LARRY ZANNINO

34 Lincoln Street   Franklin
"ZIP"

*"A little nonsense now and then
Is relished by the best of men."*
Introducing "Zip," our good-natured and happy-go-lucky Boston
"wit." With his humorous and jovial manner he won the hearts of
his fellow classmates. "Zip" was the advertisement of what a well-
dressed man should wear. Boston Latin will claim "Zip" next fall
whence he will pursue studies at some medical school.
Good luck, Larry, and may the memories of Franklin High School
always be with you.

Marshal 1, 2, 3, 4. Dramatics 1, 2, 3, 4. French Club 4. Hallowe'en Com-
mittee 1, 2, 3. Oakey Advertising Committee 4.

Larry Baione, under another of his names, in his Franklin (MA) yearbook,
1939. (Note that he had the same nickname, Zip, as corrupt FBI agent/
hitman John Connolly.

First known Angiulo mug shot, 1947.

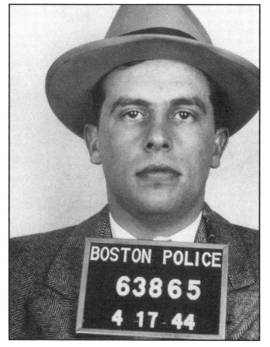

First known Baione mug shot, 1944.

CHAPTER 5

DUTIES OF A BOSS

No Mercy

Let me tell you something.
When a man assumes leadership,
He forfeits the right
To mercy.

That's exactly what this fucking thing
Is all about.
Exactly what it's all about.

Who Needs an HR Department?

We find that
One of these individuals
That we use
Becomes intolerable,
We kill the fuckin'
Motherfucker.

And that's the end.
We'll go find
Another one.

Taking Care of Made Men

First, the responsibility
Of a caporegime is to see
That all his soldiers
Make a living.

But he doesn't have
To go out of his way
To give him his fuckin' money.

More important than making money
Is the fact that the caporegime
Is a representative
Of Mr. Patriarca
In this town.

If you feel that
Any other soldier
Is being jeopardized
By any soldier's actions,
Your responsibility
Is to come forward.

New England crime boss
Raymond L.S. Patriarca after
a court appearance in
Providence, 1967.

Other mobsters called Patriarca "The Man."

Why Some Wiseguys from Another Family Must Be Run Out of Worcester

You know
The most important part
Of this conversation?

The Law over there
Knows exactly
What we are.

If we would allow
A different group
To come in
And they run roughshod
Over everybody,
The Law would lose
Respect for us.

You don't mind
Losing the respect
Of that section.
But then you lose it
In every other section.

What am I supposed to do?

The Law in that section
Tells the other Law, say,
"Hey, those fuckin' motherfuckers
Got no balls here.
They backed away from . . ."

The Need to Hide Assets

Set up a brand new
Interstate corporation.
We take these buildings . . .
Put them in the corporation.

They got to go to China
To find out who
The stockholders are.

We set up a corporation
With any name you want
As fast as possible.

Now I'm beginning to see,
We're all going
To the can.

Why Numbers Runners Never Minded Getting Locked Up for Three Months

We gave them
Three hundred a week
When all they used
To get was ninety bucks
To go and pick up
The envelope.

And you know,
Most of them
Came out
And they were all
Fuckin' rich.

Jerry and Larry Wax Philosophical about Their Duty to Order a Hit

ANGIULO:
Hey, it's you and I.
Therefore,
You and I are going
To solve a problem here.

Not because we want to do it.
Because it's our fuckin' duty to.
Okay?
Tonight?

BAIONE:
We gotta
Kill this guy,
You know.

(Postscript: The next day, Joe Porter's brother went in the trunk.)

CHAPTER 6

THE COMMISSION

Gossip and musings on the ruling
body of La Cosa Nostra

An Early Sit-Down with New York
Boss Vito Genovese

All these Italians,
They all eat fruit.
Guy comes over,
He's got a big bowl
Of cherries, bananas,
Apples, and oranges.
He keeps putting them
On the table.

On the Chicago Outfit

To begin with,
They're not like us.
They're not workers.

Over there
They work one
And they graduate you
To get in the fuckin' union
Or something.

Not that I'm knockin' it.
I'm with it.

Free Enterprise and Open Cities

Now another thing.
We're startin' to hear stories.
Who the fuck just brought it?
Skyball or somebody said that.

All of a sudden Chicago wants
To walk into Vegas
And it will not be an open city.

And the New York guys
Want Atlantic City
And the Chicago guys to keep out.

All I know is,
No matter what guys
Went to Vegas,
They always came
To the restaurant.

Joseph "Skyball" Scibelli was
Mafia boss of Springfield.

You want to invest,
Invest.
You don't want to invest,
Don't invest.

You understand?

With these people,
You can't stop.

Spilotro cannot bar
Anybody from Vegas!
I don't care
Who knows about it.
Just tell him that
Raymond and I said so.

Update on Philadelphia

All I know is
My brother Nick
Came from New York . . .
That one guy that should know
What the fuck
It's all about
And he said
To my brother Nick:

"Tell Raymond
And your brother
That these guys
From Philadelphia:
Absolutely insane.
They're gonna kill
Each other."

And this guy is on top
Of the Commission.

Cleveland Wiseguys Moving into
Boston without Permission

ANGIULO:
They come in again,
They will have them
A fuckin' problem.
Because they might
Get hurt.

BAIONE:
Come to town
And not ask permission?
They got to be
Fuckin' crazy!

On New Jersey Boss Sam
"The Plumber" Decavalcante

I hate this cocksucking
Dirty motherfucker.
These are the guys
That somebody kills,
Or they kill somebody
Immediately
Soon as they start
Talking like that.

Guy was on the Commission.

Pushy New Yorkers

You got fuckin' guys
From New York wanna
Come up in my place.

Now all of a fuckin' sudden
Youse wanna take a town
Away from me?

You tell 'em
It's for the benefit
Of everybody.

Now when he tells you
He'd rather not give it up,
You ask him to give it up
As a favor.

Chapter 7

HITMEN

I Got You, Babe
By GENNARO ANGIULO to LARRY BAIONE

I got Dominic.
I got John Cincotti.
I got Peter Limone Junior.
I got Richie.
I got my brother Danny.
I got you and I got four soldiers
In East Boston
That would kill any fuckin' body.

Peter J. Limone.

Then There's Winter Hill

We could use them.
They're the kind of fuckin' guys,
I'll tell you right now,
If I called these guys right now,
They'd kill any fuckin' body
We tell 'em to.

Why Made Guys Like Connie Frizzi Shouldn't Take Part in Hits with Non-Made Guys

Connie is
A Friend of Ours.
Therefore, we can never
Put him with these other people
And say,
"Just tell Connie who he is."

'Cause I know
What he'll do.
He'll say, "That's him!"
And stand back.
Bam!

Now we got a problem.
What do we need it for?

Cono "Connie" Frizzi, made man from East Boston.

An Old Mob Tradition—Bragging about Hits You Didn't Do
A GENNARO ANGIULO dialogue with FRANKIE THE CAD.

GENNARO:
Him and I,
My brother Nick and Frank
Buried twenty fuckin' Irishmen
To take this fuckin' town over.

We can't begin
To dig up half
The motherfuckers
We got rid of.
And I'm not bragging either!

FRANKIE THE CAD:
You're talking
About Charlestown?

GENNARO:
Shut up!
Don't say it out loud.

We're not tough guys.
We went in sharp, animals,
And talk to a guy.

He said, "No, no, what are you
Worried about?"

Okay, stay where you are.
Soon as he turns his back,
The next day,
Bam!
Boom!
Kill 'em!
Bang 'em!

CHAPTER 8

HITS GONE AWRY

By LARRY BAIONE,
with Responses from His Regime.

In testimony before a Congressional committee in 2003, hoodlum "Cadillac" Frank Salemme said of In Town hit squads: "They couldn't find their way off Hanover Street. Believe me, they would have no chance of finding this guy, little to none." Judge for yourself.

Why Joe Cataldo Jr. Hasn't Been Clipped Yet

The only reason
Joe is alive is because
Of his father.
And I like his fuckin' father.

That's the only reason.
I'd have killed this kid
Three years ago.

I think we're gonna go in
And split his fuckin' head.
Yeah, we were gonna
Send some guy
And split him wide open.

Fuckin' baseball bat
For a starter.

Soon as the old man goes,
He goes.
I swear on
My mother's soul.

How many times
We go by there,
I say:
"This asshole, lucky for his father.
It would break his heart,
Make his father die overnight."

I hope this guy lives
A hundred years old.
I will eventually
Get the motherfucker!

(Postscript: He didn't.)

Avenging the Chicken Man
By LARRY BAIONE et al.

On March 15, 1981, Philadelphia LCN boss Phil "the Chicken Man" Testa was blown to bits by a nail bomb as he entered his home in South Philly. Larry immediately knew who had clipped the Chicken Man.

BAIONE:
The fuckin' Irishmen
Killed fuckin' Phil Testa,
The Boss.

I feel that we should go all out,
And kill the fuckin' Irishmen!
Because you know why?

JOHNNY CINCOTTI:
Because it will happen
All over the country.

LARRY BAIONE:
Atta boy!
They'll be here in Boston.
They'll kill Ralphie Chong
On Hanover Street!

Ralphie Chong: fearful of Irish bombs.

RALPHIE CHONG:
Sure they will.
They're using bombs!

JOHNNY CINCOTTI:
And they don't have
The scruples
That we have.

LARRY BAIONE:
You know how I knew
They weren't Italiano?
When they bombed
The fuckin' house.

We don't do that.

You don't think Philadelphia
Is planning right now?
They'll fuck every one
Of them Irishmen.

I just hope
They need some
Fuckin' help.
Because if we don't keep
This Thing up,
We're dead!

(Postscript: It turned out the Chicken Man was blown up by his own made men—all Italianos.)

A Favor for the New York Family

LARRY BAIONE'S instructions to
DOMENIC ISABELLA and JOHNNY CINCOTTI

This Harvey Cohen,
I'm going to kill him.
It's for the family in New York.

I want to kill
Harvey Cohen
Very shortly.

You ain't done
A fuckin' thing
By tellin' me
You're goin' by
His fuckin' house
And see his car.

I want both of youse,
Start talking
To this fuckin' guy.

As a matter of fact,
Run into each other
Accidentally.

"Hey, what'd ya say?
How are ya?"
Get his confidence.

Shouldn't he be dead by now?
This is for the family
In New York.
Now I'm responsible.

Hitman Domenic Isabella could have used GPS.

You are basically
A beautiful fuckin' guy
And I'll tell ya,
I got the best regime
In the fuckin' country.

And not only that,
We volunteered.
And not only that,
The Boss and the Underboss
Give us the work.

Why did they give it to us?

Because they've got
Confidence in us.

ISABELLA:
I think I'm gonna,
I'm gonna nail him
Comin' out of the bar.

'Cause with that Jew,
He's always got
Four or five guys
Around him.

BAIONE:
I know where it is.
I've been there.

Get his confidence
And you finally keep
Talkin' to him
And make him feel
He's behind you.

And we'll hit him
In the fucking head.
We'll bring a package behind
And fuckin' we'll crack him!

Domenic Explains Why He Can't Find Cohen's House in Marblehead

ISABELLA:
There's no number
On his house, Larry.

(Postscript: The FBI tipped off Harvey Cohen and he disappeared. The favor to the New York family was never delivered.)

A Screwed-Up 1967 Hit—Killing Joe Barboza's Two Guys in Ralphie Chong's Café

By LARRY BAIONE to JOHNNY CINCOTTI and RALPHIE CHONG

RALPHIE CHONG:
Remember when
We did that work
In, in, in the Nite Lite?

LARRY:
Yeah, we made you
Go home.
I threw everybody
Out of the joint.

The bodies were dumped in South Boston.

It never should have
Happened inside the joint.

Once they get
On the sidewalk,
Crack them,
And fuck them,
And walk away.

(Postscript: Shouldn't there be a rule that Friends of Ours never begin a sentence with "Remember when?")

Walter Bennett Goes to Frankie Salemme's Garage

Another "Remember when?" story from 1967 by LARRY BAIONE to GENNARO ANGIULO

You know Frankie Salemme?
Where do you think Frankie was?
He was in the beach wagon
Inside a carton.

And he got a gun
Aimed at Walter Bennett's head.

"If you see him
Make a move,
Crack him.
Call Larry to the car.
Larry will take
And bury him."

GENNARO ANGIULO:
No problem!

(Postscript: Walter Bennett's body was never found. He was buried next to his brother Wimpy in Hopkinton. The third brother, William was shot in a car, and his body fell out into the snow.)

William Bennett, shot to death, December 1967.

Marshall Street Mayhem
LARRY BAIONE with RALPHIE CHONG

LARRY:
Why don't we go
In that fuckin' garage,
Right now?

With fuckin' machine guns!

We'll kill every fuckin' one
Of these Irishmen!

RALPHIE CHONG:
Right,
We'll go right in.

(Postscript: They didn't go right in.)

J.R. Russo Goes to Larry's Daughter's Wake
A sad memory as recounted by LARRY BAIONE

J.R. comes in.
He says,

"Larry, I don't know
What to say.
Your daughter's dead
And I loved her.
And I love you
And I don't know
What to say.

"We got a problem
With a fuckin' war."

My poor daughter!
I come back from the grave.
My fuckin' heart is broken.
But This Thing comes first.

J.R. Russo, sensitive guy.

(Postscript: There was no war.)

CHAPTER 9

A COLLOQUY ON CRAPS

GENNARO ANGIULO to his
college-boy son JASON

GENNARO:
Explain to me
If I were to put you in charge
Of the biggest crap game
In New England.

What would you do on that table
Every night?
What would be the first thing that
Absolutely got to be done?

Jason Angiulo, left, and Johnny Cincotti watch
jury entering Dog House, 1985.

Now tell me why that table
In that fucking Studio Four had
Old dice?

Here we go!
That's a fucking answer.

Hey, keep quiet!
We're talking craps now.
Fucking, motherfucking
Big mouth cocksucker,
Shut up!

JASON:
You gonna listen to me?

GENNARO:
No, you motherfucker
Now shut up.
Let me tell you something, huh?
I've been in the crap business
When you were, weren't born
You cocksucker that you are.

Don't you ever, ever ask ever that
A pair of dice that's been used
More than one and a half or two hours
Without replacing it with a brand-new set.
And that set goes in your fucking pocket
And they're thrown down the fucking sewer!

Do you understand that?
That's a fucking order
Because you're a fucking idiot.
Now just shut up!

JASON:
Yeah, let me tell you—

GENNARO:
You talk and I'll hit you
With a fucking bottle.
Hey, did you hear
The fucking order?

You go to a Vegas night,
You figure to last six hours.
You have three sets of dice.
And no set of dice will ever
Stay on that table
More than two hours.

Why, you cocksucker you,
I got a thousand sets of dice
For a Sunday game.

Thousand dice by the set.
None of you got 'em.

How about playing cards?
How many new decks you got
Every time you use them?

You use used cards,
You dirty mother!
You hear, motherfucker?

JASON:

. . .

GENNARO:
Shut up.
Just shut up.
You ever put a deck of used cards
In a blackjack game
In any fucking Vegas night
Or anywhere else again,
I'll kick you the fuck out of here.

That's an order too,
Why you fucking idiot you!

Remember what I told you.
You ever go to that joint again . . .
I'll split your fucking mind.

Get the fuck out of Boston!
You don't belong here no more.
You ever let a pair of dice stay
On a good fucking table
At any kind of game
More than two hours
Without saying,
"Give me them dice!"

Order a new set.
That's it.

I know what you are.
You're like the New York wiseguys.
Everything's okay.
Go ahead boys.
You do everything.
I do nothing.
I run . . .

JASON:
Primarily the club.

GENNARO:
Prime who?
Don't use them
Fuckin' words with me,
College boy.
They're too big.

"Primarily the club."

What club?

(*Turning to address a third party who doesn't seem to be there.*)

You know this motherfucker's
The greatest actor that ever lived.
He's got people convinced.
Sammy Granito walks in his joint
And says to me:

"Your son . . .
He is the fucking greatest."

This motherfucker don't know
A fucking thing.
He don't know that fucking much
About gambling.

All he knows is you win or lose
And you walk around
Smoking cigarettes.

Remember what I told you!

You ever let a crap table
Go more than two hours
With the same set of dice
And they ain't brand new
Every fucking time,
You better run out of here!

CHAPTER 10

WOMEN

"Panama" Is a Hen-Pecked Wimp

By JOHNNY CINCOTTI to
SALVATORE "PANAMA" MERCURIO

Do you worry
About your wife finding out
If you lose a lot of money,
Panama?

If my wife ever said
Anything to me
About losing money,
I'd throw her out
The fucking window.

Larry Recalls How Tough It Was for His Wife Isabel When He Was "Away"

Jesus, that woman
Lived on three hundred bucks
A fuckin' month.
Tell me how she did it.
I don't know.

What Good Wives Need to Know

A dialogue between DONATO "SMILEY" ANGIULO and LARRY BAIONE

I'll tell you something
That'll be hard to believe.
All right?

BAIONE:
What's that, Danny?

SMILEY:
I'll tell you something
That's hard to believe.
And you're gonna
Turn around and say:

"Who the fuck
Are you shittin'?"

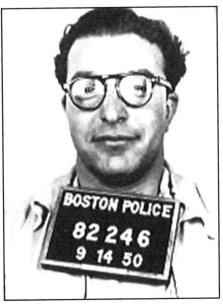

My wife does not know
From me saying to her
What I do for a living.

Donato Angiulo, nicknames included "Danny" and "Smiley."

My wife,
She has never heard from me
What I do for a living.
And she's never asked me.

BAIONE:
Well, she's not supposed
To know what you do
For a living.

All my wife knows
About me is this, Danny.

I got a slip and a hide
In the house
That I must—

SMILEY:
Hah, hah.

BAIONE:
Well, if I drop dead
Tomorrow, Dan,
This woman's
Gotta be able
To say listen
Blah blah blah
And I told her
Where to go.

You understand?

SMILEY:
That's right.

BAIONE:
And this is a
Personal thing,
And blah blah blah
And that she's gotta know
Who, what, where or how.

After all, Danny,
When you got
Three million fucking dollars,
You can't be secretive.

SMILEY:
I know exactly
What you mean.

BAIONE:
And you know, Danny,
Good wives don't want to know
What the fuck you do.

But those other wives . . .

A Disagreement over Who's Responsible for Clipping Nicky Giso's Girlfriend

GENNARO ANGIULO and LARRY BAIONE, with Consigliere NICKY ANGIULO in attendance

ANGIULO:
She is a detriment,
A jeopardy,
A danger.

It has come to the point
We got to do
Something about it.

"Hey, Nicky,
We've had it with this.
Give it a fucking cut.
You've gone too far with it.

"I can understand
This declaration
Within This Thing of Ours.

"But let me tell you, Nicol,
Do yourself a favor."

What was his fuckin' answer?
Do you want me to . . . ?

BAIONE:
Kill her?

ANGIULO:
Kill her.

Nicky Giso: girlfriend problems.

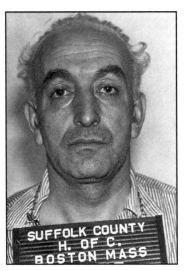

Nicky Angiulo, consigliere.

BAIONE (*pointing at Jerry, voice rising*):
There is the Boss right there.
You handle it!

ANGIULO:
Larry,
You're hollering
Like a maniac.
You better take
Your pills.

BAIONE (*loudly*):
I need pills?

ANGIULO:
You backed away.

BAIONE (*to Nicky Angiulo*):
Consigliere,
He just said to me,
"You better take
Your pills."

Did you hear that?
You yellow dog,
You didn't hear it,
Did you?

(Postscript: In 1984, Giso's girlfriend was shot in the head in the same bar on Commercial Street where Larry Baione had murdered two of Joe Barboza's crew in 1967. She survived.)

Chapter 11

THE LAM

Eternal Wisdom

By ANGELO "SONNY" MERCURIO

Power of the lam
Means you get
A lesser sentence.
I advocate
Everybody run away.

Sonny Mercurio.

In Which Jerry Recalls How Ralphie Chong's Brother, Joe Black, Went on the Lam

He goes to Naples . . .
A Sicilian.

Ralphie comes to me
In a huff.
He says some guys in Naples
Want twelve thousand in cash.

I said, "For what?"

Joe "Black" Lamattina.

"They said my brother
Went into the cigarette business
With them.
And they put up
Their fuckin' money
And my brother disappeared
And he's in Rome.

After Ralphie paid the twelve,
He said, "Tell them guys over there,
Whatever my brother
Wants to do,
Don't worry about it."

What a mistake that was!
Every month here comes
A phone call from Italy.

"Prego! Prego!
(Please! Please!)

"How much
Do you want?

"Americano
Or Siciliano?"

Cadillac Frank Salemme Defines *Lamster* for a Congressional Committee, 2003

Fugitive from justice.
I keep going back
To the vernacular.

You can take the boy
Out of Boston
But you can't take
Boston out of the boy.

And that's not
The university side
Of Boston,
Believe me.

Frankie Salemme, 1995.

CHAPTER 12

BROTHERLY LOVE

Donato's Inferno

**DONATO "SMILEY" ANGIULO has it out with
GENNARO ANGIULO**

SMILEY:
I want my cut.
I want out.

GENNARO:
When I sell things,
I'll give you
What I think
You got coming.

SMILEY:
Give me my cut
And I'll walk out of here!

GENNARO:
You get out of here!
You can't stand it no more,
Can you?

SMILEY:
I can stand anything
That stands for what
They're supposed
To stand for,
Not that turn around
And tell lies and try to take
Everything away
From everybody.

GENNARO:
Well, who are you gonna send
To get me?

SMILEY:
I don't need anybody.

GENNARO:
The Law?
You gonna kill me?
Go ahead.
What are you waitin' for?

SMILEY:
You?
You ain't worth it.
I want my end
And I want it now.

GENNARO:
Go home.
You ain't got
Nothing coming.

SMILEY:
You know the rules.
You can't take anything
Away from a man
That belong to him.

Hey, I'd rather be dead
Than listen to this.

Larry Tells Off His Deadbeat Brother Sonny Who Wants Another "Loan"

"This guy owes money.
This man owes twenty-three thousand."

Don't ever come to me
And tell me your stories.
I'm tellin' you right now.
You understand?

Don't tell me stories.
I told you this a long time ago.

Don't fuck with my money
I am not interested.
You will sell your house
Like I did.
I hocked my fuckin' house!

This is business, Sonny.

I borrow for one
And I only make one.
I cannot afford
No bullshit.
And I'm tellin' ya,
'Cause you got
A couple of cocksuckers
Down there,
I wouldn't give a buck to.

And you know it.

But you do.
'Cause you can grab
Three and four and five percent.

And all of a sudden
When they stop payin',
Don't come to me
And tell me any stories.

Do you understand?
Good.
You understand the guys you got?
Good.

I do not take
No fuckin' propositions.
I told you that
When you started.

You sell your fuckin' house, Sonny.
That's on my mother's soul.
Sonny, I done enough for you.

You know you conned me
For a lot of money
Before you was made.

I forgot all about it
When I come home
And you're not going
To do it no more.

CHAPTER 13

WHERE'S THE DAMN FBI BUG?

Maybe It's in Richie Gambale's Car

GENNARO ANGIULO:
His car's bugged,
You know it,
Don't ya?

FRANKIE THE CAD:
Richard better look
Through that
Fuckin' car.

GENNARO:
Go through it!
He better!
That car is bugged.
Guaranteed they planted it.

They went through that car
Lookin' for a pistol.
And I guarantee you
They planted it.

There's a fuckin' bug
Or beep on it.
Of course,
That's the easy way out,
Ain't it?

Next thing you know
They'll be coming in
From the parachutes.

Or Maybe It's in Louie Venios's Club Down the Combat Zone

GENNARO ANGIULO:
You can assume
He called the Mouse Trap.

The Mouse Trap
Is gotta be bugged.
If it isn't bugged,
It'd be a fuckin' miracle.

I'm surprised
At how it all started.
How did it start?
Is he sittin' talkin'
To an undercover guy
And he doesn't know
The guy is an undercover agent?

Is the phone bugged
And he gets on there,
Says how come you don't come down?

By the way,
Did you tell him
Who you were
On the phone?

Or Is It on the Pay Phone at the Drug Store on Hanover Street?

A Dog House dialogue

SKINNY KAZONIS:
They all use
That phone.

GENNARO ANGIULO:
I know they do.
They figure
Because it's a pay station,
It's okay.

FRANKIE THE CAD:
Yep, stay the fuck
Away from it.
That fuckin' pay system,
That's been tapped.
Yeah, that's where
It's all coming from.

Or Could It Be in the Fan Up on the Roof?

GENNARO ANGIULO issues an order to FRANKIE THE CAD

Frank,
Tomorrow, tonight
Call the electrician
And give him ladders.

Tell him to go outside
And take that fan apart.
Go all the way into that fan.

And take the air conditioner
Out of there
And look in the air conditioner too.
Okay?
Before we wind up
In the fuckin' nuthouse.

Frankie the Cad Takes Matters into His Own Hands

By GENNARO ANGIULO

Look at Frankie!
He's looking for the feds
On the fucking roof!

Or Maybe It Was the White Van?

By GENNARO ANGIULO

A bell just went off
In my head.
Richie says a white van
In the Ramada was around
The corner from his house.

Is this the same white van
That's following Jason?

White van.
Well, you know the number
We gave Jackie.

White van.
I found another van
Just like it.

It's in Nahant.
That was the one.
It had different three numbers.

It Must Have Been Jimmy Jones' Phone!
By GENNARO ANGIULO

They just nailed
Jimmy Jones!
Motherfuckers,
I told them last Friday!

"What are youse
Doing there?
Is that the only place
You know where to work?"

Fuckin' nitwits!

They grabbed G.
They grabbed Chelsea.
They grabbed everybody
Today.

Jimmy "Jones" Angiulo.

Tapped Jimmy Jones's phone,
He called all them
Fuckin' guys.

C H A P T E R 14

NEITHER A BORROWER NOR
A LENDER BE

How to Handle Somebody Who's 106 Weeks and $50,000 in Arrears

A Socratic dialogue led by GENNARO ANGIULO with SKINNY KAZONIS and MIKEY ANGIULO

GENNARO ANGIULO:
If, out of the goodness
Of your heart,
You made a deal with him.

And he paid,
Only to ask
For another loan.

What would you do?

SKINNY KAZONIS:
Take him
To Household Finance?

MICHELE ANGIULO:
I'd hit him
In the fuckin' head.

GENNARO ANGIULO:
I'd like to meet him
In a dark alley
With a fuckin' ax.

You know, an ax?
You don't waste time
With a fuckin' ax.
You got to throw it.
Pray it hits him
Right between the fuckin' eyes.

Larry Loses Twenty Large at His Own Barbooth Game in Lowell
By FRANKIE THE CAD

It happens to be our game
If you're interested.
And he goes
To his own fuckin' game!

He blew twenty large,
The fuckin' idiot.
The whole city knows
He lost twenty thousand.

He won't tell me.
Oh yeah, he's gotta tell
'Cause he's gotta pay
The twenty thousand.

Frankie "the Cad" Angiulo.

Jerry Demands the Money He's Owed by Louis Venios in the Hospital

Get me my fuckin' money!
Louis didn't bring the money.
You understand?

When Louie comes out,
If he ain't got two thousand,
You go get the fuckin' money.

"I gave it to you."
Just like that.
Got that, friend?

I don't know nothing about Louis.
Okay, pal?

Bring me my money!
That's it.
All of it.

Mikey Follows Orders and Visits Louis Venios in the Hospital

By MIKEY ANGIULO

He looked up at me.

"You fuckin' guys come
Right into the hospital, huh?"

"Louie, my brother wants to know,
Are you alive?"

Mikey Angiulo: Checking
up on Louie.

A Demand To Louis's Son-In-Law, Walter LaFreniere

By FRANKIE THE CAD

You tell me
You're going to be here,
Be here.

Don't let me
Come up the joint
Looking for you,
Okay?

What's the matter with you?
You just don't give a fuck?

By the way, you owe
A thousand at the game,
Don't you?

And tell the other guy
I'm looking for him.

Howie Carr · 79

Frankie the Cad Brooks No Excuses from Abe the Bookie
A dialogue

ABE THE BOOKIE:
I'm just starting
To get on my feet.
I'm telling you the truth.

I don't make nothing on horses.
I'm just starting
To make something
On dogs.
And I'm working hard!
And I'm not drinking!

FRANKIE THE CAD:
You'd better not!

ABE THE BOOKIE:
I don't smoke.
I don't go out.
I do nothing but trying to get even
And make some money for myself.

FRANKIE THE CAD:
That's what got you in debt
To begin with.

ABE THE BOOKIE:
The drinking did.
I did it.
I'm not blaming anybody else.
Give me a little opportunity, pal.
And you'll be paid completely,
And we'll be friends for life.

FRANKIE THE CAD:
No problems, Abe.

ABE THE BOOKIE:
Thank you!

Smiley and Frankie the Cad Pick on Another Deadbeat Bookie Singing the Blues

DEADBEAT BOOKIE:
I've been in the red
So fuckin' long,
I'm still makin' up
The eighteen thousand
From when I was
In East Boston.
I haven't made a . . .
I'm getting' out.

SMILEY:
Da-da-da-da—

DEADBEAT:
I ain't makin no money!
What the hell do you think?
I'm not mad,
I'm jealous because I'm not makin'
Any money.

Fuckin' aggravation.
The both of ya's.
I, I ain't comin' here
No more on Saturdays.

Ya's always pickin' on me!

Sometimes You Just Gotta Pay What You Owe

Wisdom from LARRY BAIONE to JOHNNY CINCOTTI

They're going to hit him.
Yes, they are, Johnny.
What I'm trying to do
Is prevent that.

If they weren't hot at him,
I'd say, "Fuck it kid.
Wait 'til they get mad at you."

Am I right or wrong?

Cincotti, John

Johnny Cincotti, one of
Larry's favorites.

Gennaro Angiulo on Offering a Deabeat a Carrot . . .

It's the same old story.
It's how you ask for your money.
You should be tough.
But don't threaten.

. . . Or a Stick

You ain't gonna cry, baby,
And you're never gonna
Miss a week.

I'm gonna tell you
The kinda fucking people
We are.

Larry Baione Is Owed $59,000
By LARRY BAIONE

How much trouble
Did I have
With this mother?

I threatened his fucking father,
His fucking brothers.

"You fucking cocksucker,
You'll pay this fucking . . ."

They're down to fifteen thousand!

Lecture to a Lackluster Nephew on Debt Collections
By GENNARO ANGIULO to JOHNNY ORLANDELLA

You're all fuckin' idiots
In my opinion.

Remember what I tell ya,
A man takes money on a Tuesday,
He don't bring it on a Friday,
Stop right then and there
Cashin' him!

"C'mere, don't tell me a fuckin' story.
Go get my fuckin' money!
I'm not interested."

Got that straight?

CHAPTER 15

JOE PORTER'S BROTHER IS IN THE TRUNK

Joe Porter (real name: Patrizzi) was a Revere wiseguy who got whacked in late 1978. His brother Angelo vowed revenge when he got out of state prison in early 1981. He was stalking Freddie "Cement Head" Simone when Larry Baione straightened it out.

Joe "Porter" Patrizzi.

PATRIZZI—By accident, of Revere and Malden. Nov. 11. Joseph (Porter), beloved father of Joseph Jr. and James both of Revere. Son of Mrs. Helen and Peter Petrosino of Malden. Brother of Mrs. Diane Puopolo of Everett, Angelo of Revere, Mrs. Darlene Wienrib of Newton. Funeral on Thursday at 8 a.m. from the Salvatore Rocco and Sons Funeral home, 331 Main St., EVERETT. Funeral Mass in St. Anthony's Church, Everett at 9:15. Relatives and friends invited. Visiting hours Tuesday 7-9, Wednesday 2-4 and 7-9.

Joe Porter paid death notice—"By accident."

Joe Porter's brother Angelo:
headed for the trunk.

83

Why Joe Porter's Brother Has Got to Be Cracked
By LARRY BAIONE to FREDDIE SIMONE

Freddie,
This kid's gonna
Kill you.

Don't think
He ran away.
He's layin'
And he's waitin'
And he'll crack
One of you.

Freddie "Cement Head" Simone:
on the Hit Parade.

Sonny Boy Steps Up and Joe Porter's Brother Sleeps with the Fishes

LARRY BAIONE breaks the news to
JOHNNY CINCOTTI and RALPHIE CHONG

BAIONE:
Shh, no shh, Johnny.
I told you, didn't I,
About Joe Porter's brother?
Well, they clipped him.
Don't say a fuckin' word now.

CINCOTTI:
Did they find him?

BAIONE:
No, they didn't find him.
They put him in his trunk.
Nine of them.
Nine of them.

Sonny Boy Rizzo, Revere wiseguy.

They lugged him from the fuckin' Topcoat.
Nine fuckin' guys.
He went in for a top coat
And nine of them did it.

Sonny did.
Sonny Boy.

You know all the fucking *camurist* (troublemakers)?
And he's in his trunk.

The Super Boss had told me on the QT.
Jerry say, "I gotta tell you something.
They clipped Joe Porter's brother.
Larry, listen to me now."

"Listen what?"

He says, "Got him in his trunk."

RALPHIE CHONG:
It's been ten days.

BAIONE:
But they got him.
They got him.
Freddie was scared to death.
The kid would have clipped him
In two fuckin' minutes.

RALPHIE CHONG:
He wanted to clip Freddie.
The kid wanted to, ahhhhh . . .

BAIONE:
Freddie fucked him in the ass!

(Postscript: In a later decision turning down an appeal by one of the convicted wiseguys, the First U.S. Circuit Court of Appeals pondered Baione's final ambiguous statement: "Freddie fucked him in the ass."

The court wrote: "We assume that this is not to be taken literally but we are not sure what it connotes. The most we can legitimately infer is that Patrizzi was killed before he could kill Simone.")

CHAPTER 16

THE LAW

FBI Special Agent Edward Quinn

Quinn, Quinn
All over again.
You know Quinn at all?
Thin-looking motherfucker.

Jerry Angiulo arrested by Quinn, left, and an unidentified FBI agent.

Did you ever see
Those guys from South Boston
That wear the scally caps
From the fucking docks?

Thin, thin guys,
Black beardish.
Always with a dark beard.
Without the beard on
And the fucking eyebrows.

The real Irish.
That's Quinn.

I'm beginning to hate
This fuckin' motherfucker
More every minute.
He's a cute son of a bitch.

Quinn,
The dirtiest motherfucker
That ever lived.

Running into "Mr." Quinn Outside the Grand Jury

I says,
"I know who you are
But I can't remember
Your first name."

What was his
Fuckin' answer?

"My name is
Mr. Quinn."

"Oh, I know that."

Now he knows
I'm hitting on him.
He knows it.

"What I want to know
Is your first name."

Like, nice and easy,
I'm saying to him,
"You know I wanna know,
You cocksucker,
Where you live, Quinn.
That's what."

He knows it.

On U.S. District Court
Judge A. David Mazzone

That fucking Mazzone
Right now is got a knot
On his fucking asshole.

And in my opinion,
He is the dirtiest Italian
Motherfucker that ever lived.

Mazzone is a dirty weak motherfucker.
He is a dirty rotten motherfucker.
Remember that.
Don't ever forget him,
Even though he remembers you.

On the Eightieth Birthday of Superior Court
Judge Wilfred J. Paquet

A fuckin' meathead!

Jerry Gets Pinched on Independence Day, 1972

Piloting his yacht back into Marina Bay in Quincy, Jerry is cited by a young Coast Guardsman for violations in a "No Wake" zone. At the dock, U.S. Navy boatswain's mate (ret.) Angiulo goes off on him, with a memorably obscene final line.

What are you,
Nuts?
That's the ocean
Out there.

The other boats
Shouldn't be there
Then.

Who are you,
The son of a bitch chief?

Who the hell
Are you
To be promoting
Boat safety?

If I had you
In my Navy,
I'd teach you
A few things.

I've eaten up
Guys like you
Before!

You say anything
About this,
I'll have your job!
Your life will be miserable!

Walk around me,
You son of a bitch!
Don't you ever speak
To me again,
You son of a bitch!

(*Takes the Coast Guard citation, crumples it up, and throws it back in the officer's face, then declaims with great passion.*)

And take that violation
And stick it up
Your sister's cunt!

(Postscript: Jerry might have been able to apologize, shake hands, and go on his way, but a cop on the docks recognized him. He ended up doing a short stretch, first in the Plymouth County House of Correction, before being transferred to softer accommodations in Barnstable County.)

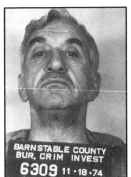  

Jerry in county jail in Buzzards Bay.

Jerry in county jail in Plymouth.

Jerry in county jail in Billerica.

Fixing a Case
By FRANKIE THE CAD

I straightened out
That pinch.

That pinch
Is all over.

Sixty-one hundred dollars.
The whole fuckin'
Shooting match.

To "Father Flanagan" at the Arraignment of Gennaro Angiulo

ANGIULO:
Hey, Mr. O'Sullivan.
You don't say hello.
It's been a long time!
You've come a long way.

O'SULLIVAN:
We've both come
A long way.

ANGIULO:
"We've both come
A long way."
Right!

Buona fortune a me!

That means good luck—
To me!

O'SULLIVAN:
You'll need it.

Federal prosecutor Jeremiah T. O'Sullivan, a/k/a "Father Flanagan.

CHAPTER 17

A FATHER AND HIS SON

Giving Jason the Needle about the Grand Jury
GENNARO ANGIULO to JASON ANGIULO

GENNARO:
There's a kid
That's worried to death
He might go to jail
Tomorrow.

JASON:
Fuck you, Dad.

GENNARO:
Look at him,
Goes around
With fuckin' roses.

Why is that basket
Shaking like that?

You got the willies
Or something?

JASON:
You know how much
That weighs?

GENNARO:
Why are you shaking?
Something wrong with you?

JASON:
No.
Why do you say that?
Joke is a joke, right?
I'll make my own jokes.

GENNARO:
I'm not joking.
You're shaking.

Jerry Again Chides Jason about Screwing Up "Insulation"

Frank and I
Made you the Boss.
But you were only
The Boss
With insulation—
Skinny, Johnny O, Candy.

How did you allow yourself
To sit at the table
With Louis Venios's son-in-law,
That he could ask you
For two thousand bucks?

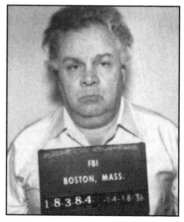

John "Candy" Candelino: Insulation for Jason at card games.

New "Insulation" for Jason—A Kid from Nahant Named Richie

A discussion between GENNARO ANGIULO and LARRY BAIONE

BAIONE:
He's going to be with him.
He's gonna tell people
He is with Jason, isn't he?

Now, we know, I know
I don't know, that he's up
On cocaine.
I don't think that
Is such a problem.

ANGIULO:
That is what
They're telling me.

BAIONE:
Well, God forbid,
If he is.
And he's gonna say
He's with your son.

Suppose he got nailed
Some day with the cocaine.
Jerry, he's no strong man.
You got to decide that, Jerry.

He's being insulated
Through Richie.

ANGIULO:
That's it.

BAIONE:
How strong is Richie?
Who the fuck is Richie?

ANGIULO:
I would say
That Richie's got
That kind of strength.

If you talked about Tony Conigliaro,
I'd tell you
I wouldn't trust him
From here to there.

You ask about his brother Billy,
I'd say, "That motherfucker!"

But this kid, I would say
That if he happened
To be the insulation,
I got the faith
In the kid Richie.

My Son Is Now a Man

That's the end
Of the conversation,
Man.

Before you got this summons,
I could call you boy.
Now I call you man.

So we understand
Each other.
And remember another thing.
You eat like a man.
You spend money like a man.
You understand?

Ain't going to take much
For you to be a man,
Right?

And you take it easy now.
All I just ask is,
You just stand up.
Don't you worry
About a fuckin' thing.

CHAPTER 18

FIFTY LARGE TO WINTER HILL

After Howie Winter's arrest, Jerry goes to the Holiday Inn in Somerville to give $50,000 in cash to the remaining Hill crew, to tide them over.

What is a fuckin' guy
Like me doing sittin' here
With fifty thousand
In my jacket?

I said now let's get serious.
Because I'm gonna tell you why
I'm giving it to ya.

You ain't got bread to eat.
You ain't got no bread to eat.
Neither have you
And the other guy's
In the fuckin' can.
He's not here.

I hope youse can use this
In a spot
Where you can straighten
Yourselves out.

CHAPTER 19

GENNARO J. ANGIULO, ATTORNEY AT LAW

Jason's New Mouthpiece

Put that fucking bottle of wine down!
Do you think
I should go up there
With you tomorrow
And deal with this kid
As co-counsel?

I'm gonna appear for my son.
Father of my prick in the can.
He'll be around a long time
If I'm his lawyer!

How to Answer Once the Feds Give You "Immunity"

Even if we were
To get immunity,
Go up and say,
"Yeah, I run a crap game,
What about it?"

"What do you do?"

"I give out money to people.
What about it?"

"You file for the money?"

"Absolutely, I don't file
For a fuck!"

We're just assuming,
Got immunity.

"Who's the people
That gambled?"

"Are you kidding?
I couldn't remember them
If I wanted.
Thousands,
Millions of them."

Don't Be Lying Under Oath

Remember what I told Skinny
When he left here last night?

"You tell that fucking kid
That if they ask him,
'Did he speak
To William J. Kazonis about this?'
He's to say,
'Yes I did.'"

That's the only way
To overcome them.
You understand?

"What'd you tell him?"

"I told him everything
You were trying to do
To me."

You know,
It's a very ticklish question
That I told a guy one day
That had immunity,
Sitting here.

I said, "You're going today.
They're gonna ask you,
'Were you talking
To Mister Angiulo about this?'

I said, "I want you to say yes."

Like a tough guy he got up.
He said, "Not me!
I ain't getting you in trouble."

"You fucking idiot, if you don't think
They don't know
You're coming through that door,
And everything you answer
To the grand jury, I'm telling you
To answer, you're totally more insane
Than they are."

"Jeez, I never thought of that."

So they know Skinny's up there.

"Once You Start L-Y-I-N-G"

If they say,
"Do you run a game?"
The answer is
Definitely: "No."

Once you start L-Y-I-N-G
The answer is always yes or no,
There's no explanation.

Do you "run?"
I said, "Run."
Okay?

"Do you go to a crap game?"
Now when they come out
With that question,
"Do you go to a crap game?"

You just come from
Fucking Atlantic City!

What the fuck
Is he talking about?

Billable Hours

I'm here
For an evaluation.
I ain't here
For fuckin' conversation.

CHAPTER 20

"THE HILL IS US"

In which LARRY BAIONE convinces JERRY MATRICIA, an associate of JOHNNY CINCOTTI's, that he needs to repay the more than $50,000 he stole from Winter Hill in TONY CIULLA's race-fixing scheme—or else.

(With CINCOTTI, RALPHIE CHONG and NICKY GISO also present.)

BAIONE:
Now Jerry, I have to ask you
Some questions.
Sit over here.
Jerry, Johnny likes you very much.

You understand?

I don't know you.
I love Johnny very much.
I like you.
Same for Ralph,
Same for Nicky.

But one thing we do, Jerry.
If you fuck someone
That's friendly with us,
If you fuck someone
That's close to us,
I'm going to give you a shake now,
So that you understand me.

Do you know that the Hill is us?
Maybe you didn't know that,
Did you?

Did you know Howie and Stevie,
They're us?
We're the fuckin' Hill with Howie.

You know that they're with us.
You didn't know that?

MATRICIA:
Up to now,
I didn't know.
I know it now,
Now that you—

BAIONE:
Well, tell me
What you fucked them for.

MATRICIA:
Fifty-one.
Fifty-one five.

BAIONE:
And you don't want to pay it?
You still owe the money.
You never gave nothing to nobody,
Right?

Stevie Flemmi, age 39.

Howie Winter, age 28.

How much you have to take
To give something?

Give it to Johnny.
And Johnny will get in touch
With me, Stevie, and them.

These kids haven't got thirty cents,
Between you and me,
To start off with.

These are not big money guys.
They owe their fuckin' life.
Did you know that?
You probably didn't know that.
They got their own fuckin' headaches.

You know, you're with Johnny.
And you're with the best guy.
You couldn't be with any better guy.
Just put that in your fuckin' head.

But Johnny will not tolerate you
Fuckin' people
Because you're with him.

I know you're out
In a fuckin' scuffle.
But you better curtail.

You make sure,
You make a score,
I'm going to see
Whitey and Stevie
Get the money.
And Howie.

You understand?

After all, you fucked them.
You out and out fucked them.
But you don't fuck them
Because they're with us.

Are they with us?
Are they with us?

MATRICIA:
A thousand percent!

BAIONE:
These are nice people.
These are the kind of people
That straighten a thing out.

Am I right or wrong?
They're with us.
We're together.

And we cannot tolerate them
Getting fucked.
Okay?

(Postscript: In 2013, on the witness stand in a different organized-crime trial in Boston, Matricia described the evening in question thirty-two years earlier:

"I was a—scared for my safety that night. I'm talking to a guy who looks like he's gonna kill me in two minutes. His reputation precedes him. I just agreed to whatever he said. That night I would have said I killed Kennedy to get out of there alive.")

CHAPTER 21

RACKETEER-INFLUENCED AND CORRUPT ORGANIZATIONS (RICO) ACT

The Injustice of It All

I wanna tell you
Something.

Why should I go to jail
In this fucking thing?
You know how many
Fucking things I did worse
Than this fuckin' shit?

Picked up the fucking gun!
I mean, huh?
For what, huh?

Ruminations on the Insidious Power of RICO

Remember,
They're not saying
This or that.
They're saying
Angiulo . . .

It could be me, you,
Him, him, and him too.

Nobody knows.
Under RICO,
No matter who the fuck we are,
If we're together,
They'll get every fuckin'
One of us.

They'll take every fuckin'
Motherfuckin' cocksucker thing
Every one of us owns,
Including your fuckin' eyeballs.

Now we're fuckin' idiots.
We never looked up
The thirty-two specific crimes.

In other words,
If you break
One of those crimes
This year and within
The next ten years,
You break the other one too.
They will take
Your fuckin' head off.

On the Meaning of *Enterprise* under RICO

An enterprise!
Remember that word.
Enterprise!
And it isn't
The USS aircraft carrier either.

Enterprise!

See what you're doing
Right here?

You're making an *enterprise*.
All it takes
Is one guy.

RICO Is Everywhere!

This is all a big joke
Till the day the fuckin' roof
Crashes in.

Last night
In Westchester, New York,
How many guys they pick up
In one shooting match?

Twenty-nine?

That ain't bad, boys.
I can see us all now
In the federal building,
Fucked, and ahh,
And all the joint is bugged.

You know what I mean.
Don't mention me.

All It Would Have Taken Was Fifty Large

This RICO Act
That's before
The Supreme Court.

There it is, right there.
You know what
I'm so fuckin'
Aggravated about?

We had to be
Total fuckin' idiots.

Well, let me
Tell you something.
It's gone.

We blew the biggest
Fuckin' thing
In the country.

For fifty Gs,
We could've got
The best argument team
In Washington.

For fifty cold.

I know this for a fact.
No matter where the fifty
Had to come from,
Send 'em down!

Everybody's sleeping!

CHAPTER 22

CAVEAT EMPTOR

Why You Gotta Be Careful, Part I
GENNARO ANGIULO to RALPHIE CHONG

You know I know that
You and everyone,
We all think alike.

You know there are
Certain guys that
Can walk in here
With a fuckin' score
Of a half a million bucks.

You know what I would say?

"Thank you very much.
See you later."

It's happened before,
You know?
You tell me who
You hang with, Ralph,
I'll tell you what you are.

Why You Gotta Be Careful, Part II

Well, I'll tell you something, buddy.
Maybe, just maybe,
I got in my fuckin' mind
Right now another story.

You know sometimes
When people keep telling you things,
Keep telling you things,
Even though we're friendly,
They love us,
They'll do anything in the world.

Today, tomorrow,
Tomorrow and tomorrow . . .

CHAPTER 23

A POLEMIC ON POKER

After Larry loses a poker game to a black guy, the fill-in dealer is relieved of his duties.

I swear to God!
Fuckin' motherfucker!
You are a fuckin' cocksucker.
You fucking punk
Get up!

I don't want you here.
Go home,
You fuckin' rat motherfucker!

Seven hundred, you fuckin' asshole.
Aces for . . . eights.
For four fuckin' cards
You fuckin' dirty motherfucker.
Queens and eights
You give him!

Every fuckin' card you made him
A fuckin' straight!
You dirty rat motherfucker
That you are!

Get out!
Go home!
Screw!

Get the fuck out of here,
You asshole!
Just continuous,
Like they got it in for you.

That last fuckin' card,
I'm fucked!

I can't believe it.
I swear to God,
Eighty percent of the time
I'm the best fuckin' hand
Going in.

And God forbid
I get the worst hand
And tried to draw
A fuckin' card.

He give him
A fuckin' straight,
The dirty motherfucker
That he is.

Fuck! Fuck!
Punk!
He's glad, the asshole.
He hates our guts,
This motherfuckin'
Cocksuckin' asshole.

Jealous, vindictive
Little prick that he is.
Every card he give ya,
He betters your fuckin' hand,
Right from the first card.

Jesus.
Mother.
But you can't look in the fuckin' hole
And find another pair.
It's impossible.
No!

Vinny found them, though.
He showed a fucking flush.

Three nines.
He showed me a straight,
Fuckin' little motherfucker.
Cocksucker!
Fuckin' dirty motherfucker!

I said,
"Nobody in the fuckin' world . . ."

(Postscript: Even though the prosecution handed reporters transcribed copies of the above rant before playing it in court for the jury, the Boston papers couldn't agree on how many obscenities Larry had used. The *Globe* said thirty-seven, the *Herald* counted forty-one.)

CHAPTER 24

FACES IN THE CROWD: RANDOM MUSINGS FROM SUPPORTING PLAYERS

Dan Smoot Don't Talk to No Lawyers
By DAN SMOOT

Truth is,
I wouldn't tell
Youse three nothing.

I wouldn't trust
Youse around the corner.

Joey DiFronzo Has a Question after Being Shot in the Head on Hanover Street

Does this mean
I'm going to be
Retarded?

Joey DiFronzo Recants Earlier ID of His Assailants after Recovering from Wounds

When you get
Shot in the head,
You get amnesia
Easy.

(Postscript: A few months later, DiFronzo was ambushed again, on Hanover Street, and shot five times. He did not survive.)

Stevie Flemmi on the Meaning of Wealth, 2018

If you're broke,
You're a joke.

If you have money,
You're funny.

"The Proverbial Street Life"

FRANK SALEMME reflects on JOE "THE HORSE" SALVATI, who was framed by the FBI and did thirty-five years in prison for a murder he didn't commit.

Joe's a full-time asshole,
Believe me.
And that's the truth.

"Don't play off
Like you're some kind
Of abused hero."

I told him that in Walpole.

Now he's making himself off like . . .
Sure, you got screwed,
So has everybody.
That's the life you chose, kid.

Frank Salemme after arrest in NYC, 1972.

You want to be a gofer,
Opening and closing the doors
In the after-hours joints,
That's the price you pay.

He's got to bite the bullet.
That's the life,
The proverbial street life.

Chapter 25

HANDLING THE HILL

Reconfiguration of the Winter Hill Gang after Howie Winter's Arrest

Whitey's got the whole of Southie.
Stevie's got the whole of the South End.
Johnny's got niggers.
Howie knows this.

Howie Winter, after state arrest, 1978.

Alas, Poor Howie—Now He Understands that Jerry was Right about Fat Tony

When a guy like Howie
Goes to the can,
Who was the guy
Responsible for all of it?

And after what his closeness
To me and the other guy was,
Maybe for our own reasons too,
Sends word:

"I never listened before
But now I'm learning.
I want you to know,
I ain't got ten cents in cash.
I have these lawyers.
I never knew in my life
What could happen like this.

"And I used to listen to you
But I never really believed it.
But now I see what you mean.
These guys will take it,
Better than a half a million dollars
From me to defend myself."

The only guy
That I owe anything to
Is Mr. Howie Winters.
Nobody else.

And I know
What I owe Howie.
There's no other discussion.

Other people that got
Involved with him,
None of my business.

Giving the Hill the Bad News about RICO . . . and Another Reminder about Who Warned Them about Fat Tony

Gennaro Angiulo's re-creation of a conversation at the Holiday Inn in Somerville.

Now before I leave this table
I'm gonna tell you somethin'.

You, Johnny Martorano,
You will be indicted within one month
And the charge will be the RICO Act
And you will face twenty fuckin' years.

Tony Ciulla.
Remember what I told ya?

Johnny Martorano,
Winter Hill.

Before I could say a word
To Stevie and the other guys,
Whitey popped up.

"Wait a minute," he said.
"Let's get one thing straight.
You warned us about this culprit
And I want you to know that,
Jerry sittin' here."

Stevie spoke up.
"I'm gonna tell you something Jerry.
He's right.
Because I never had two good words
With Tony Ciulla."

Fat Tony Ciulla.

I said, 'Good.'

"Tell me in as many words
And I don't even want to fuckin' know
Who dealt with Tony Ciulla
When I sent youse word
He was no fuckin' good?"

He says "Howie,
Johnny and Jimmy Martorano."
I says okay.

Whitey you can find out
A little more than me.

Gonna indict you, you, and you
With you.
I'll tell ya somethin'.
Don't stick your fuckin' nose in, Jerry.

I'll tell ya,
They were dead serious.

Johnny said, "You know
I don't got that much to do
With it myself."

"Hey, Johnny, under RICO:
Twenty fuckin' years!
Remember what I tell ya."

What's It All about, Whitey?

GENNARO ANGIULO's recollection of his conversation about "obligations" with WHITEY BULGER

Is that right, Whitey?
You're *separated*?
I don't know what that means.

I must have the wrong story then.
Howie sent me word you're separated.
You took over obligations
And he took over obligations.
Then he sent me word that you guys
Agreed to take over my obligations.

Forget the figures.
Tell me.
Is it so or isn't it so?
Did you take the obligation?

Gotta say yes.
Jesus Christ, it don't make sense.
I've been waiting for two fucking months
For you people to come down.

Nobody had even sent me word
That you could have—couldn't pay.
I don't understand.
Since you accept the obligation,
What's it all about?

Smiley's Follow-Up Conversation with Whitey
As recounted by GENNARO ANGIULO

Smiley looked at him and said,
"Whitey, I know what you mean
When you say you're broke.

"You mean you can't get your hands
On one hundred thousand overnight.
That's what you mean.
But don't tell me you're broke.

"I know fifty guys that claim
They give you one thousand a month,
Four hundred a week,
Three hundred a week.

"That's fifty thousand a month.
What the, what the hell
Are you talking about?

"You're talking about
Ten million like the old days.
Well you ain't got that.
I know that."

Smiley and Whitey in the garage on Lancaster Street,
West End.

Larry Defends Whitey and Stevie Against Jerry's Suspicions About Them

Dialogue among LARRY BAIONE, SMILEY and GENNARO ANGIULO

BAIONE:
Danny, when these people
Talked to you,
You're the one
That's been talkin' right?
A few times?

I got permission to ask him this, Jerry?

Larry visits Whitey in the garage.

JERRY:

. . .

BAIONE:
They act arrogant or tough
When they talk to you?

SMILEY:
Never happened.

BAIONE:
Do they act like, well, Danny, ah, ah,
Yeah, we're gettin' a thousand a month
But we told him to turn in.

It's not like, well, fuck you!
In other words, and you turn in
To who we say?

SMILEY:
Talkin' like we talk.
No animosity, no . . .

JERRY:
Larry, for you to ask
That question,
Then you must have misconstrued me
Complete.

You know if that would have happened
With him, what I would be saying to you
Right now?
I wouldn't be telling you a story,
I'd . . .

BAIONE:
You'd holler, Jerry.

Where's Whitey and Stevie?

Jesus Christ all fuckin' mighty,
Why haven't these guys
Been in touch with me?

I don't understand it.
Fuck me, maybe
They don't like me.

They got a right not to like me.
It's no problem.
Because I remember,
One of them said,
"There's a guy,
We kill people for him."

(Postscript: Whitey and Stevie were giving the Angiulos the swerve
on the Hill's $245,000 debt because in return for payoffs to certain
FBI agents, they had been assured of not being indicted. They knew
the Angiulos were going down.)

Surveillance photo of Stevie and Whitey in South Boston.

CHAPTER 26

CARMEN TORTORA IS GOING AWAY

Saga of a Mook's Final Night of Liberty

Act I: Carmen Is Recorded on an FBI Bug by a Rat Named Paul Alexander

TORTORA:
Where's my fuckin' money?

ALEXANDER:
I don't have any money
To give ya, Carmen.

TORTORA:
I'm gonna split
Your fuckin' head open
If I don't' start getting
Some money.

This fuckin' bullshit,
Fuckin' hidin' . . .

Carmen Tortora, in Medford, finally about to be initiated into the Mafia, 1989.

I'll cut your
Fuckin' throat.
Now get me
Some motherfuckin' money
Down there!

ALEXANDER:
I haven't been
Working at all, Carmen.

TORTORA:
I don't give a shit
About you're working or not.
Go out and work
And get me
My fuckin' money!

I want my fuckin' money.
This weekend
Or the next time
I see ya,
I'll send the guy
To split your fuckin' head open.

I'll tell them to cut
Your motherfuckin' head off.
I want money this weekend!

ALEXANDER:
I don't have anything.

TORTORA:
You're living, ain't you?
How you eating?

ALEXANDER:
I'm borrowing.

TORTORA:
Then go borrow money
For my fuckin' money.
You have been hiding
Long enough.
Next time I see you,
I'll split your fuckin' head.

It's that simple.
You are not going
To hide no more
Because I'll send them
Right up to your house
To put you in the hospital
For six months!

Post-Conviction, Larry Explains
Why Carmen Had to Plead Out
By LARRY BAIONE to RALPHIE CHONG

He can withdraw his plea,
Yeah, but he'll get
A hundred years
If he goes to trial.

He's dead.
Ain't got a fuckin' chance.
Hasn't got a fuckin' chance.

He's got a fuckin' fourteen page
"I'll kill you, you cocksucker.
Your family, I'll kill everybody
You know.
You pay the fuckin' vig,
And you took two hundred fifty,
You owe six hundred.
And I'll chop you
In little fuckin' pieces."

Forget about it!
Why do you think
I told him to cop out?

Hey, that's part of the game.
He's thirty-three years old.
He's a big boy.
He's got good shoulders.
He'll go in and do
His fuckin' time.

All This Brugliamente for Two Hundred Fifty Bucks!

By LARRY BAIONE

Two hundred fifty dollars.
Two hundred fifty dollars.
Sent a man away
For two hundred fifty dollars.

You know, if it was
Twenty-five thousand,
I could understand
The guy panicking.
He can't get it up.

But two hundred fifty
Motherfuckin' . . .
Cocksucker that he is.

You know he went
To the feds
And they wired him.

And oh, how he set him up.
"Don't hurt my wife!"

This is an asshole
He knows from the corner.
He had himself wired up
For two hundred dollars.

Larry Reminds Carmen How to Handle Himself in Prison

Wait a minute.
No matter who
Pats you on the shoulder,
Have no conversation.

"How are ya?"
Ah.
"You know Larry?"

"Ya, I know him casual."

No conversation.
Nothing we ever did,
And nothing we ever
Discussed.

Because someone
Might be trying
To test ya.

Someone might be trying
To send word to Larry
And say this guy does a lot
Of fuckin' talking over there.

You understand?
Remember Joe Porter, kid?

He was an asshole.
He wasn't you.

Hey, you was there with me.
The way you did your bid,
Do the same bid.

I seen how you . . . beautiful.
But get on that fucking farm!

Larry Dissuades a Despondent Carmen from Getting Hammered

LARRY:
Go up there.
Call me.
Call me from the court,
Will you please?

CARMEN:
My wife or me
Will call you.

LARRY:
All right.
I hope it's you, kid.

You're my fuckin' guy.
Just remember that.
Don't ever forget that.

I wish I had three more
Like you.
Three more like you.

CARMEN:
I'm gonna have
Five or six more martinis.
Then I'm gonna go down.
I suppose we'll meet again but . . .

LARRY:
No, go home.

A Post-Incarceraton Request from Carmen
LARRY BAIONE fills in GENNARO ANGIULO

LARRY:
Carmen's in New Hampshire
State Prison.
And his wife called me yesterday.
And she said,
"Larry, Carmen's going out of
his mind . . . Can't stand that."

I said, "Listen, Bonnie,
that's the way it is."

"No," she says,
"you don't understand.
He wants a TV in the worst way
Because he don't read . . ."

Carmen Tortora under arrest
again, 1990.

I says, "It'll be up there today," I says.

What do you think she said to me?

GENNARO ANGIULO:
Send a machine-gun cake?

(Postscript: In 1989, while on parole, Carmen Tortora was inducted
into the Mafia during the infamous Guild Street initiation in Medford
that the FBI bugged. He was convicted and sent back to prison. The
other four Mafia thugs were ordered to forfeit between $758,200 and
$1,116,200 that they had made illegally. In another indication of his
utter failure as a career criminal, Tortora was only assessed $2,500
in forfeitures. He was paroled in 2001. He is now seventy-seven
years old.)

CHAPTER 27

LOUIS VENIOS' SON-IN-LAW

A s mentioned in the introduction, when the bug was installed at 98 Prince Street, Jerry was lounging on his new yacht in Florida. All the FBI was picking up was Smiley and Frankie the Cad casually hassling bookies who owed money. To get Jerry back to the Dog House, the feds started issuing subpoenas. He was shocked to learn that his son Jason, as well as Skinny Kazonis, had been summoned to the grand jury, in addition to Louis Venios's son-in-law, Walter LaFreniere, to whom Jason had directly loaned $2,000.

LaFreniere was a bartender at Venios' Combat Zone bar, the Mouse Trap, not a wiseguy but a "civilian." Jerry panicked that Venios's son-in-law would flip and take down both Jason and Skinny . . . and maybe even Jerry himself. He immediately flew back to Boston and started convening one sit-down after another.

Suddenly the FBI's Dog House bug was generating indictable gold, night after night.

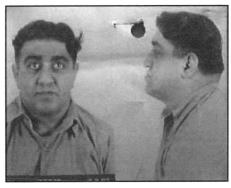

Louis Venios, Combat Zone wiseguy.

Talking Walter LaFreniere Blues

Oh, my fuckin' life?
Now you got me
A fuckin' problem!

Who called LaFreniere first?
Did you ever have
A conversation?
You're all mixed-up again.
Why'd you call him
In the first place?

Hey, Smiley,
This kid's a rat.
Let's get it straight.

I don't want no opinion:
"He's working on it
With Joe Balliro."

We'll have no opinions here.
Did he show up,
This kid?

Look at Skinny.
He's very nervous.
This kid is starting
To aggravate him.
Why?

Skinny, why are you
Sweatin' like a faggot?

Drink up, Skinny.
You might be going away tomorrow.
Obstruction of justice.

Louis, what are you,
A fucking idiot?
This cocksucker,
A fucking junked-up
Motherfucker.

Fuck what Louie thinks.
I knew all of a sudden
This was something
Very fuckin' new.

Keeps his father-in-law
Waitin'.

Nobody ever told us this.
You know what we thought?
We thought that junked-up
Fuckin' idiot cocksucker . . .

Who the fuck knows
What way he'll go?
He's liable to go
To fuckin' Charles Street
For thirty days
And start climbing the walls.

Kid's the type too,
He's got a broad.
He's got everything.

Fuckin' Louie.
This is his son-in-law.
He's gotta be
Totally fuckin' insane.

Get rid of that fuckin' kid.
He's your son-in-law.
Get rid of that fuckin' motherfucker.
That cocksucker will put
All of us in jail one day.

All junkies do.

I don't even know
He's got a girl.
Nobody told me
He's got a fuckin' girl.
Nobody ever fuckin'
Told me he's livin' anywhere.

All they told me
Is Louie kicked him
Out of his house.
That's the end
Of that fuckin' story!

Unconscious Stool Pigeon

He don't want
To go to the can.
Can't cut it.
Just a question of time.

From what you just told me,
He'll probably go to jail.
But I don't even give him
Two fuckin' weeks,
He'll be sendin' for Quinn.

This might be a fuckin'
Unconscious fuckin'
Stool pigeon.

You understand
What I'm saying to you?

I go for the first idea.
He's talkin' to somebody
Who told the feds.

The feds summon him in
And he says,
"I owe Richie
A ton of fucking money.
My fucking father-in-law,
Louis Venios . . ."

Bu beep bu
Bo bub u ba.

And that's how it gets back.

You know
What happened?

Gennaro Angiulo
Fell asleep.

Jerry Misses a Message from God, Part I

I ain't had a fuckin' night's sleep
Trying to figure out
How fucking stupid we got.
And I'm not gonna blame
Me alone.

We've been sleepin'.
I've been jerkin' off
In Florida
For three fuckin' weeks!

Why, I don't know
Where the fuck
We're at now!

Soon as that kid
Got a summons,
That was the beginning.
That was the beginning.
We all fell asleep.

It was like,
It was like God
Was sending us
A fuckin' message
And we couldn't
Read it.

Who the fuck
Gives a fuck?

Jerry Misses a Message from God, Part II

I remind you
I only came in early
One fuckin' day
And I said,
"They're here."

Remember how we beat
Four years, five years ago?

No phones.
No cars.
No drivers.

We got careless
That's what happened.
And we got
Exactly what we deserved.

We have become
Fuckin' idiots.
And in our zeal,
We fell asleep.

Remember the old days
When we were
In the cellars?
Hear a knock here,
A crash there,
Out the fire escape.
Over the top!

What happened?
Come in,
Take what you want.
Have a party!

Fuckin' stupid
We became.
I'll tell you the truth.
I know who fell asleep.
Me!

You know why?
I started listening
To some stories
From lawyers:

"Feds are giving up
On gambling."

They're giving up on gambling?
They're giving up on gambling,
Like I did!

Talking Never-Should-Have-Gone-to-Florida-for-the-Winter Blues

I get up
Every fuckin' morning.
I'm gonna take
My fuckin' time.

I do what I want.
Go where I want.
Go to Florida,
Come back
And get myself
In a trap!

We better never
Fall asleep again.

Why is this
Worrying me?
This kid owes money
On the shark.

Gotta be protected.
This kid should never have gone
To the grand jury
By himself.

We got caught
With our pants down.
We got careless.

I got a decision to make.
I want to have it
All in front of me.

Louis, I can believe.
This kid?
Double talks.

A Bilingual Dirge about Walter LaFreniere

Put three and three
In your fuckin' mind.
He's at the fuckin' games!

Ce la cornet pui' cornuta di Christo!
(It's Christ's worst kind of fucking!)

I hit it right on the head!

Mannagia la cornata!
(Damn the fucking!)

Nephews—You Just Can't Get Good Help No More!

You know,
We must admit
That we are
Fuckin' idiots.

All our lives
We never worked
The way we made
Those two work.

Nowhere in the world
Did we ever work
Where our phones were.

Fictionizing

The dirty part of this,
They're no fiction here.
They don't have to fictionize.
He'll give 'em the pieces,
They'll put the pieces together.

CHAPTER 28

JERRY MEETS THE PRESS

Serenading Reporters During a Morning Recess in U.S. District Court, 1985

(Sung to the melody of "Just a Gigolo")

I'm just a racketeer.
That's all I ever hear.
People know the game
I'm playing.

When they lay me to rest,
With a lily on my chest,
The gang will go on
Without me.

At a State Grand Jury with His Brothers, 1964

What do you think we are?
Monsters or something?

My tie straight?
Wait 'til I say something
To make me smile!

Cheese!
Cheese!
Cheese!
Cheese!
Cheese!

Wait a minute.
If you're going to take
My picture,
Take my good side.

Five Angiulo brothers: left to right, Anko, Mikey, Nicky, Jerry and Smiley.
(Frankie was running late.)

In U.S. District Court, 1985

ANGIULO:
Hey,
I been up all night,
Racking my brains over this.
Does anybody remember
The third line
To "Hey diddle diddle"?

TV REPORTER:
"The cow jumped over the moon."

ANGUILO:
That's it!
The cow jumped over the moon.

Chapter 29

"THE BEST REGIME IN THE COUNTRY"

Larry Baione's soldiers included Ralphie Chong, Johnny Cincotti, Domenic Isabella, and Freddie "Cement Head" Simone. Carmen Tortora was waiting to get made. (See *Carmen Tortora Is Going Away.*) Larry's son Joey also wanted in, but it wasn't in the cards. Perhaps it was just as well.

Joey's Plea to His Dad

Joey says to me,
"Daddy, not for nothing,"
He says, "But you know
I—I—I know you're,
'Cause Domenic's
Always with you.
And the shylock vig thing
Is enough.

"Why don't I let you
Pick it up?"

"It's too late Joey."

So I give Joey like,
He gets three fifty a week cold.

I says, "You got a piece of me."

He says, "Well, let me earn it."

How do I let him earn it?
Like Carmen?
Go talk to a guy
And give the money
Or I'll cut off
Your fuckin' head!

Who's the Boss?

A stern lecture to DOMENIC ISABELLA

Who the fuck are you
To make a decision?
You'll make no
Fuckin' decisions!

You know when you make
A decision?

When they put
Fucking stripes on you!

I'm a caporegime
And I'm talking to you
As a soldier.

Don't you ever dare
In your fuckin' life,
Ever tell me
That you're neutral
With an outsider,
Whether he's right
Or wrong.

Didn't you ever hear Jerry
When he made his speeches?

If you have to give the edge,
It's the soldier that's right.

Remember one thing.
I didn't become
A caporegime
For political reasons.

I never asked.
I never went
And wiped asses.

And I never went
Down to Providence.
No one helped me,
Jerry, or nobody.

Ralphie Chong Makes the TV News
Again and Larry Is Pissed

Like the Brinks thing,
He was walkin' down
The fuckin' street!

"What are you walkin'
Down the street for?
Don't you see all the TVs?"

He said, "Yeah."

"So why did you come out
Of the house?
Did you know
They'd be around
The North End?
The Law."

I said, "Why the fuck
Did you walk around
Hanover Street
After you was
On national TV?"

What was Ralphie thinking of?

Johnny Cincotti Gets "Snappy" with His Caporegime

A dialogue between LARRY BAIONE and JOHNNY CINCOTTI

BAIONE:
Who the fuck are you?
I'm just saying to you, Johnny,
Listen when I talk.

CINCOTTI:
I am listening.

BAIONE:
Three or four times
You were loud
And you got carried away,
Johnny.

Take it easy.
Take it easy.

You're a good man.
You got a long way to go.

All I can do
Is try to teach you.
Maybe I'm an idiot.
Maybe I'm—

CINCOTTI:
No Larry.
You're far from an idiot.

BAIONE:
Well, maybe I'm not
An idiot.
But Jerry Angiulo
Will call me
In his fuckin' joint,
In front of Ralphie Chong
And say that all my brothers
Talked about something
Here tonight.
And we want your opinion.

And he said, "We all agreed
Blah blah blah'"

And I turned around and say,
"Nah, it's wrong, Jerry."

And what do you think he said?
"Larry's right. Fuck 'em!"

And I don't say that to try to . . .
I only say what I feel.

You understand?

CINCOTTI:
Yeah.

BAIONE:
I want you to understand,
Johnny.
I like you very much,
Johnny.

You're a very smart kid.
Just remember one thing.
As long as I'm alive
And I'm your caporegime,
You'd better treat me like that.

CINCOTTI:
I understand that.
I wouldn't raise
My voice to you.
I don't raise my voice—

BAIONE;
No, John.
Yes you do, Johnny.
You get snappy, Johnny.

CINCOTTI:
I don't get snappy.
I maybe–

BAIONE:
You got snappy right now
About the stairs tonight.
Very snappy.

Remember one thing
I told Ralphie one night here,
Didn't I?

I says, "Ralph, I'm your
Fucking boss and don't pull
That shit again!"

Ralphie didn't say a word
To me, did he?

CINCOTTI:
Nope.

BAIONE:
But Johnny,
You keep getting
A little fucking loud.

That's not nice.

Johnny Forgets Larry's Birthday

By LARRY BAIONE

You're lackadaisical.
I asked you to get me
A little fuckin' thing
For my TV.

You was going to get it
The next day.
I says, "I don't mention it."
He wanted to get it
For my birthday.

I said, "No, Johnny's
Buyin' it."

Chapter 30

WHERE THE HELL IS RICHIE GAMBALE?

Jerry wants to set up the hit on Walter LaFreniere

Checking with Frankie the Cad

GENNARO:
Where was Richie Gambale, Frankie?

FRANKIE THE CAD:
He was up the corner today.

GENNARO:
He was huh?
High-class motherfucker,
This kid.

Richie Gambale.

Checking with Mikey Angiulo

Get me Richie!
I want to see him!

Checking with Doc

Is Doc down the restaurant?
If he's down the restaurant,
Tell him to call Richie.
And tell Richie I want to see him.

I personally don't give a fuck
Where he is.
Just tell him I want to see him.
Richie Gambale.
Got it right here.
The number.

Richie Finally Shows Up and Fails to Give a Good Account of His Dealings with LaFreniere

Richie, that wasn't what
You just told me.
You gave an entirely
Fuckin' different story
A few minutes ago.
You said it.

What did you say to him?
Stop jumpin'
These fuckin' hurdles.
I want to know
What his mind is,
Right now!

Jerry Tells Richie Not to Go Near LaFreniere's Girlfriend's House

If they ever catch
One of our cars near
That fuckin' broad's house . . .
Two fuckin' minutes
And they'll put him in
Protective custody.

He'll never know
What hit him 'cause
Of this fuckin'
Motherfuckin' situation.

Jerry Expresses His Frustration about Richie to Larry Baione

I'm glad you didn't
Come in last night.
'Cause I was so
Fuckin' aggravated.

You would never
Believe it.

I got a guy sittin' here
That wants to tell me
How a guy escaped.

"He's missin'!"

"YOU UNDERSTAND AMERICAN?"

An epic poem in five stanzas about the LaFreniere hit

Introduction

Richie Gambale finally arrives at the Dog House after giving the Boss the swerve. Jerry is not pleased.

You're a big fuckin' man.
You know that?
You don't even come
And see anybody no more.

Stanza One: The Eternal Question

Did I tell you that
A certain guy
Might get called back
To the grand jury?

Did I tell you
What could happen
If he got called back?

What is your opinion?
I want to hear it.
That you never came back to me
To say to me,
I thought this whole shit over.

Will he or won't he stand up?

What do you want?
I want to know from you
What you want.
What do you want Richie?
I want fuckin' answers from you.

Shhh, shhh, shhh, shhh—
Never say a word!
You don't have to make the decisions,
That's why I'm the Boss.
You don't have to make
No decisions.
What I want to know is
Your fuckin' mind, Richie.

Let me put it to you
This way, Richie.
If you had this kid
In the Mouse Trap
And you are takin'
Three or four thousand
A week.

Then if he goes to the grand jury,
You're gonna get indicted.
And I want you to know,
If you don't worry about it,
Why the fuck should I worry about it?

What the fuck,
I don't even know him,
Except through you.

Motherfucker!
Motherfucker!

Stanza Two: Richie Gives the Wrong Answer

GAMBALE:
I think he'll stand up.

ANGIULO (*Voice rising*):
Your answer is no!
Strangle him!
And get rid of him.
Hit him in the fucking head.
Richie Gambale . . . fuckin' . . .
Let me tell you why, okay?
Make you feel better.

In the last six weeks,
The feds have had
Jason Brion Angiulo
And Skinny Kazonis.
Mean anything to you?
Has to be a spy in the game.

Stanza Three: What Richie Ain't Got

You ain't got a hot car.
You ain't got a gun.
You ain't got nothin'.

You think I need tough guys?
I need intelligent tough guys.
Huh?

You're not gonna get him?
You're gonna have to!

I feel that my son
Might be in jeopardy.
I feel that Skinny
Might be in jeopardy.

Well, what do you want me to say?
Do you want me to say,
"Do it right or don't do it?"
Richie, you want to be careful
Because you can be killed.
Because the only guy
He's gonna bury
Is you.

The fuckin' life, it stinks!
I don't need that fuckin' shit!

Okay, buddy?
You get him where you want him.
Don't ever tell me
Something happened
And you had to pass.
Because you will be
In more fucking trouble
Than you were to start with.

You understand?

Now I don't want a problem.
I don't need this.

Stanza Four: A Direct Order to Richie

I'm gonna tell ya
How I feel about it.
I feel about him
That if you took him
And he got in the car,
Tell him to take a ride, okay?

Get out of the car
And you stomp him.
Bing!
You hit him in the fuckin' head
And leave him right in the fuckin' spot.

Do you understand?

Tell me what your plan is tonight.
I want to hear it.

You used to go to the fuckin'
Motherfuckin' Mouse Trap
To get your fuckin' money.

See if he's in the Mouse Trap.
Meet him in the Mouse Trap.

Don't call him at ten o'clock,
And you ain't gonna meet him
Until five in the morning,
'Cause he'll tell twenty fuckin' people
He gotta meet Richie.

You understand that?

Stanza Five: Final Instructions

Meet him tonight.
I hope it's tonight.
That's why I'm sendin' you
Because I know
You gotta supposedly call him.

Understand?

Not a bad spot,
Out of that fuckin' car.
You ain't got a hot car.

Just hit him in the fuckin' head
And stab him, okay?
The jeopardy is just a little
Too much for me.

You understand American?

Okay, let's go!

(Postscript: Richie Gambale never whacked Walter LaFreniere. LaFreniere refused to testify before the grand jury. He did eighteen months for contempt. In other words, he stood up.)

CHAPTER 32

"ANGIULO SEEMS TO BE COMING UNGLUED"

A prose interlude from an FBI 302 report dated March 11, 1983. Mob hitman Stevie Flemmi reports to fellow mob hitman Zip Connolly (who moonlighted as an FBI agent) about the different reactions of Jerry and Larry to their impending indictments.

Gerry Angiulo took source aside from the place where they were sitting at the table in the back of Francesco's and whispered to source that seven indictments were supposed to come down on them in the next couple of days. Angiulo whispered to source that Joe Jordan owed him a big favor and reached out for Gerry to tell him of the seven indictments. Angiulo stated that Jordan told him that he (Angiulo) had five murders which he had to be concerned about and Jordan told him, "you'll be very surprised when you see whose going to testify against you. It will make your hair stand on end."

Source advised that Angiulo seems to be coming unglued and it was obvious to him that the federal investigation is taking its toll on him. Source further added that Larry Baione, although somewhat concerned about a possible indictment, feels that he will never be brought to trial because of his heart condition. Source stated that Baione does not act like a man with a heart condition and is constantly talking about hurting people or ranting about people who owe him money.

Chapter 33

PORK CHOPS AT FRANCESCO'S

Slam poetry by Gennaro Angiulo after his arrest at dinner by FBI agent
Ed Quinn's squad on September 19, 1983.

> I'll be back
> For my pork chops
> Before they're cold!

(Postscript: Gennaro J. Angiulo was finally released from the Bureau
of Prisons on September 10, 2007.)

Jerry Angiulo strikes a defiant pose.

Francesco's in 1983.

CHAPTER 34

FOUR MEDALS OF HONOR

Gennaro Angiulo and his brothers have their bail hearing in U.S. District Court after a night at the Charles Street Jail.

Giving the Needle Again to Father Flanagan of the Organized Crime Task Force

Hey, Jerry!
Don't you say hello?

No football cards
For you today,
Jerry!

It's been a long time
Since that pool hall
In Watertown,
Jerry.

We've both come
A long way,
Mr. O'Sullivan.
Right?

Telling Father Flanagan about the Disheveled State of Himself and His Brothers

Let us not lose
Our sense of humor,
Sir.

You have the only four
Underdressed men
In the courtroom
And that's an accomplishment.

To a Courtroom Artist Drawing His Sketch

You're making me look good.
How much would you charge me
For a copy of that picture?

Jerry Angiulo in court.

An Exhortation to the Press

How many of you been to high school?
How many of you been to college?

Write this one good, boys.
It's me today,
It could be you tomorrow.
They're usurping power
Like you've never seen!

Statement to U.S. Magistrate Lawrence Cohen
When Asked His Name

My name is
Gennaro J. Angiulo.
Joseph is the middle name.

I was born in Boston,
With the aid of a midwife.
I live in Nahant now
With my wife and two children.

We all live happily
At 9 Vernon Street.

I served in the U.S. Navy
During World War II,
And I received
Four Medals of Honor
In the Pacific area.

(Postscript: After Jerry's antics, the magistrate didn't take long to issue a decision:)

CHAPTER 35

"THE SORRIEST GUY IN THE WORLD"

Larry Baione is convicted of racketeering

First Thoughts to His Beloved Wife Isabel after the Jury's Guilty Verdict

They framed me!
Don't worry about it.
They can't do anything more.
I haven't died yet.
I hope the jury dies tonight!

Presentencing Lamentations from the Jailhouse

By LARRY BAIONE to a reporter for the Lynn *Item* in February 1987

I'm a big gambler.
Sure, I regret it.
But those were tough times.

I like to bet—
Cards, dice, all of it.
I'd bet you on an ant race
If you wanted it.

I'm a dying man.
I walk wobbly.
If they let me
Go home, home now,
I'd have maybe two years.

But in here, less.
I know I'm going to die
In jail.
That's what the government wants.
They're going to let it happen.

Random Thoughts to Random Cops and Others Before His Sentencing

(Stage notes: Larry appears in a wheelchair, oxygen tubes attached to his nostrils, accompanied by a medical aide in white scrubs.)

On His Post-Verdict Statement That He Hoped The Jury Died That Night

I am the sorriest guy in the world
That I said that.

To FBI agent ED QUINN

I hope you're happy, Mr. Quinn!

On Prosecutor JANE SERENE's Claims That He Continued Loansharking from His Sickbed in Lynn Hospital

She has no proof whatsoever
That I shylocked
From the hospital!

I did not have no piece,
Your Honor,
Of no card game!

A Final Plea for Mercy from "Daddy" to Judge David Nelson

What you're going to do
Is sentence a dying man,
A dead man.
Death is ahead of me.

You're the judge up there
And my whole life depends
On you
Right now.

I want my people to go home
And be able to say:

"We might someday see
Daddy on the street."

I'm guilty of swearing
And gambling.
I'm not lily white.
I'm no altar boy.

But why am I now
The most vicious guy
In the world?

It was just a lot of blabbin'.
Everybody was stinkin' drunk.

I know I'm going home
In a box.
I might live two years.
I might live five years.

I'm beggin' for my family.
I'm not guilty of these charges,
Your Honor.

My fate is in your hands.
Give my family
Some consideration.

I'm begging for my family
My fate is in your hands.

You live in hope
And you live in despair.
But if you live in hope,
You might live
A little longer.

(*Repeats refrain*)

I'm guilty of swearing
And gambling.
I'm not lily white.
I'm no altar boy.

(Postscript: After finishing his plea, Baione collapsed back down into his wheelchair and whispered to his attorney, "How'd I do?" Judge Nelson then sentenced Larry to thirty years in prison.)

CHAPTER 36

THE BOSS TAKES A LOAD OFF

To the Press after the Judge's Announcement that He Would Be Sentenced on March 20, 1986

Hey, they can't do that!
That's my fuckin' birthday!

Pointing at the Press on Sentencing Day

Organized crime,
If ever I saw it.

To Prosecutor Jeremiah "Father Flanagan" O'Sullivan

This case
Is all bullshit,
Mr. O'Sullivan!

You can go back
To the poolroom
In Brighton
And sell football tickets
Again!

(*Turning on his heel to return to his seat, then turning back around to yell*)

And I can prove
Everything I say!

As a Recess Drags on, Turning Back to the Press

Wanna go
To the bathroom,
Anybody?

To a Young Woman in a Pink Jump Suit

Hi, babe!
How ya been?

When "Father Flanagan" Tells the Judge that Murder Is the Way the Organization Protected Itself

Bullshit!

To the Press, as the Lawyers Argue Over Where Jerry Should Serve His Sentence

How about the Pine Street Inn?
I know a guy there.
Or a halfway house
In Lawrence?

To His Brothers before His Sentencing

As long as I take the rap,
Everything will be
All right.

After a Possible Sentence of Up to 140 Years Is Announced after the Verdict Is Read

(*With a theatrical shrug*)

It ain't that bad!
We worked it down.
To one hundred forty
Instead of one hundred seventy.

Nobody ever gave them
That good of a fight!

To the Jury as They Departed the Courtroom

Thank you!

Final Words to the Judge after Finally Being Sentenced to Forty-Five Years in Prison

Thank you, Your Honor.
Ya mind if I sit down?

Jerry reacts: "How many years?"

To a U.S. Marshal Before Returning to Charles Street Jail

If you don't mind,
Let's go someplace
Safe.

EPILOGUE

Jerry Angiulo was imprisoned for twenty-four years before being released in 2007 at the age of eighty-eight.

He spent much of his incarceration at the Federal Medical Center Devens in Ayer, Massachusetts, just under an hour from Boston. His Bureau of Prisons (BOP) number was 03583-016.

All of Angiulo's codefendants served much shorter sentences, and many were dead by the time Jerry was freed.

His brother Nick, the "consigliere," died in 1987 before he could be tried. Jerry was permitted to attend Nick's funeral, and was photographed in the cemetery, dressed to the nines as usual, even as an incarcerated federal inmate.

Mikey Angiulo, the gang's go-fer, served three years in prison for gambling and died in 2006, aged seventy-nine. His BOP number was 14050-038. His wife Connie survived until April 2024, when she passed away at age ninety-four.

Larry Baione continued citing his health problems in his appeals from prison. His son Joey wrote a letter pleading for mercy to Judge David Nelson, saying "My father's no angel but he'll soon be with them if you don't release him."

Baione finally died in 1996, at the federal prison hospital in Springfield, Missouri, at the age of seventy-six. Two years later, J.R. Russo, the very brilliant guy with a carbine, died at the same prison, at age sixty-seven, of a lung disorder.

Through the decades, Jerry filed appeal after appeal, eventually *pro se*—representing himself, quite a comedown for the Boss. In his final complaint before his release, in 2002, Jerry accused the FBI, Whitey Bulger and Stevie Flemmi of framing him, which was true—up to a point.

In 2013, four years after Jerry's death, Flemmi testified at Whitey Bulger's murder-racketeering trial in Boston. A decade earlier, he had pleaded guilty to 10 murders and been sentenced to life in prison.

Flemmi testified that around the time of the Angiulo bugs, he and Bulger had been making cash payoffs to six FBI agents—John "Zip" Connolly (who at the time of the trial was in prison in Florida for the 1982 mob murder in Miami) and John "Vino" Morris (the former head of the FBI training academy in Quantico, Virginia), as well as Michael Buckley, John Cloherty, John "Agent Orange" Newton, and Nick "Doc" Gianturco.

None of them, not even Connolly, were ever stripped of their FBI pensions. Connolly was released from prison in Florida in 2021 because he was supposedly dying of cancer. As of 2024, he remains alive in Massachusetts—and collecting his full FBI pension.

As for Jerry Angiulo, after his release, he returned to his waterfront mansion in Nahant that he shared with his common-law wife, Barbara.

During Jerry's incarceration, his younger son, Gennaro Jay Angiulo, built up a major towing company in Revere—GJ Towing. At an earlier parole hearing, Jerry had told authorities he planned to go to work for his son at GJ Towing.

But by 2007, it was clear the end was near for Jerry.

In May 2009, his younger brother Donato "Smiley" Angiulo died at the age of eighty-six. He'd been released from federal prison in 1997 after serving eleven years. His BOP number was 14057-038.

Frankie the Cad was the last of the Angiulo brothers to die, in 2015 at the age of ninety-four. To the end, bachelor Frankie had lived across the street from the Dog House, at 95 Prince Street. He had been released from prison in 2000 after serving fourteen years. His BOP number was 03586-016.

For his funeral, one of Frankie the Cad's beloved antique Cadillacs was parked outside St. Leonard's on Hanover Street.

His kidneys failing, Jerry broke his hip in a fall in the summer of 2009. He died at Mass General Hospital in Boston on August 29, 2009. Sen. Ted Kennedy had died four days earlier, at age seventy-seven.

Jerry's funeral took place on September 3, 2009—the eightieth birthday of Whitey Bulger, who had paid those thousands of dollars in bribes to a half-dozen of the FBI agents who put the Angiulos behind bars.

At the time of Jerry's death, Whitey Bulger had been a federal fugitive for more than twelve years, having fled Boston ahead of his indictment in December 1994.

Bulger would finally be arrested in Santa Monica, California, in 2011, where he had been living under the alias "Charles Gasko." At his federal trial in Boston in 2013, Bulger would be convicted of eleven murders.

Five years later, in 2018, Whitey would be bludgeoned to death in a federal prison in West Virginia by mob-connected inmates from New England. They would plead guilty to murdering the serial-killing FBI informant in May 2024.

Two more of Jerry Angiulo's Friends of Ours would be exposed as FBI informants. In 1984, Ralphie Chong was indicted with other lesser wiseguys in the gang. But as they did with Whitey a decade later, the feds gave their prized rat Ralphie a heads' up and he was permitted to flee to Italy, like his brother Joe Black before him.

Following a leisurely ten-year sojourn in Sicily, Ralphie Chong returned to the U.S. in 1994 and got what Sonny Mercurio had described as a "lesser sentence—power of the lam!"

At sentencing, Ralphie told his judge that he never heard of any organization called "the Mafia."

Ralphie Chong served six years before being released in 2000. He died in 2017 at the age of ninety-four. They even had a wake for Ralphie at Langone's—"the loneliest wake you ever saw," said someone who knows.

Ralphie Chong's paid obituary read, "The red roses on his casket represent his love for his mother Rose, his love for his family and his love of the ponies."

His BOP number was 20747-038.

As for Sonny Mercurio, like Ralphie Chong he too turned out to be a rat for the FBI when he wasn't advocating for the power of the lam.

Mercurio was the FBI's primary informant about the 1989 Guild Street Mafia initiation, which was supposed to reunite the feuding In Town Mafia factions as Jerry and Larry were beginning their prison sentences.

For his invaluable snitching, Mercurio had some of his later drug-dealing sentences reduced in 2000. In court, he told the judge he had come to regret his life as a stool pigeon for the corrupt FBI.

"I deserve nothing," Sonny said sadly. "When you're a rat, you deserve nothing."

Sonny ended up in the Witness Protection Program in Arkansas, living in a one-room apartment under the alias of "Anthony Valenti." He got a small monthly check from the FBI, which he spent gambling at casinos in nearby states.

After Sonny's death at age seventy in December 2006, his paid obituary said, "His generosity and charisma were legendary, his valor profound."

The only significant figure in *You Understand American?* who survives is Stevie Flemmi. He remains in the BOP's Witness Security Program at an undisclosed location.

Stevie Flemmi turned ninety on June 9, 2024.

Jerry Angiulo's casket arrives at St. Leonard's, 2009.

The Hells Angels served as Jerry's honor guard.

In what was likely his last visit to Boston, Flemmi testified in a 2018 murder trial against former New England Crime Family boss Frank Salemme. Under cross examination, Flemmi admitted that he had taken part in "probably about fifty murders."

Salemme was convicted on Flemmi's testimony and sentenced to life in prison. He died at age eighty-nine in 2022 at the federal prison hospital in Springfield, Missouri, where his fellow Boston mobsters Larry Baione and J.R. Russo had expired decades earlier.

Jerry Angiulo's funeral Mass took place at St. Leonard's on Hanover Street in the North End. His widow, Barbara, arrived at the church in a black Rolls-Royce. A flatbed truck was parked out on Hanover Street for the almost 200 floral tributes.

There was a Navy honor guard from the nearby USS *Constitution*. The pallbearers were members of a Hells Angels chapter from New Hampshire. His coffin was draped in an American flag.

The funeral eulogy was delivered by Jerry's younger son, Gennaro Jay Angiulo.

"Don't mourn his passing," the thirty-eight-year-old Angiulo said. "Celebrate his life. Because in the words of the great Frank Sinatra, Jerry did it his way."

He continued: "Anyone who knew him well enough called him Jay. Everyone else called him Boss."

Jerry's son got a standing ovation for his tribute.

His mother, Barbara, died in 2020 at the age of 80. In the paid obituary, she was described as Jerry Angiulo's "life partner." Her life was detailed "from her start as a cocktail waitress at Jay's Lounge where she met Dad in the 1960s."

Her survivors included "her cherished grandson, 'The Prince,' Gennaro Francesco Angiulo."

So not only would Jerry's name live on, but also Frankie the Cad's.

A year later, in 2021, the Prince's father, Gennaro Jay Angiulo, would be convicted of masterminding an under-the-table payroll fraud scheme at his towing company that defrauded the government of more than $3.3 million.

The U.S. attorney asked for a twenty-seven-month prison sentence. But the judge gave Gennaro Jay Angiulo a slap on the wrist—eighteen months of home confinement, as well as ordering restitution of $1.77 million and forfeiture of $430,000.

His lawyer said, "He is not his father."

Nor is anyone else, for better or for worse.

DOG HOUSE MEMORIES

The Dog House, 98 Prince Street, North End.

Larry Baione's headquarters, 51 North Margin Street.

Frankie, Mikey and Smiley Angiulo watch as their jury and press make visit to the Dog House during federal trial, 1985.

Funeral procession for the Angiulos' mother,
Giovannina, in 1975.

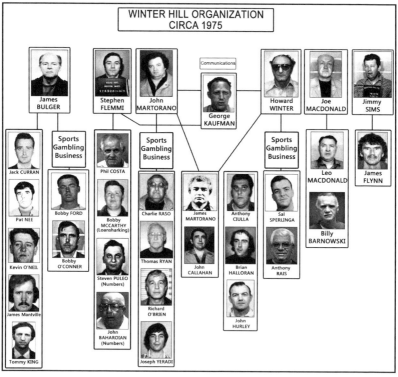

The Winter Hill Gang, from a federal trial.

North End restaurant, scene of many In Town and Winter
Hill sit downs.

Jerry Angiulo's Three Codefendants in His 1968 Murder Case in Boston, All of Whom Were Also Acquitted

Bernard Zinna, shot to death in Revere, 1969.

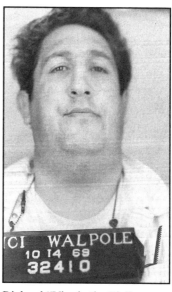

Richard "Vinnie the Pig" DeVincent, shot to death in Medford, 1996.

Marino Lepore, who apparently died a natural death.

Gennaro J. Angiulo
1919-2009

HOWIE CARR BIBLIOGRAPHY

The Brothers Bulger, 2006

Hitman, 2011

Hard Knocks (a novel), 2012

Rifleman, 2013

Ratman, 2013

Plug Uglies, 2014

Killers (a novel), 2015

Kennedy Babylon, Vol. 1, 2017

What Really Happened, 2018

Kennedy Babylon, Vol. 2, 2018

Paper Boy, 2023

You Understand American?, 2024

PLUG UGLIES
A Scrapbook of Boston Organized Crime

New York Times Best Selling Author of *Brothers Bulger* and *Hitman*

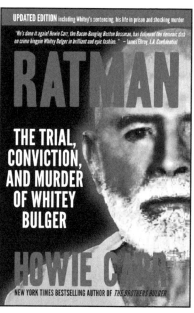

UPDATED EDITION including Whitey's sentencing, his life in prison and shocking murder

"He's done it again! Howie Carr, the Racco-Banging Boston Bossman, has delivered the demonic dish on crime kingpin Whitey Bulger in brilliant and epic fashion." — James Ellroy, *L.A. Confidential*

RATMAN

THE TRIAL, CONVICTION, AND MURDER OF WHITEY BULGER

HOWIE CARR

NEW YORK TIMES BESTSELLING AUTHOR OF *THE BROTHERS BULGER*

RIFLEMAN

THE UNTOLD STORY OF STEVIE FLEMMI, WHITEY BULGER'S PARTNER

HOWIE CARR

NEW YORK TIMES BESTSELLING AUTHOR OF *THE BROTHERS BULGER*

PAPER BOY
READ ALL ABOUT IT!

MY LIFE IN MEDIA

"How do you know you're doing your job as a journalist? When the Mob decides to assassinate you. Not many of us can claim that honor, but Howie Carr can—that and much more. What a life. It's all here, and well worth reading."
—Tucker Carlson

HOWIE CARR

NEW YORK TIMES BESTSELLING AUTHOR OF *THE BROTHERS BULGER*

2012.[84] A further issue is that those organized groups that have enjoyed longstanding ties to Iranian state elites and military institutions tend to be better organized, armed, and paid, and more experienced and trained, and thus benefit from an asymmetrical advantage over their more recent volunteer compatriots.

The dynamic in Syria is fundamentally different, for several reasons. The Badr Organization are redoubtable Twelver Shi'a Islamists[85] (with a view to my typology, they are largely ideologically aligned, though differences remain). They are comparable to their one-time Iranian patrons, and were organized along similar lines to Iran's own Basij paramilitary forces, cultivating highly integrated political and organizational relationships between the two over the course of some three decades. The first decade revolved around fighting under the broader tutelage of Iran's Revolutionary Guards against the Iraqi army, both harboring the shared aim of toppling Saddam Hussein's Ba'athist regime.[86] More recently, Badr's commander-in-chief, Hadi al-'Ameri, was not only pictured on the battle front with the Quds Force's Major-General Qassem Soleimani, driving the campaign to free Amerli from ISIS control, but has repeatedly attested to the fraternal and longstanding nature of their relationship, and his approbation of Khamene'i's leadership of the Islamic *umma*.[87]

The nature of the Badr Organization (especially its experienced cadres), and the role of Iranian personnel in training thousands of Iraqi volunteers with the coordination of the Baghdad government, has obviously placed the Islamic Republic's allies in a favorable position within the umbrella of the Popular Mobilization Units. But this should not be thought of as synonymous with control by the external power, because one needs to consider the volunteer nature of the initial surge in membership, not to mention the sheer number of political, social, and religious actors embroiled in the organization's ranks, which see themselves as defending Iraq's national interest—albeit mediated and inflected through a Shi'a-majoritarian lens. Moreover, training can be understood in terms of fraternal solidarity and political alliance, without implying obedience, or even control, since there is a convergence of interests between the political entrepreneurs inside Iraq and the Iranian state in consolidating their power in the battle against ISIS.

This complex web of interpersonal networks and organizations is not reducible to the simplistic dyad of patron-client: it ranges from the

Sadrists to powerful (predominantly Shiʻa) tribes, the traditional religious establishment, and factions within the Iraqi state itself. Moreover, formidable volunteer forces have been organized within the ʻatabat (the shrine cities, particularly Karbala and Najaf) in what is a historical trend dating back to at least the late eighteenth century. It is worth noting that at that time, notwithstanding crucial differences, according to Meir Litvak, urban gangs developed as:

> a mechanism for providing communal and personal security for members of a community in response to the absence of permanent governmental authority in the frontier situation, or where the formal government was invested with very little legitimacy.[88]

In short, these forces have developed and thrived in response to domestic security dilemmas.

The Syrian NDF, by contrast, was only founded in late 2012, and was born largely of necessity, as members of the mostly conscripted army began to either defect to opposition forces such as the Free Syrian Army (FSA) or abscond altogether. Reflecting the character of the Iran-Syria relationship itself, the NDF is the outcome of an exercise in knowledge transfer between two authoritarian allies overlaying a domestic security dilemma as individuals and groups invested in the survival of the Assad regime, or fearing the outcome of the regime's collapse, as well as elements looking to exploit the vacuum resulting from state withdrawal, organized themselves with the aid of an external actor, namely the Islamic Republic. The NDF has little to no sectarian or ideological affinity with the Islamic Republic, and does not possess a longstanding relationship with the external power that played a role in its initial training and organization. In this instance, the Islamic Republic acted as a facilitator, helping train, streamline, and organize the pro-regime Popular Committees,[89] which had answered Bashar al-Assad's call to take responsibility for security on behalf of the regime and to police dissent within their local communities.[90] There is very little ideological affinity at work; the relationship is defined partially in fiscal terms, and partly in terms of knowledge transfer and training.

Insofar as "sectarianization" was at all a factor, it might be said to be one of the repercussions of a far more profound political antagonism at the domestic level: the ruling Alawite families' (not Alawites *tout court*) and their tribal allies' repression of the predominantly (but by no means exclusively)

Sunni opposition and the militarization of this political conflict,[91] not an ideational one binding Syria's ruling clan to the Islamic Republic's political elite. As Thomas Pierret has argued, a key element underlying regime resilience in Syria is the kinship/sectarian ties that define its elite security apparatus and military forces.[92] By contrast, Iran's Revolutionary Guards have grown frustrated with Syria's NDF—which, according to numerous accounts, is manned, at least in part, by semi-criminal thugs, often disparagingly referred to simply as the *shabiha*,[93] who had become notorious in previous decades for smuggling, looting, extortion, and brazen corruption. Some of these behaviors have carried through to the present, often alienating the communities within which they were supposed to maintain order.[94] But, as Aron Lund has argued, one needs to be careful not to gloss over the actual diversity and local nature of such pro-Assad armed groups fighting in Syria, which have included "plain-clothes police, intelligence personnel, Ba'ath Party members and paramilitary groups, government-linked tribal figures, and young men recruited for money by intelligence contacts or pro-regime businessmen."[95] In short, local dynamics are absolutely key to understanding the composition of pro-Assad forces and their alliances in disparate regions across Syria.

Furthermore, in the case of Syria's NDF, questions remain about the extent to which the Assad regime is able to control these myriad and highly decentralized paramilitary groups. It is for this reason that the Islamic Republic has played an integral part in organizing, mobilizing, and arming numerous, predominantly foreign, militias and collaborated with trusted partners such as Lebanon's Hezbollah, the Badr Organization, and more recently established organizations such as the Iraqi Kata'ib Sayyid al-Shuhada, Liwa Abu al-Fadl al-'Abbas, and Kata'ib Hizbullah to fight Assad's adversaries. In comparison to Syria's NDF, a case in which ideological affinity is negligible, Hezbollah, Badr, and the other Iraqi groups harbor a significant degree of overlap, even while financial and other material incentives certainly continue to play a role.

The nature of Iranian engagement is thus intimately intertwined with the nature and characteristics of the regimes in power (in both the Iraqi and Syrian cases an ally), their social base and client networks, and the variegated regional-demographic balances of the societies—but also, to be sure, the confessional distribution across state institutions, especially those endowed with the capacity for coercion. Moreover, while the Iranian-Syrian alliance neither originated in nor fundamentally rests on sectarian considerations, the Islamic Republic has, curiously, relied upon a "sectarian" explanation for the presence of IRGC personnel in Syria, while repeatedly denying participation in the wider conflict, claiming instead that the latter were in Syria in a purely advisory capacity. The official, "sectarian," explanation offered for the presence of alleged retirees and active members of the IRGC in Syria has been the defense of the Sayyida Zaynab and Sayyida Ruqayya shrines in suburban Damascus, under the banner of the so-called Defenders of the Sayyida Zaynab Shrine. In this way, the Iranian authorities seek to portray their role as strictly delimited in geographical terms—the "sacred geography" of the shrines—while disavowing the larger and unmistakably political purpose behind sending advisors and senior personnel to directly partake in the defense of strategic locations along the Syrian-Lebanese border: Hezbollah's logistical support channels, or key cities such as Homs and Aleppo, vital to the very feasibility and survival of the Assad regime.[96]

While one prominent IRGC commander, Brigadier-General Hossein Hamedani, went as far as to claim that Iran had established a "second Hezbollah" in Syria,[97] the command structure and the *esprit de corps* differ dramatically from those that have traditionally bound Hezbollah to its Iranian patron. It is for this reason that the Islamic Republic has essentially subcontracted a great deal of the fighting in Syria to Iraqi, Afghan, and Pakistani co-sectarians. This is not merely a matter of retaining plausible deniability, but also, in the bluntest of terms, reducing the costs, both political and economic, of Iranian involvement. The Iranian state is not accountable in the same way to its own social base or the wider public when it comes to the death of foreign Shi'a fighters hailing from Lebanon, Iraq, Afghanistan, or Pakistan. When senior members of the Revolutionary Guards are killed in action their deaths must be accounted for, commemorated, and sacralized in the public sphere. This fact had, until October 2015, constrained the extent of the Islamic Republic's commitment to placing Iranian "boots on the ground," to use a hackneyed phrase.

The analogy with Vietnam invoked by some pundits is thus off base, since Iran, after four years of conflict, had proven highly reluctant to commit large numbers of ground troops, instead preferring to retain its forces' suppleness and versatility through advising and overseeing pro-Assad Syrian militias and foreign co-sectarians. In this instance, therefore, it can be said that the Islamic Republic has contributed to the framing of political mobilizations in "sectarian" terms. As of June 2015, estimates are that close to 400 Iranian and Afghan fighters have been killed in Syria since 2011,[98] and despite the death of several senior personnel in quick succession in October 2015, the figure remains relatively modest in the overall scheme of things, even while official denials of Iranian involvement have long lost any semblance of credibility.

The introduction of Russian troops and aerial sorties against Syrian opposition forces—that is, Great Power cover—has increased Iran's willingness to employ Iranian members of the IRGC in ground campaigns. This, however, has and will in all likelihood remain relatively measured. Given the demographic balance, there is no prospect of a mass mobilization along the lines of Iraq's Popular Mobilization Units, by means of which Iran could position allies within a larger sociopolitical movement. To paraphrase Mao, in times of weak central statehood and acute insecurity, Iraq's Twelver majority affords the Islamic Republic the ability to embed allies within a broader sociopolitical movement, like fish in the sea, while at the same time claiming to support Iraq's national defense and territorial integrity (the broad social base can, however, temper the extent of that influence); Syria, in contrast, provides no such opportunity, and therefore the Islamic Republic has vacillated between outright denial and the "sectarian" explanation adduced above in order to justify the hard-headed pursuit of its strategic interests.

Conclusion

In this chapter I have tried to provide a tentative explanation of the drivers of Iran's security policy, its support for armed sociopolitical organizations in Iraq and Syria, and its contribution to the logics of sectarianization in the civil conflicts currently racking those two countries. The nested and interlocking web of security dilemmas and their interplay at the systemic and meso-levels, which emerge in weak states in times of acute crisis, can engender the conditions for a convergence of shared interests between foreign and domestic actors, and the presence of political entrepreneurs and violence specialists willing to step into the fold, mobilize, represent, and connect communities in the face of security threats and activate the us-them boundaries that shape the nature of conflict in turn.

The Islamic Republic's desire to protect and augment its strategic depth in light of its dated conventional military, and the specific genealogy of its war-making capabilities forged during the Iran-Iraq war, in tandem with its allies' own local practices of war-making, have contributed to the logic of sectarianization and shattered the illusion of a monopoly on violence in both Syria and Iraq. The nature of Iranian political and military engagement in these two countries, despite practical similarities, diverges considerably, and is indissociable from the nature of the regimes in power, questions of demography, and the historical trajectory, composition, and social bases of the militias and their antagonists. Moreover, if we view the militias, especially in the Iraqi case, as forms of contentious politics that embody case-specific mobilizing structures, repertories, and framing processes, and that mediate between political opportunities, organization, and action, it complicates simplistic notions of proxy war and the client-patron dyad, which often cast a pall over prevalent analyses.[99] We can consequently better grasp the extent and constraints placed on Iranian political and military engagement in these conflicts, as well as the strategic policies upon which they rest, and the political conjunctures at which so-called sectarian mobilizations wax and wane.

Under the most precarious of circumstances, confessional identity has come to represent plural communities in their totality, while domestic actors competing as guarantors of security have established material and organizational ties with an external power—the Islamic Republic of Iran—in ways that are unprecedented in the histories of either Iraq or Syria. While, as I have attempted to show, these relationships, and the paramilitary groups that have proliferated in Syria and Iraq, lie neither in supposedly primordial sectarian affinities nor in Iran's putatively exceptional, ontological compulsion to dominate the region, there is nonetheless a very real danger of generating path dependencies whereby deficits of security are transfigured into totalizing sectarian animosities, and perceptions of enmity displace relations of amity and become increasingly difficult to challenge and overturn.[100] If we wish to avert this scenario from taking hold and becoming a new normal on both the narrative-symbolic and structural-sociopolitical levels, it is critically important that we understand the nature of regional-level security dilemmas, so that the sectarian polarization of communities across the Middle East might one day be defused and trust in a pluralistic future for the region might be renewed.

SECTARIANIZATION, ISLAMIST REPUBLICANISM, AND INTERNATIONAL MISRECOGNITION IN YEMEN

Stacey Philbrick Yadav

Difficult as it is to imagine amid the brutality of the ongoing war in Yemen, there was nothing inevitable about the sectarian dimension of the conflict that is currently destroying the country. The aim of this chapter is to challenge accounts that substitute nominal description for explanation, shifting away from the notion of the Yemeni war as a "sectarian conflict," and toward an analysis of the *sectarianization* of the conflict, as it has unfolded through institutions and discourses. In particular, I will show that key "transitional" institutions that developed with outside support during and after Yemen's 2011 uprising have been premised on forms of misrecognition that have paradoxically helped to produce the sectarianized conflict that they now aim to resolve. In particular, I will focus on the Gulf Cooperation Council (GCC) transitional framework—including the power-sharing government, provisional elections, and the National Dialogue Conference (NDC)—as mechanisms through which misrecognition of sectarian dynamics has been concretized. And I will explore the role of this framework as a central antecedent of the war through which sectarianized conflict is becoming increasingly entrenched.

Misrecognition, Institutions, and Meaning

The concept of misrecognition is distinct from "misunderstanding," inasmuch as it obscures the relations of power through which it is actively made. As Pierre Bourdieu has argued, misrecognition is premised on "the structural homology between the field of ideological production and the field of class struggle" and in ways that "produce euphemized forms of the economic and political struggles between classes."[1] This is effected both through institutions—as sets of rules and norms—and a dominant discourse that functions as "a structured and structuring medium tending to impose an apprehension of the established order as natural ... through the disguised (and thus misrecognized) imposition of systems of classification and of mental structures that are objectively adjusted to social structures." In this way, "internal systems of classification reproduce overt political taxonomies in misrecognizable form," and enable these new (misrecognized) taxonomies to do the work of class struggle.[2]

The GCC-brokered transitional agreement and consequent transitional framework represented just such a form of institutional misrecognition, in ways that reflected the coordination of "*khaleeji* capital" and that were supported by critical allies and transnational institutions.[3] One of the principal effects of this misrecognition has been the sidelining or obscuring of existing (and longstanding) political grievances by repackaging them as, among other things, sectarian conflict. This process fundamentally misread political possibilities that emerged, during the Arab Spring protests, from moments of solidarity across sectarian lines and originating along Yemen's cultural and economic periphery, undermined those solidarities, and ultimately contributed to the conditions of war that now obtain and appear intractable. This is not to say that the current conflict in Yemen lacks any sectarian dimension, but rather to argue that this dimension was fundamentally produced through international institutions and discourses, as detailed in the sections that follow.

More specifically, the transitional framework that emerged in response to the protests erased the possibilities of an emergent convergence between Islamists of divergent sectarian affiliations. Despite mutual misgivings and a tense relationship throughout the 2000s, the process of shared collective action during the 2011 uprising revealed substantial overlap between rival Islamist organizations. Members of Yemen's predominant Islamist opposition party, the Yemeni Congregation for Reform (Islah), and the populist (Shi'a) Zaydi movement led by the Houthi family both advanced claims regarding republican citizenship and political accountability that were compatible, if not congruent.[4] The institutional arrangement put in place in 2011 rewarded and empowered one of the two groups at the expense of the other, amplifying grievances that were systematically misrecognized as "sectarian" by international actors and concretized in a specific set of institutions built on the political exclusion of potential "spoilers." At the discursive level, a sectarian framing of longstanding political and economic grievances unfolded in a context of greater regional polarization and escalating conflict between Saudi Arabia and Iran, in particular. The erasure of overlapping consensus between rival Islamist groups has not only fueled war, but has virtually guaranteed that postwar reconstruction will replicate the kinds of institutional "fixes" that contributed to this deterioration in the first place.

Islah and the Houthis before 2011: Convergent Republicanism

The relationship between Islah and the Houthi movement unfolded uncomfortably throughout the 2000s, in the context of the former's participation in a broad-based oppositional coalition and the latter's participation in an insurgent movement targeting forces loyal to then-president Ali Abdullah Salih.[5] Islah is a complex organization, composed from its founding in 1990 of dissimilar factions of modernist Muslim Brothers, non-denominational Salafis, and some Zaydi tribesmen who have either adopted a nominally Sunni identity or else find the social conservatism of the party to be sufficiently attractive on its own terms.[6] Prior to the current war, the Houthi movement, for its part, might best have been understood as a populist Zaydi revival movement that worked to defend and advance the cultural rights of Yemen's Zaydi Shi'a minority in ways critical of the regime, the Islah party, and traditional Zaydi elites alike.[7] While the conflict between Islah and the Houthis dates to developments in the North that pre-date the formation of either organization in its current form, the tension has centered less on doctrinal or denominational belief than on the issue of cultural and political rights in the context of a republic. Leaders of the Believing Youth, the movement that would eventually transform into the Houthi insurgency, criticized what they saw as regime support for Salafi evangelism in the Zaydi heartland of the far north, symbolizing the republican state's non-neutrality on issues of religious and cultural identity and practice.[8]

Throughout the 1980s and 1990s Salafi religious institutions (or "scientific institutes," known for the teaching of the religious sciences), supported by Islah and putatively financed by Saudi Arabia, contributed to the eroding coherence of the Zaydi community through the "conversion" of lower-status Zaydis from outside the religio-political elite to a non-denominational and putatively more egalitarian Sunnism.[9] This occurred not only among the rank-and-file, but among tribal shaykhs, who saw this as an opportunity to offset the legacies of historical *sayyid* (descendant of the Prophet) privilege under centuries of Zaydi rule in the North. By aligning their tribes with Islah, a party both distinct from but tied to the regime for most of the 1990s, these leaders "hoped the pro-shaykh and anti-*sayyid* thrust of Islah would strengthen their positions and bring material benefits."[10] This hope was not in vain. The fragmentation of the predominantly Zaydi North shaped not only the Houthi critique of Islah and the regime's acquiescence in Islah-supported evangelism, but also the populist flavor and institutions of the movement and its antecedent Believing Youth, with a network of schools and youth outreach programs designed to undercut the appeal of Salafi egalitarianism by promoting a more inclusive culture among Zaydis. In this regard, the movement "exhibited a mode of associationism and activism that was particularly modern and different from traditional Zaydi practices."[11]

Despite the Houthi movement's stark break from the traditional Zaydi elite, President Salih justified successive waves of armed conflict with the Houthis through a republican rhetoric that claimed the state's "defense of all Yemenis against the particular denominational and historical assertions of Zaydis who claim direct descent from the Prophet."[12] This framing, Lisa Wedeen argues, served to "divide [Islah] party members" and promote "ambivalence toward the conflict," thereby contributing to the formation of "a broad coalition of acquiescent, if not fully supportive, Islahis."[13]

As widespread human rights abuses committed by the military in civilian communities were reported, Islah was called upon by its opposition allies to take a position on the movement, and on the civilian destruction that Salih's forces left in their wake. The politics of Islah's position-taking were shaped by the Islamist party's participation in the Joint Meeting

Parties (JMP) opposition coalition, and it was through this institution that other parties endeavored to "discipline" Islah and compel its renunciation of Salih's violence against civilian communities in the province of Saada. This was accomplished through an inventive invocation of the concept of *fitna* (religiously proscribed conflict among Muslims), by which Islamists were called upon to enact their commitments by showing solidarity with those oppressed by the regime.[14] While JMP stopped short of endorsing the Houthi insurgents outright in deference to Islahi equivocation, alliance representatives framed the government's conflict with the Houthis as confirmation of the need for the kinds of reforms the alliance was advancing through civil means (through proposed electoral reforms, transparency and accountability, press freedom, etc.). Both JMP activism and the Houthi insurgency, in other words, were framed as challenges to the Salih regime's personalized capture of state resources and undermining of republican accountability. As Muhammed Qahtan, the Islah party's most prominent Brotherhood centrist, put it at the time, "when an individual pursues an armed campaign against citizens, it is outside the constitution and the law. If we are held to the standard of the constitution and the law, then the regime needs to be bound by it, too."[15]

Adopting Sectarian Rhetoric or Rhetorical Wars of Position

Regime elites, for their part, adopted a sectarian rhetoric that sought to conflate specific political demands advanced by the Houthi leadership with Zaydism generally, and the putative anti-republicanism of the *sayyid* family of 'Abd al-Malik al-Houthi as *ahl al-bayt* (privileged descendants of the Prophet Muhammad), more specifically. As one senior member noted to me at the time in language characteristic of the dominant discourse, "inside every Zaydi, there is a little [Zaydi] imam waiting to come out."[16] Regime discourse in the 2000s consistently sought to cast doubt on the Houthis' republican commitments, raising the specter of the disproportionate power of *sayyid* families as a class under North Yemen's pre-republican Zaydi imamate. This harking back reminded a cross-sectarian Yemeni community of republican state-building following the 1962 revolution and North Yemeni civil war, a time when "the honorific *sayyid* became a swearword."[17] In effect, the discursive struggle to frame the Houthi conflict in the 2000s can be read as a struggle among the inheritors of Yemeni republicanism, with an effort to sever the Houthis' substantive grievances from their origin in a movement spearheaded by a titular *sayyid*.

Amid this, three distinct institutional relationships shaped Islah's ambivalent relationship to the Houthi movement in the mid- to late 2000s, and, taken together, highlight both the difficult road by which Islahis arrived at recognition of the Houthi movement's republican aims and the ease with which the post-2011 settlement eroded this recognition. To understand this deterioration, some discussion of each of these institutional relationships—between Islah and the regime, Islah and its JMP allies, and rival factions within Islah—is in order.

The Islah party is neither a Salafi party nor a straightforward analogue of the Egyptian Muslim Brotherhood. Instead, it is a loose, often internally contradictory amalgam that was established alongside the unification of North and South Yemen in 1990, largely as a bulwark against the (anticipated but never realized) expansion of socialism from the south.[18] The Islah party's leadership has included a Brotherhood-influenced modernist faction dominated by urban professionals of midlands origin, tribal figures from the far North (some of whom are at least nominally of Zaydi Shi'a background), and Salafis of an activist persuasion.[19] While its membership is not drawn exclusively from the parts of the former Yemen Arab Republic, it is fair to consider Islah a "Northern phenomenon," if not always a straightforward extension of Northern power over the South (as some of its Southern critics claim). This makes the Houthi–Islahi tension very much an intra-Northern conflict, which developed according to a logic somewhat (but not entirely) distinct from the Hirak, or Southern Movement, building in areas of the former People's Democratic Republic of Yemen during the same basic period.[20]

Yemen's Salafi movement itself is internally varied, but the Salafi faction within Islah has been reasonably centralized around the leadership of a few specific shaykhs and managed through participation in a wide network of higher educational institutions, al-Iman University not least among them. While Flagg Miller has documented the inventive way in which Islahi evangelists have adopted regionally specific poetic and oratorical styles to expand their appeal outside the North, he nonetheless notes that this has been made more difficult by the decisively anti-Southern countenance of the party's most popular (and populist) shaykh, 'Abd al-Majid al-Zindani.[21] This is mitigated somewhat by the party's Brotherhood faction, demographically drawn from the more educated and urban communities in the midlands (especially Taiz and Ibb) and Sana'a, where many enjoy professional ties with Yemenis from different partisan, ideological, and sectarian backgrounds.[22] While its influence has been contested in recent years, the tribal faction within Islah has often played a rather decisive role as "kingmaker" in conflicts between the two more ideologically driven groups. It is also the case that some tribes have "split the difference," with one leader joining President Salih's ruling GPC and another in Islah. Whether these splits were acrimonious, or a calculated division of risk, is a source of speculation and no small amount of gossip.

For most of the 1990s and 2000s these internal factions within Islah mapped onto different party institutions, offering each group a reason to view membership as beneficial and forestalling the (often looming) risk of party fracture.[23] The Salafi wing, under the leadership of Shaykh 'Abd al-Majid al-Zindani, enjoyed prominence on the party's internal *majlis al-shura*, its consultative body constituted through intra-party elections, though this dominance was considerably challenged following the 2007 internal elections. The speaker of the parliament was Shaykh Abdullah bin Hussein al-Ahmar, the paramount shaykh of the Hashid tribal confederation until his death, also in 2007. He enjoyed symbolic prominence through his role as the head of a group of Islahi MPs, though Yemen's parliament itself was a largely ineffectual institution. His power was far more often expressed in informal adjudications of disputes between the Brothers and the Salafis, or between President Salih and elements of the opposition. The Brothers, for their part, were active in the leadership of the political directorate, the party's day-to-day decision-making body, responsible for crafting its platform, participating in inter-partisan forums, etc. Women associated with this faction have also played a particularly significant role in leadership of the women's directorate, a parallel set of institutions within the party, and their leadership successes were instrumental to a particularly momentous internal shake-up in the party's 2007 *majlis al-shura* elections.[24]

These internal factions within the party have often functioned in complementary ways, drawing on their distinctive strengths. The Brotherhood faction—many university graduates and people with professional training, which ties them to activists from other parties and from the broader associational sector—is best positioned for the mundane work of party-building. The tribal leadership has finessed a challenging relationship with the regime, and dampened the impact of the Brothers' opposition platform. This was a double-edged sword in the 2000s, limiting the potential of the party as an effective opposition, but also perhaps protecting it from the kind of suppression faced by others in the JMP, especially the Yemeni Socialist Party. And the Salafi wing has typically been effective at mobilization and evangelism, though the evangelical outreach of Islahi leaders is certainly a kind of politicized evangelism that should be distinguished from more quietist Salafi trends who reject participation in electoral competition as profane.[25]

The formation of the JMP alliance and the party's shift toward more overt opposition to the Salih regime strained the relationship between the factions, however. Islah's participation in the JMP was anchored firmly in the Brotherhood cohort and was a natural extension of its general commitment to a politics of accountability based on shared notions of republican citizenship. This was inconsistent with some of the anti-Zaydi rhetoric of the Salafi evangelists, as well as with the party's critique of the Zaydi principle of *khuruj*, or compulsory uprising against an unjust ruler.[26] Leading Salafis in the party, for example, criticized Zaydi opposition to the Salih regime as disobedience to the ruler—an alleged violation of their understanding of Islamic ethical norms—even as Brothers within the party were seeking more strident (if unarmed) forms of opposition to Salih. The formation of the JMP alliance thus strained an already fissiparous relationship between the Brothers and the Salafis in Islah in ways that exposed a lack of consensus on key republican commitments to accountable governance. This tension became particularly acute following the death of Shaykh Abdullah in 2007 and the weakening of the tribal cohort as a whole. While the senior shaykh had often been able to mediate between the two factions, his absence produced an ever more fragile and bipolar dynamic within the party. A campaign of *takfir* (accusation of apostasy)—waged both inside the party and through extrapartisan institutions through which Islah's Salafi leaders worked with counterparts aligned closely to the regime—sought to discipline members who more openly embraced opposition, including leaders such as Muhammed Qahtan, Islah's most prominent Brotherhood centrist.[27]

Yet Islahi centrists committed to the JMP were hardly progressive, at least in the eyes of their socialist and leftist nationalist counterparts in the alliance. They continued to express deep skepticism about the Houthi movement and, over time, about Zaydis more broadly. Indeed, internal tensions within the JMP on questions of substantive politics produced an alliance committed first and foremost to questions of procedural reform and accountability, often painfully silent on substantive issues of great concern to many Yemenis. That said, the procedural reforms endorsed and advanced by the JMP (and thereby Islah) were substantially congruent with claims put forward by Hussein Badr al-Din al-Houthi and his followers in the early years of the movement.[28] Central to the Houthis' claims were that the republican state had an obligation to uphold equality among categories of citizens, and ought not systematically to privilege one group (Salafis) over another (Zaydis) in the context of republican citizenship.[29] This approach was consistent with the Zaydi elite's republican reorientation following the 1962 revolution and civil war in North Yemen, whereby Zaydi *sayyids* grappled with the reconstitution of political authority and emerged as what Gabrielle vom Bruck has described as committed constitutionalism.[30] As a populist Zaydi revival movement that sought to wrench leadership of Yemen's Zaydi community away from the more traditional elite leadership, the Houthi movement was founded and developed entirely in the context of such post-1962 republicanism, and while regime and (some) Islahi discourse obscured this, the events of 2011 brought it temporarily to the fore.

Transformative Impact of Collective Action

When youth activists and others converged on protest spaces throughout Yemen in the winter and spring of 2011, their demands were articulated against the Salih regime, but also against the formal opposition parties that they increasingly came to characterize as a central component of the regime itself. Younger Islahis played an important role in protest activity, and through this practice came into sustained contact with differently situated Yemenis, including Houthis. In a series of workshops and trainings with youth activists from across the political spectrum that I attended between 2011 and 2013, I observed the effects of this collective action as distinct from the intra-partisan dynamics observable among JMP leaders.[31] In interviews, activists cited the quotidian work of maintaining protest spaces as constitutive of a shared activist identity that was deeply republican in its focus. While there was no broad agreement on the question of secularism among these activists, there was a clear rejection of sectarianism (expressed as *ta'ifiyya*, *madhabiyya*, or even sometimes *'unsuriyya*),[32] and there were moments of explicit political coordination between Houthi and Islahi youth that were characteristic of the potential of both political movements to advance republican aims within the parameters of their (different) Islamisms. While the two groups were undecided on the question of federalism, they joined together to articulate a notion of a "civil state" consistent with a modernist reading of *shari'a*. They did so in way that was premised on republican notions of political accountability, popular sovereignty, and rule of law.

This disjuncture between a convergent Islamist republicanism among Islahi and Houthi youth and emergent tension between senior leaders of both groups (detailed below) is consistent with what Atiaf al-Wazir has characterized as "the introduction of youth as new political actors" forged through the process of collective action.[33] Al-Wazir claims that in relation to other youth-led initiatives characteristic of this "exceptional time," such convergence:

> may not be sustainable over the long term and will remain subject to elite dynamics. Still, the urge for self-realization and the vision of a just social order that defined the spirit of 2011 ... will create a permanent repository of resistance and repertoires of contention with which political elites will have to reckon.[34]

The argument here is that the institutional misrecognition produced by the transitional framework and the discursive framing of the 2015 war have been just such a reckoning, albeit with some corrosive effects.

The Transitional Framework and Institutional Misrecognition

Structural features of Yemen's transitional process played a significant role in amplifying the sectarian framing of Islahi–Houthi tensions and undermining some of the incipient solidarities forged through collective action. Three features of the GCC framework, in particular, have been central to this process, emerging from and further sedimenting institutional misrecognition of Islamist republicanism.

First, the composition of the transitional government gave disproportionate power to existing political parties, i.e. members of the JMP alliance. This decision ought to be understood in a broader regional context, where the fractured nature of political opposition under more repressive conditions in Syria and Libya, for example, colored thinking about Yemen. The JMP offered international negotiators the "advantage" of a pre-formed and relatively deeply institutionalized opposition with which to broker an agreement. Transitional planners were resistant to recognizing the scope of opposition to the framework or the ways in which it was being challenged on the ground, particularly when those challenges were nonviolent.[35] Instead, they deferred the challenge of inclusivity to non-binding "outreach" initiatives to be carried out by the narrowly construed transitional government in preparation for the NDC, a centerpiece of the transitional framework.[36]

Because Islah was a central player—arguably, *the* central player—in the pre-organized opposition alliance, it was also the greatest single beneficiary of the brokered transition. The former ruling party, of course, also managed to do well, insofar as the Yemeni transitional framework preserved significantly more power for existing regime elites than transitional frameworks in Tunisia, Egypt, or Libya. By contrast, the total exclusion of the Houthi movement from any formal role in the transitional government was the first institutional step in eroding republican solidarity among Islamists.

Deepening this rift was a second institutional step that identified (not incorrectly) the potential role both the Houthis and the Southern Movement (Hirak) might play as spoilers in the transitional process. The fact that these two groups were understood as potential spoilers underscores the significance of their exclusion from the transitional framework. But their identification by the UN and the US government as targets for sanctions and asset freezes displaced sole responsibility for this onto the movements themselves, without inquiring into the broader processes of exclusion that made spoiling attractive, and were themselves premised on institutional misrecognition. The demands of these movements—and of many independent groups not aligned with either group—in relation to the transitional framework were deemed illegitimate.[37] Thus the short-term advantage enjoyed by Islah and former regime elites was shored up behind an international regulatory framework that adjudicated the legitimacy of opposition movement demands on the basis of opaque criteria.

The final institutional mechanism by which transition planners undid the possibilities for shared republican commitments and contributed to the sectarianization of the conflict was, paradoxically, the NDC itself. It is paradoxical because this was the only transitional institution in which the Houthis played a direct role, yet their inclusion in the most toothless of the transitional institutions underscored their exclusion from institutions of transitional governance with the power to shape policy. In effect, their participation in the NDC offered voice, but not power, a condition which was apparent before but appeared to become intolerable after the conclusion of the NDC.

The tension between Islah and the Houthis came to a head in the NDC working group on Saada, the province that was most thoroughly destroyed by the Salih regime's counterinsurgent campaign and represents both the area of greatest Houthi control and the historic center of Islahi evangelism. Conflicts between the two groups at the NDC were accompanied by the eruption of armed violence between Islah-aligned tribal militias and Houthi militias in and around the city of Dammaj, home to the Salafi religious institute, Dar al-Hadith. As Lisa Wedeen argued with regard to the conflict in Saada under President Salih, "regimes can rely on spaces of disorder as a mode of reproducing their rule."[38] This argument can be extended to the transitional process if we view the "regime" in question as one constituted through the internationally brokered empowerment of select elites along terms that benefit the regional foreign and domestic policy interests of Yemen's Gulf neighbors.[39]

Elite framing of the conflict between Houthis and Islahis as a "sectarian conflict" may have originated with the response of the GPC (Salih's party) to both movements in the 2000s, but it was dramatically amplified by Saudi involvement in Yemen's domestic political deterioration from 2009. Offering air support to Salih's troops in Saada, the Saudis justified their participation in the campaign as a roll-back of Iranian influence in Yemen, despite the fact that "there are more than enough grievances in Yemen and Saada to perpetuate the fighting without drawing in regional dynamics."[40] By linking what was a fundamentally domestic Yemeni political struggle over institutions and rights to a conflict between regional actors itself framed in sectarian terms, the Saudis helped to amplify the nominal existence of sectarian difference to the status of a causal story, offering the descriptive fact of the Houthis' Zaydi identity as the substantive *reason* behind the conflict. Before the uprising, self-serving Yemeni elites did little to disrupt this, despite privately acknowledging that allegations of Iranian support for the Houthis were "unfounded."[41] During the transition, youth activists who were frustrated by partisan manipulation of the sectarian dimension had few avenues through which to challenge it, given the shutdown of internal party deliberations across the political spectrum during the transitional period.[42]

ISLAMIST REPUBLICANISM IN YEMEN

Sectarianization, War, and Post-War Prospects

Journalistic and policy accounts of the "march to war" in Yemen typically begin with the Houthi move on Sana'a in September 2014. Both Yemeni activists and many academic Yemen specialists challenged interpretations of the Houthis' aims as "sectarian" early in the process, often citing the ability of Ansar Allah (as the Houthis' political wing is known) to mobilize crowds across sectarian lines in opposition to the transitional government.[43] The substantive demands of the Houthi movement on the eve of September 2014 were focused on the exclusions produced by the transnational framework's institutional elitism, and failure to enact anti-corruption reforms long promised by the partisan opposition, which was rewarded by the transitional framework. In this context, the fact that the Houthi militia's primary missions when they entered Sana'a were symbolic attacks on the homes of prominent Islahis can be read less as sectarian animus (in which case, we might have expected them to be far less discerning in their targets) than as grievance with the institutional asymmetry of the transitional framework and their misrecognized exclusion as anti-republican spoilers. The reconstitution of the transitional government through the National Peace and Partnership Agreement in November 2014, however, was not a sign that political elites conceded that Houthi republicanism had been misrecognized by transitional planners and now welcomed their political inclusion. It was instead a reflection of the limits of Islah's position in relation to President Abdrabbuh Mansour Hadi, and a further shoring up of the relationship between President Hadi and Yemen's neighbors that alienated both Islah and the Houthis by further pitting them against one another.

As Houthis and Islahis locked into a stalemate, and government functioning was even further paralyzed, the new constitution-drafting committee released its recommendations in January 2015, including a provision for a federal redistricting plan that would have significantly limited the ability of the Houthi movement to advance cultural autonomy in traditionally Zaydi areas. During the takeover of Sana'a that almost immediately followed in January 2015, and into the early months of the war that spring, Houthi militants detained and arrested prominent Islahis, but there was little to suggest a widespread campaign against Sunni communities as such. At the time of this writing, however, military campaigns led by Houthi militias and their Salih-loyalist allies,[44] and by the Saudi-led coalition fighting on behalf of the transitional government, have engaged in collective punishment along sectarian lines. While some sectarian targets have had a transparent political logic—such as the destruction in May 2015 of the shrine to Hussein Badr al-Din al-Houthi, the founder of the movement—others have been far more indiscriminate, as when entire cities in the Northern highlands have been declared "war zones" by coalition forces, or cities with a predominantly Sunni demographic composition have been held under siege for months by Houthi–Salih forces.[45] These everyday realities of the war in Yemen have torn the social fabric in ways that may be irrecoverable.

Conclusion: Misrecognition in the Postwar Context

Contemplating a postwar Yemen is a painful exercise. The scale of human suffering produced by nearly a year of unceasing civil and international war, and the destruction of much of the country's critical infrastructure, will be a generation-long reconstruction challenge. It is unclear as of this writing what kind of polity (or polities) will emerge. But the long-term effects of the institutional and discursive misrecognition reflected in the post-2011 "transitional" framework designed by Western governments and their regional allies will not be displaced by the war and are likely to be deepened by any kind of postwar agreement that we might currently envision. In effect, the sectarian conflict that so many sought to avoid, and openly decried during the Arab uprisings, has been produced through war and has shaped lives and livelihoods in ways previously unimaginable.

A Yemen polarized along sectarian lines is now a social fact with which postwar planners will have to contend, despite building resentment of the Houthis even among their supporters.[46] The desire of Saudi Arabia to dictate the international response to the conflict—through its role at the UN and through its bilateral relationships with the USA and France in particular—is unlikely to change, given the Saudis' ever-present anxieties regarding Iran, which shape the kingdom's domestic and foreign policy.[47] The Saudi fixation on Iran has thus become both a lens and a strategy—a way of understanding the conflict in Yemen, and a way of setting aside, and ultimately destroying, the possibilities of convergent republicanism on Saudi Arabia's border.

11

SECTARIANIZATION AS SECURITIZATION

IDENTITY POLITICS AND COUNTER-REVOLUTION
IN BAHRAIN

Toby Matthiesen

The small island nation of Bahrain provides one of the most salient case studies of the sectarianization process.

Bahrain has a long history of organized political opposition that has taken the form of street protests, strikes, trade unions, and underground political parties, as well as in a parliament with limited powers (1973–1975 and since 2001). Anti-colonial nationalist and leftist movements of various ideological persuasions that mobilized many Bahrainis since the 1950s were cross-sectarian. The parliament of 1973–1975, under the influence of communists and Ba'athists, started to challenge the authoritarian system of government of the minority Sunni Al Khalifa family and the pervasive powers of the security services.[1] As a result, parliament was disbanded in the summer of 1975, elections were postponed indefinitely, and political opposition was driven underground. The decline of these cross-sectarian and secular political movements and the rise of Islamic groups were key factors in the growth of sectarian politics in the country.

Thereafter, Sunni Islamic movements such as the Muslim Brotherhood as well as Shi'a Islamist movements, such as the Da'wa Party, Hizbullah (the Line of Imam (Khomeini), or Khat al-Imam), and the so-called Shirazi movement (named after its spiritual guide, Muhammad Mahdi al-Shirazi), gained a foothold in Bahrain. The state built up Sunni Islamic movements as a counter-weight to the Shi'a Islamic movements that gained in prominence after Iran's 1979 revolution. Sunni Islamic groups, therefore, by and large did not mobilize in opposition to the monarchy. And while the uprising in 2011 started as a cross-sectarian mobilization, and the opposition tried to use national and not sectarian slogans, many Sunnis were frightened by it, and more or less supported the crackdown. Particularly as repression started to target the Shi'a as a group, many Shi'a, including some elite Shi'a families, started to see the state as an adversary. The regime used all means at its disposal, including the media, the security forces, and even vigilante groups, to scare the Sunnis with the specter of a Shi'a takeover, and to portray the uprising as led by Shi'a radicals who wanted to establish an Iranian-style Islamic republic.

Sectarianization in Bahrain is thus a deliberate and long-term strategy by the regime to undermine the possibility of a broad-based coalition demanding democratic change. But sectarianization and disproportionate policing of Shi'a residential areas has also sustained and strengthened opposition to the state amongst Shi'a Bahrainis, thereby undermining security and perpetuating sectarian divisions.

Securitization through Sectarianization

Scholars of critical security studies, in particular from the Copenhagen school, have coined the term *securitization* to describe the process by which political actors transform subjects that do not constitute existential threats to the survival or the territorial integrity of the state into matters of national security, thereby securitizing subjects and legitimizing extraordinary measures to "deal" with those "threats." Perceptions and speech acts, i.e. the ways politicians think and talk about certain "threats," are key.[2] Immigration; religious, ethnic, and linguistic diversity; a cosmopolitan and educated population—these can all be seen as assets and strengths for a country's success. Or they can become securitized. In this process, immigrant populations or particular ethnic, linguistic, or religious groups can be exposed to intense surveillance and repression, in turn leading to radicalization and alienation of those communities from the state and from the wider society. If these groups share some linguistic or ethnic affiliation with a powerful neighbor—as has often been the case in European history, for example—then securitization is even more straightforward and effective.[3]

The process of securitization has also been used as a policy by authoritarian states in the Middle East, particularly in the Gulf region, to deflate demands for social, economic, and political reform, voiced before and after 2011. Initially peaceful protests and demands by opposition groups soon became securitized. Sectarianization has been used in a number of Middle Eastern and South Asian countries with religiously heterogeneous populations, such as Lebanon, Syria, Iraq, Iran, Yemen, Pakistan, Afghanistan, and in the Gulf. Syrian and Iraqi leaders have been particularly skillful at this. The deliberate sectarianization of the Syrian uprising has been one of the main reasons why Bashar al-Assad has survived in power for so long since 2011.[4]

Cosmopolitanism and Gulf Cities

The cosmopolitan port cities of the Gulf region have long depended on religious, ethnic, and linguistic diversity to become the global hubs for goods, peoples, ideas, and arms that they are today.[5] Before 1979, and especially before the oil boom, the highly mobile, cosmopolitan, and internationally connected Shi'a merchant families formed the backbone of economic networks that led to the growth of Kuwait, Manama, Dubai, Bushehr, and other Gulf port cities.[6] Rulers of port towns vied for trading families—both Sunni and Shi'a, both Arab and Persian—to settle in their particular territory.[7]

Throughout much of the twentieth century Shi'a communities in Kuwait, for example, were allied to the ruling Al Sabah family, and could be relied upon to support the regime in conflicts with Sunni merchant families and a nascent Arab nationalist-led movement pushing for a constitutional monarchy.[8] In fact, earlier periods of securitization in the Gulf states focused more on the threat of leftist and Arab nationalist movements, particularly around the time of British withdrawal from the Gulf in 1970/71. From the 1950s onwards such movements posed probably the most serious domestic threats to the Gulf ruling families. One in particular, the Popular Front for the Liberation of the Occupied Arabian Gulf (PFLOAG), had transnational appeal and led the armed Dhofar uprising in Oman in the late 1960s and 1970s.

PFLOAG and similar groups were all cross-sectarian, and in particular the communist movements were distinctly cross-ethnic (including both Arabs and Persians). Securitization of these threats often led to the build-up of counter-forces, which included both Sunni and Shi'a Islamic movements. Moreover, in the smaller Gulf states, Iranian nationals (both Sunnis and Shi'a) were nationalized in order to counter the threat of Arab nationalism and of Arab migrant workers. Subsequently, Arab workers were themselves slowly displaced by migrant workers from South Asia, who were perceived as less politicized and less likely to make common cause with their Arab co-workers.[9]

Divide and rule, particularly the playing-off of different ethnic, sectarian, and tribal groups against one another, was thus a longstanding strategy of Gulf rulers. This may previously have been less visible because it did not single out one particular sectarian or ethnic group over a prolonged period of time. Since the Iranian revolution of 1979, however, the Shi'a populations on the Western (overwhelmingly Arab) side of the Persian Gulf have become securitized.

In Saudi Arabia the securitization and sectarianization of the Shi'a population goes back further still. Military forces that were loyal to the House of Saud and were trying to spread the Wahhabi dogma first conquered the Eastern Province (al-Ahsa/Hasa and Qatif) in the eighteenth century, and finally brought the region under direct control of the Al Saud family in 1913. Driven by missionary zeal, their treatment of the local Shi'a, who constituted the majority of the sedentary population in the area, was supposed to exemplify their determination to spread what they perceived to be the true and pure form of Islam. And so Shi'a mosques were destroyed, clerics killed, and at one point some of the Shi'a notables were forced to convert. Ever since, and in particular since 1979, the specter of popular Shi'a opposition has been portrayed as an issue of national security, delegitimizing any demands for equal citizenship rights from the Shi'a, with the aim of scaring the Sunnis (and the elite Shi'a families) so that they stand firmly behind the ruling family.[10]

A similar history of conquest lies at the core of the contemporary political system of Bahrain. The Al Khalifa family conquered Bahrain in the late eighteenth century, and subsequently took over many landhold-ings and properties. The local population, most of whom were Arab Shiʻa (called Baharna), became tenant farmers and were subject to an array of discriminatory taxes that drove them into destitution. Apart from agriculture, the main pillars of the economy were trade and pearl diving, all capital-intensive activities that concentrated wealth in the hands of a small upper class. The Al Khalifa family thus became the largest landholders, and also controlled other economic areas together with their allies, which included a few Shiʻa families but mostly Sunni families, some of whom had entered the island alongside them.

This resulted in a situation where the Baharna became a kind of underclass and developed a tight-knit community structure centered around popular religious practices and a feeling of oppression, which frequent Shiʻa mourning rituals brought out into the open. Communal conflicts and sporadic uprisings were a facet of modern Bahraini history.[11] Sectarian discrimination existed in Bahrain in the sense that Shiʻa had fewer chances than Sunnis to get jobs in the government and the security forces. Cultural and religious differences between the two sects persisted, too. On the other hand, however, intermarriage was not unheard of. Given the small size of the island, and in particular the emergence of Manama as a new commercial and political center, and the migration of many Bahrainis from their villages to Manama, a high degree of cross-sectarian interaction and cooperation became the norm. This became particularly pronounced when Sunni and Shiʻa Bahrainis cooperated in a struggle against British colonialism and the paternalistic authoritarian rule of the Al Khalifa from the 1950s onwards.[12]

Cross-Sectarian Solidarity and Contentious Politics

With the development of an oil industry, modern education, and the ever-increasing connectedness of Gulf port towns to other areas of the British Empire—from Egypt to India and beyond—anti-colonial move-ments and ideas, some coupled with socialist ideas, spread to Bahrain. The Bahraini national movement developed in part in response to sectar-ian tensions. In September 1953 urban riots and clashes between Sunnis and Shiʻa erupted during ʻAshura (a day of mourning for the death of Husayn, grandson of Muhammad, in Karbala, Iraq, in 680 CE—and a historical memory that divides the Sunni and Shiʻa sects of Islam). These clashes deepened the "construction of Sunnis and Shi'as as a modern political community."[13] As a reaction to the sectarian clashes, however, and to channel feelings of alienation away from communal chauvinism and toward resistance to the British presence, leaders from both sects formed the cross-sectarian nationalist political movement in Bahrain, the High Executive Committee (al-Hay'a al-Tanfidhiyya al-'Uliya), which became the driving force of popular protests in Bahrain in the 1950s. The High Executive Committee (HEC) was particularly dangerous to the British and the Al Khalifa because it incorporated various sections of society. In 1956 the leaders of the HEC were arrested and exiled, and many others were imprisoned at home.[14]

At the height of these mobilizations, in 1955, the Bahrain National Liberation Front (Jabhat al-Tahrir al-Watani al-Bahrayn, BNLF) was founded as an alliance of Bahrainis with a number of Iranian and Iraqi communists in exile in Bahrain. The BNLF had a substantial Shi'a and ethnically Persian base, but was avowedly anti-sectarian and anti-nationalist. In its 1962 program, for example, it described sectarianism as a tool employed by the British and the Al Khalifa to divide the local population. In an editorial in its mouthpiece *al-Jamahir* it claimed that the colonialists "exploited confessional differences (*furuq madhhabiyya*) by establishing an economy of sectarianism (*tijara al-ta'ifiyya*) to divide the people."[15]

The pan-Arab nationalists, the other main ideological trend at the time, had a more Sunni makeup, and its mother organization, the Movement of Arab Nationalists (Harakat al-Qawmiyyin al-'Arab, MAN), was initially quite avowedly anti-Iranian.[16] In 1965 a broad-based workers' uprising, in which the BNLF was key, paralyzed important sectors of the economy. It was suppressed harshly, leading to several casualties. In response to the uprising, the British government facilitated the appointment of Ian Henderson, a colonial police officer who had been key in the suppression of the Mau Mau rebellion in Kenya in the 1950s, as head of security in Bahrain. He would oversee the creation of a special investigations unit to track domestic opponents. This unit was also key in protecting the regime after the ruling monarch, Shaykh Isa, aborted the parliamentary experiment from 1973 to 1975 following Bahrain's independence from Britain in 1971.[17] The BNLF, and another initially Arab nationalist but increasingly Marxist–Leninist group, the Popular Front in Bahrain (al-Jabha al-sha'biyya fi al-Bahrayn), that had grown out of the MAN, were essentially cross-sectarian. They were both opposed to Britain's presence and the rule of the Al Khalifa, and at times advocated armed resistance. They were thus a serious threat to the regime, in particular because they were popular among both the working classes and the intelligentsia, especially students. The main threats to Bahrain and other Gulf monarchies in the 1960s and 1970s were thus leftist movements that successfully managed to bridge religious and ethnic divisions.

Sectarianization was a regime strategy aimed at undermining these cross-sectarian and secular opposition groups. The encouragement of religious and "traditional" forces, mainly clerics, was another such counter-revolutionary strategy, but one which likewise had the effect of strengthening communal sectarian solidarities, and heightening a sense of religiosity. Shi'a clerics worked against the communists during the 1973–1975 parliament, while the ruling family sponsored Sunni Islamic charities and clerics, including some associated with the Muslim Brotherhood, as a counter force.[18] So the sponsorship of religious forces and the rise of sectarianism went hand in hand, and were thus well under way even before the Iranian revolution of 1979. Repression and surveillance as well as the backing of loyalist and rival opposition forces were mechanisms the regime deployed to undermine cross-sectarian political movements.

Sectarianization through Policing and Social Engineering

Until the late 1970s this cross-sectarian and multi-ethnic composition of the opposition ensured that surveillance and repression did not target one particular ethnic or sectarian group in the country. But in the late 1970s and into the 1980s, when Shi'a Islamists, inspired by the new Islamic Republic of Iran, started to become the most powerful political opposition force on the island, security forces started to disproportionately target and police Shi'a villages and urban quarters.[19] The security forces, largely made up of foreign mercenaries and exclusively Sunni, had thus always been the main tool through which the regime shielded itself against possible threats, but the Shi'a had not always been singled out for repression. With the intensification of this disproportionate policing, however, a sense of alienation and victimhood amongst many Shi'a became more pronounced, and the state and its institutions became increasingly seen as hostile and Sunni-dominated. The split deepened throughout the 1980s, when relations between the Arab Gulf states and

Iran were at a low point and some Bahrainis went into exile in Iran. This trend became even worse during the Bahraini "Intifada" (1994–1999), when an uprising centered in Shi'a-dominated villages challenged the state, and dozens of activists were shot dead.[20]

From its inception the Bahraini police had a large number of non-Bahraini and mainly Sunni staff. They often hailed from other parts of the British Empire, such as Pakistan or Jordan, as well as from Syria and Yemen. The local Shi'a were by and large excluded from both the police and the army. The state has excluded the Shi'a from these sectors because, even though inclusion would result in less political alienation on the side of the Shi'a, Bahrain's Sunni rulers fear that this would "be inviting those citizens deemed most dangerous to walk in, so to speak, through the front door."[21]

This policy reinforced a sense of exclusion, and when these security forces were used against Shi'a protests or opposition groups, the Shi'a increasingly saw them as Sunni forces. Today, the mainly Shi'a opposition accuses the Bahraini government of trying to alter the demographic balance of the country from a Shi'a majority to equal percentages, or even a Sunni majority. The Sunni immigrants who come to work in the security sector are an important factor in this social engineering. They not only confront people at the checkpoints at the entrances to Shi'a villages, at demonstrations, or during raids, but also fulfill an important demographic role by their very presence. As such, they actively sectarianize Bahrain, by participating in the altering of the demographic makeup of the island.

The Urban Geography of Sectarianization

The security forces have also, since 2011, been used to further entrench preexisting divisions between urban, recently urbanized, and rural areas, and between broadly pro-uprising and pro-regime areas. The heavy policing of pro-uprising neighborhoods and villages—and the at times total lockdown of such areas for days or weeks—and the extensive use of tear gas as a form of collective punishment have become features of daily life on the island.[22] These practices are the result of transformations in Bahrain's urban geography over the past decades, which have seen the massive reclamation of land from the sea and a radical transformation of built-up areas, fueled by and fueling real-estate speculation. These developments had negative byproducts for villages that were formerly by the sea and for the quality of life in many other areas (falling groundwater levels, pollution, etc.). And many of these villages are the areas that the poorer Shi'a live in. In essence, this "spatial-demographic revolution," as it has been termed, has been a key driver of the uprising, and policing has since 2011 reinforced spatial divisions that Bahrain's urban planning attempted to achieve in the first place.[23]

While earlier protest movements from the 1950s to the 1970s were centered in the cities of Manama and Muharraq, the so-called "1990s Intifada" and the post-2011 uprising have followed the inverse pattern. Since mid-March 2011 the protests have been largely confined to the villages and outlying suburbs of Manama, while the urban centers of Manama and Muharraq, and the business district, are policed so heavily that protesters refrain from going there, except for brief flash-mob-like actions that are quickly dispersed.[24] The occupation of the Pearl Roundabout, which was a briefly successful attempt to reclaim public space, ended with the destruction of this iconic structure and the creation of a (heavily guarded) traffic intersection.[25]

The crackdown and the ensuing heavy policing have thus further entrenched divisions on the island, and driven protests out into the periphery. There, however, they continue on an almost daily basis. A dialogue process that included parts of the opposition has stalled, arguably because the ruling family was not prepared to make significant concessions.[26] The opposition boycotted elections for municipal councils and the lower house of the bicameral parliament, which highlighted the political polarization of the island.[27] The marginalization of protest out of the commercial center also has a decidedly sectarian dimension. Unlike in the main cities, the villages are often quite neatly divided between the different sectarian communities, and so protests in mainly Shi'a villages will be largely out of sight of many Sunnis. As such, this spatial dimension of protest and policing also has a sectarian dimension, and hardens sectarian divisions, particularly when we take into account the sectarian composition of the security forces.

Sectarianizing the Narrative of the Uprising

Apart from policing and straightforward repression, a discursive sectarianization strategy, which took shape through the official and semi-official media, social media, and government statements, was pivotal. As in other Middle Eastern countries, the media in Bahrain is tightly controlled. It is freer than in some neighboring countries, but political pressure, ambiguities of financing, and restrictive laws severely limit the Bahraini media's range of motion. The government directly controls Bahrain television, the Bahrain News Agency, and a number of newspapers, while the rest of the newspapers can be seen as semi-official.

Most Bahraini media outlets thus portrayed the uprising as led by a violent mob seeking to overthrow the government. The only newspaper that can be classified as independent and that did cover the uprising in a positive light was *al-Wasat*, and it was temporarily closed in response. All the other newspapers went along with the government narrative. Bahrain television immediately portrayed the protests as foreign inspired, linked to Iran, and a threat to the nation.

From quite early on in the uprising the regime drew connections between the 2011 protests and the failed 1981 coup attempt by the Islamic Front for the Liberation of Bahrain (al-Jabha al-Islamiyya li-Tahrir al-Bahrayn, IFLB). The former leader of the IFLB, Hadi al-Mudarrisi, did indeed appear on Shi'a satellite channels based in Iraq and called for the overthrow of the Al Khalifa, and this in turn was used by the regime media to further the narrative that this was a foreign-directed conspiracy. Regime media also spread messages that the (Shi'a) protesters and "rioters," as they were usually called, were deliberately attacking Sunni civilians. This was done to instill fear in the Sunni population that, in the event of a successful revolution, they would face a similar fate to the Sunnis of Iraq. The use of social media was another—and perhaps the key—tool, in sectarianizing the narrative around the uprising,[28] spreading rumors and uncertainty, particularly amongst Sunnis and expatriates in Bahrain, and to instigate a witch-hunt on protesters.[29] This push to rally the Sunnis around the ruling family and the regime was also related to factionalism in the ruling family itself.

A related development, and one that was given much coverage in pro-regime media, was the emergence of loyalist "opposition" blocs, in particular the National Unity Gathering. While presenting some demands to the government, and classifying themselves as in "opposition" to the government, the group and a similar youth movement called al-Fatih Youth, was in effect used as a counter-revolutionary force. Despite the importance of its counter-mobilizations at the al-Fatih mosque at the time of the Pearl

Roundabout protests, it then failed to establish an independent position for itself on the Bahraini political scene. Highlighting this fact, the National Unity Gathering failed to win a single seat in the 2014 parliamentary elections, despite the boycott of the elections by the opposition.[30]

Royal Factionalism

On February 17, 2011 it seemed as if the security forces had retreated and left the Bahraini street to the protesters. Less than a month later a state of emergency was declared, Gulf Cooperation Council (GCC) troops—mainly from Saudi Arabia and the United Arab Emirates—moved in, and security forces started perhaps the largest and most pervasive crackdown in the history of the island. While the Bahraini crown prince, Salman bin Hamad Al Khalifa, was trying to reach a negotiated agreement with the opposition, in particular with the Shi'a political party al-Wifaq, other members of the Al Khalifa family, and the security apparatus, were preparing for a "security solution" to the mass protests.

The intensity of this crackdown can be explained in part by factional politics within the ruling family. The faction that has its power base in the various security institutions felt deeply threatened by the protest movement. The security minded-factions of the Al Khalifa family are led by the prime minister, Khalifa bin Salman Al-Khalifa, as well as by a faction of the ruling family that is known as the Khawalids. The Khawalids stem from a different branch of the Al Khalifa family than the king and the crown prince—they are descendants of Khalid bin Ali Al-Khalifa, and feel disenfranchised in the succession to the throne. They were sidelined by the British but have regained increasing importance over the past decade, and they now hold key positions: the royal court minister, Khalid bin Ahmad Al-Khalifa; the commander of the Bahrain Defense Forces (BDF), Khalifa bin Ahmad Al-Khalifa; and the minister of justice, Khalid bin Ali Al-Khalifa, are all Khawalid.[31]

Prime Minister Khalifa bin Salman, who has been in his position since 1970, was a focal point of the protesters, who called for his resignation. So while the king and his son, the crown prince, could have expected to survive in their positions and even potentially be strengthened through a political settlement, the prime minister and the Khawalid faction would have been weakened, and might have lost their positions. So the "security solution," which they subsequently imposed on Bahrain, and which led to the deaths of dozens, the exile of many others, and the dismissal and imprisonment of thousands, was partly a result of elite fragmentation and rivalry.[32]

The securitization of Bahrain has shifted the power dynamics in intra-ruling family struggles more toward the security-minded branches of the family. Shi'a are being marginalized even more in key state institutions, while naturalization of foreign Sunnis is ongoing. So the Shi'a, whom King Hamad and the crown prince had wooed in the decade before 2011, are becoming less and less important as potential bases of support in intra-regime power struggles. In essence, the security sector has learned to live, and indeed thrive, off the demonstrations and the ongoing uprising. (This is, of course, not a phenomenon unique to Bahrain, as multiple chapters in this volume attest.) The prime minister, who as mentioned above had been a key target of the uprising, has emerged as the symbolic defender of the Sunnis, an image his followers have been spreading on social media and in gatherings with members of the Sunni constituency in Bahrain.

The Crackdown

Bahrain could not have gone down the securitization route without the strong support of external backers, who for decades have assisted the security apparatus and provided political cover for rights abuses and authoritarianism. This includes, most critically, the former colonial power in Bahrain, the UK, whose response to the crackdown has been one of almost unwavering support for the Al Khalifa family, and its criticism of the crackdown even more muted than that of the USA, who maintain a key naval base in the country.[33]

The GCC and other Arab and Sunni allies (such as Jordan and Pakistan), as well as important business partners of the GCC in the West, also provided much-needed political cover. Bahrain was also helped by the sheer amount of world-historic events unfolding in a short span of time. Attention quickly shifted elsewhere in March 2011, particularly to Libya, where the uprising against Muamar Qadhafi gained pace and drew in the international community. In her memoir, former US Secretary of State Hillary Clinton acknowledges that the United Arab Emirates had threatened to pull out of the coalition against Qadhafi if the United States had taken a harsher stance toward the Bahraini regime.[34] Saudi support for that military intervention was likewise linked to US acquiescence on the crackdown in Bahrain.[35]

Despite their large numbers, the protesters were no match for a brutal crackdown by heavily armed security forces. Despite the regime's claims to the contrary, the vast majority of protesters were unarmed. The small island's geography, with no natural hideouts, does not lend itself to armed struggle. In addition, the sheer numbers in the security forces were overwhelming (and thousands more have been recruited since 2011). Because they are largely made up of foreigners or naturalized officers, who feel little sympathy with the uprising, there was little danger that they would defect or resist orders. Moreover, the arrival of GCC military units (and most likely Jordanian Special Forces) tilted the military balance even further in the regime's favor. Finally, the regime escalated its sectarian rhetoric and reinforced divisions that split the island's population more or less along sectarian lines. This ensured that while the majority of the population felt alienated by the crackdown, a significant percentage of citizens (mainly Sunni) supported or at least tacitly accepted it.[36] A related but more subtle narrative that was propagated by the regime was that Bahrain is an inherently multicultural place, with a large number of expatriates. Allowing free elections would empower a Shi'a majority led by nativist Islamist parties that might undermine this multiculturalism.[37]

The widespread arrest campaign in response to the uprising disproportionately targeted Shi'a Muslims. So did a campaign to lay off workers who had participated in the strikes that had been called by the major trade unions in support of the uprising. While Sunnis also participated in the strikes, strikers were overwhelmingly Shi'a, and the punishment was therefore directed at Shi'a trade union members.[38] There was also a witch-hunt on social media, but supported by the state broadcaster Bahrain TV, to identify everyone who had attended protests on the roundabout in order to enable their dismissal from government jobs and government-affiliated companies. According to conservative estimates at least 4,500 people, 2,500 from the private sector and 2,000 from the public sector, were fired for responding to the strike calls and for participating in protests. Several dozen medical personnel were also fired, and some even arrested, tortured, and given long prison sentences, for continuing to treat wounded people from the protest sites when the government had ordered a ban on such treatment.[39] Again, while some Sunnis were also caught up in this, these measures specifically targeted the Shi'a professional classes, inflicting a heavy economic punishment on top of the physical and ideational repression.

The Radicalization of the Sectarian Fringes

The heightened sectarian atmosphere in Bahrain had a dangerous byproduct: it provided a fertile breeding ground for extremist ideas. A number of Bahrainis or descendants of migrants from other countries working in Bahrain, including in the security sector, went to Syria to join the uprising, and some later joined ISIS. Abdelaziz Kuwan, for example, grew up as the son of Syrian parents in Bahrain, and then went to study *shari'a* in Saudi Arabia. He went to Syria to fight in 2012, later joined ISIS, and was motivated by his hatred of the *rafidha*, the "rejectionists," as some Sunnis derogatorily call the Shi'a, a hatred he internalized while in Bahrain and Saudi Arabia.[40] One of the most important ISIS ideologues and organizers, Turki al-Binali, is a young Bahraini cleric, whose family has very close ties to the Al Khalifa family. As a Sunni Bahraini from a family perceived to be loyal to the Gulf rulers, he could travel across the region in the years preceding the establishment of ISIS to mobilize people and establish networks of support. Several other members of his family have also joined ISIS.[41]

While at the time of writing ISIS has not managed to carry out an attack on Shi'a mosques in Bahrain, it is clear that this is one of the aims of the ISIS franchises in the Gulf and the Arabian Peninsula. They have carried out one devastating such attack on a Shi'a mosque in Kuwait, several on Shi'a civilians in Saudi Arabia's Eastern Province, one on an Ismaili mosque in Najran, and several on Zaydi/Houthi targets, including mosques, in Yemen. ISIS has thus emerged as a radical sectarian actor that is taking the sectarian rhetoric promulgated mainly in Saudi Arabia but increasingly used across the region, including in Bahrain, to its logical conclusion. The prospect of sectarian violence in Bahrain is thus real, even if the sophistication and level of political experience, as well as the restraint of the opposition, have prevented this so far.

In response to the crackdown fringes of the Shi'a opposition have also embraced armed struggle as a viable form of resistance. Much speculation abounds over whether the grand announcements of the government that it regularly dismantles Iranian- or Iraqi-trained cells and intercepts large weapons shipments or finds weapons caches are true. Most likely many of these reports are fabricated or doctored to fit the regime's anti-Iranian narrative that sees all opposition as foreign inspired. But some of these allegations may well be true, and sophisticated attacks on security forces are becoming more common.[42] These have led to casualties amongst security forces. Some of these fringe groups have adopted Shi'a revolutionary rhetoric and abandoned the earlier more egalitarian discourse and demands of the February 14 uprising. While they are openly advocating the overthrow of the Al Khalifa regime by any means possible, they are not anti-Sunni per se, and cannot be equated with Sunni jihadi groups whose aim it is to kill Shi'a civilians and start a civil war between Sunni and Shi'a in the Gulf. Nonetheless, the prospect of the militarization of the fringes as a result of sectarianization is real.

Conclusion

The post-2011 Bahrain uprising should not be explained with reference to a simple sectarian narrative of a Shi'a majority rising up against a Sunni minority. The uprising was fueled by a whole range of grievances, not all of which were directly related to sectarianism. Bahrain's political economy was and is based on a small group of elite families that get access to benefits and largesse handed out by the Al Khalifa family, which sits at the top of the political pyramid. These loyalist elite families are often Sunni, but several important Shi'a families are also amongst this class. The marginalization of a Shi'a underclass and of the Shi'a villages is more the product of uneven development on the island, and a political economy based on the exclusion of the majority and the rewarding of a minority of loyalists, than of sectarian discrimination per se.[43]

There was some support for the February 14 uprising from various Sunni constituencies, and Sunni leftist opposition leaders such as Ibrahim Sharif, who have been jailed for their role in the uprising, undermine the sectarian narrative pushed by the regime and largely adopted by mainstream media in the West and by Gulf-funded Arab media. The portrayal of the uprising as Shi'a in nature was thus a regime strategy to prevent a truly cross-sectarian opposition movement that could lead to its fall.

Bahrain was not the only country whose autocratic leaders used sectarianism to divide the opposition and deflect attention toward foreign enemies who were allegedly "stoking sectarian conflict." Saudi Arabia has done so, but Iraq's Nuri al-Maliki and the Ba'ath regime in Syria have mastered this as well. As a result, the various uprisings and wars in the regions are increasingly connected, while at the same time powerful states try to further their aims and push their narratives across borders. The Saudi-Iranian rivalry has come to be one key fault line, and because both countries mainly use proxies that broadly conform to their sectarian outlook and use sectarianism in foreign policy, the Sunni-Shi'a narrative has become the dominant frame to analyze conflicts in the Mashriq (the eastern Arab world), while also becoming a way in which actors understand and legitimize their actions. A sectarian identity entrepreneur, whether he is an MP in Kuwait, a rebel leader in Syria, or an editor-in-chief in Beirut, can be sure to get support from his patrons by buying into that sectarian master frame. Bahrain's revolutionaries might not be particularly sectarian, but Bahrain is of such regional and geostrategic significance that its political future is tied up with the future of the wider region. So for now, Bahrain cannot escape the machinations of its two large neighbors (Saudi Arabia and Iran) as well as of its international patrons (the United States and Britain). The sectarianization of the Bahrain uprising has thus increasingly turned into a self-fulfilling prophecy. It is important, however, to remember that sectarianism originated as a ruling strategy, as a conscious decision by colonial powers and Middle Eastern elites to structure society according to ascriptive group identities in order to divide and rule. It has, by and large, worked, in the sense that it has kept these elites in power, but the costs to the wider region and to Muslims around the world have been enormous.

12

THE ARCHITECTURE OF SECTARIANIZATION
IN LEBANON

Bassel F. Salloukh

The popular uprisings that swept across the Arab world starting in Tunisia in December 2010, and the domestic and geopolitical responses they elicited, securitized sectarian identities where these had often over-lapped with other—in many cases more pertinent—class, regional, or tribal affiliations.[1] In the process, invariably polyphonic and cross-cutting identities were reimagined and reconstructed along chauvinistic and reductionist sectarian fault lines. Many Arab societies have been vivi-sected along newly securitized vertical cleavages, leaving a number of states and regimes in utter ruins. By contrast, Lebanon's political system seems immune from this sectarian wave, but for all the wrong reasons.

Of all the Arab states, Lebanon has had the longest and most uninter-rupted experience with the sectarianization of political identities and con-flicts. But the institutionalization of sectarian identities in Lebanon's political system is a legacy of the country's process of state-formation, not of primordial forces.[2] It was the socioeconomic upheavals of mid-nine-teenth-century Mount Lebanon, when a commoners' rebellion against feudal lords overlapped with Ottoman reforms, elite attempts to quash subaltern demands, and European intervention in the politics of the Ottoman Empire that collectively forged a new sectarian political order, which replaced the traditional order anchored on rank and routine.[3]

Practically and geographically, this new sectarian order took shape in December 1842, when the Ottoman and European powers divided Mount Lebanon into two unbalanced districts, or *qa'imaqamiyya*, along explicitly Druze and Maronite religious lines. This sectarian reimagining of Mount Lebanon was reinforced in 1845, when Şekib Efendi's *Règlement* introduced new administrative councils based on sectarian identities to the *qa'imaqamiyya* system. However, the tensions inherent in the unstable double *qa'imaqamiyya* system soon expressed themselves in both class (Maronite–Maronite) and sectarian (Druze–Maronite) conflicts that ultimately exploded in the bloodbaths of 1860.[4] The subsequent promulgation of the June 9, 1861 *Règlement Organique* of the *mutasarifiyya* of Mount Lebanon (1861–1914), to end what by then had developed into a full-fledged communal war, institutionalized a more intricate form of sectarian representation. As Ussama Makdisi notes, "Every article in the *Règlement* indicated that the new order was to be sectarian."[5]

The Ottoman and European powers imposed on the inhabitants of Mount Lebanon "a single identity, where one's sect defined one's involvement in the public sphere and one's ability to be appointed to office, to govern, to collect taxes, and to punish."[6] By 1864, when Mount Lebanon's new political regime was finalized, its administrative council consisted of four Maronite members, three Druze, two Greek Orthodox, one Greek Catholic, one Sunni Muslim, and one Shi'a Muslim, proportionally mirroring the area's demographic balance of power as shown in Table 12.1. Instead of the previous overlapping and malleable identities of rank and religion, the new order was based on fixed sectarian affiliations, historically constructed but now reimagined as primordial givens.

In the next section I unpack how these historically constructed sectarian identities were institutionalized into Lebanon's multiple pre- and postwar power-sharing arrangements, giving rise to the sectarianization of identity politics, communal relations, and modes of political mobilization. This is followed by an analysis of the technologies of sectarianization that make up the complex ensemble of institutional, clientelist, and discursive practices collectively sustaining the sectarian system's political economy and ideological hegemony. The discussion then draws on the experience of the summer 2015 garbage crisis protests as an example of the myriad forms of resistance to the sectarian system, and how the sectarian elite deploy their institutional, material, and coercive capabilities to contain and sabotage such resistance. This is followed by an analysis of the impact of the overlapping domestic/external contests over post-Syria Lebanon, and sectarianized geopolitical contests after the popular uprisings, on the country's sectarian politics and tensions. The chapter closes by highlighting the postwar power-sharing arrangement's *cul-de-sac*, suggesting the need for its imaginative rethinking.

Table 12.1: Percentage of Christian and Muslim Sects: 1913–2011[7]

Year	1913	1932	1975	2011
Christians				
Maronite	58.3	28.8	23	19.31
Greek Orthodox	12.6	9.8	7	6.75
Greek Catholic	7.7	5.9	5	4.375
Other	0.8	6.8	5	4.292
Total Percentage	79.4	51.3	40	34.9
Muslims				
Shi'a	5.6	19.6	27	29.375
Sunni	3.5	22.4	26	29.375
Druze	11.4	6.8	7	5.479
Total Percentage	20.5	48.8	60	65.1
Total Population	414,963	786,000	2.55 million	4.8 million

Institutionalizing Sectarianism in Lebanon

There was nothing inevitable about the export of the Mount Lebanon sectarian order into the politics of the 1920 French-created state of Grand Liban, one that included the *mutasarifiyya* and its mainly Muslim hinterlands plus Beirut. That this ultimately transpired was the result of French Mandate policies, the instrumental policies of sectarian identity entrepreneurs or *zu'ama*,[8] and attempts to reconcile different visions of a polity deeply divided along overlapping religious, regional, socioeconomic, and cultural lines.[9]

Indeed, the sectarianization of politics in Lebanon was ultimately the result of elite accommodation in a nascent but deeply divided society. This elite institutionalized historically constructed sectarian identities into a static power-sharing arrangement, one that served their own political and economic interests. In this respect, Lebanon is an example of a corporate consociational power-sharing arrangement. Unlike its liberal variant, which assumes political identity as malleable and endogenous to political institutions, corporate consociation takes identities as primordial and unchanging, and hence exogenous to institutional arrangements.[10] With its emphasis on predetermined sectarian identities and fixed sectarian quotas, Lebanon's brand of corporate consociation is a textbook case of how *not* to engineer power-sharing arrangements in plural societies.[11] Two elite pacts have hitherto shaped Lebanon's pre- and postwar corporate power-sharing arrangements, in the process sectarianizing everything from political identity, state institutions, and popular mobilization to family law, civil society associations, the media and public sphere, and the practices of everyday life.[12]

The 1943 National Pact, or al-Mithaq al-Watani, represented an unwritten gentlemen's agreement between the Maronite president, Bishara al-Khouri, and the Sunni prime minister, Riyad al-Solh.[13] Negotiated with the help of Great Britain, Syria, and Egypt, it essayed a reconciliation between the state's binary political ideologies: Lebanism and Arabism. Consequently, the National Pact described Lebanon as an independent state with a *visage arabe*. To the Christians this meant that Lebanon was geographically part of the Arab world, but was not itself an Arab state. The Muslims, on the other hand, assumed Lebanon's Arabness a matter of fact and history. The National Pact also committed Muslims to renouncing any demands to reunite with Syria and to accepting the continued existence of Lebanon as an independent and sovereign state, provided it considered itself part of the Arab fold and Christians renounced external—namely, French—tutelage.

Institutionally, the National Pact created a fixed sectarian quota system whereby public offices, cabinet portfolios, and parliamentary seats were intricately divided among the different sects. The all-powerful presidency was reserved for the Maronites in what was supposed to be a genuine partnership between Christians and Muslims in the administration of state affairs, while the premier was to be Sunni and the speaker of parliament Shi'a. By contrast, the constitution deposited in the presidency substantial executive prerogatives, elevating it to the single most powerful office in the post-independence state. This created a dissonant duality between the spirit of the National Pact and the letter of the constitution.[14] The presidency possessed formal and informal powers that allowed the president to dominate the state's political, security, financial, and judicial institutions. Furthermore, the president's prerogatives were buttressed by Maronite control over the most sensitive security and military posts in the state. The president's Maronite protégés headed the Sureté Générale, the army, and military intelligence (Deuxiéme Bureau).

In parliament, and to address Christian fears about becoming a permanent minority in a mainly Muslim Arab world, the ratio of Christian to Muslim deputies was fixed at 6:5. Yet within this ratio, and in every electoral district, seats were divided among the different sects along a fixed, predetermined sectarian quota depending on the district's demographic balance of power. A simple plurality electoral system in often gerrymandered districts enabled the sectarian political elite to predetermine the results of the elections to a large extent.[15] Cabinet, a grand coalition where posts are distributed proportionally among the different sects, was equally dominated by the presidency. Per Article 53 of the constitution's 1947 amendment, the president was empowered to appoint cabinet ministers, designate one of them premier, and dismiss them.[16] The president could also, with cabinet's consent, dismiss parliament.[17]

The sectarianization of politics in Lebanon was not limited to the distribution of public offices and the architecture of political institutions alone, however. The constitution consecrated confessional groups and sects as the main pillars of Lebanese society. It granted sectarian communities substantial non-territorial autonomy in administering their own affairs, especially those pertaining to religious and cultural matters. For example, Article 9 obliges the state to "pay homage to God Almighty" and to:

> respect all religions and sects and guarantee the freedom to exercise all religious rites under its protection provided these do not disturb public order. It also guarantees for all, irrespective of their sects, the respect of their personal status laws and religious wellbeing.[18]

On this view, then, family law was the preserve of state-recognized sectarian courts. Religious elites prohibited the state from promulgating an optional civil marriage law, lest this undermine the sectarian system's ideological hegemony.[19] Lebanese citizens are thus intentionally made subjects of sectarian communities. Their recognition by the state is derivative of their membership in predefined sectarian groups. It follows, then, that secular citizens or atheists have no place in this sectarianized social system. Similarly, Article 10 of the constitution declares that "education is free ... as long as [it does not] jeopardize the dignity of any of the religions or sects."[20] The same article makes sacrosanct the right of all religious groups to establish their own private schools. Other civil society organizations—such as scouts, sport clubs, and philanthropic organizations—are divided along confessional and sectarian lines.

These foundational constitutional articles made Lebanon a collection of disparate sects, each with their own "visions of Lebanon."[21] Consequently, sects, rather than state institutions, monopolize people's political allegiances, while the sectarian political elite use their control of state resources and access to public offices to create sophisticated clientelist networks mobilizing and controlling their protégés. The result is the hardening of confessional and sectarian identities at the expense of other potential identities (class, regional, or cross-sectarian). The sectarianization of politics in Lebanon was thus never a product of timeless primordial identities or a sectarian political culture; it is, rather, the consequence of a complex ensemble of institutional, clientelist, and discursive practices operating to produce and reproduce docile sectarian subjects driven by sectarian incentive structures.[22]

Paradoxically, the October 22, 1989 Ta'if Accord that ended Lebanon's 1975–1990 civil war retained and expanded the political system's sectarian architecture, thus further entrenching the sectarianization of political identities and conflicts. A postwar power-sharing arrangement replacing the 1943 National Pact, it consecrated sects as the main pillars of political identity and mobilization in postwar Lebanon. It recalibrated the sectarian system in a manner reflecting the new domestic and regional balance of power, but did not entertain dismantling it.[23] In fact, the Ta'if Accord acknowledges the persistent fears that all Lebanese sects feel about being dominated by other confessional groups or coalitions of sects. To ameliorate these fears, and in typical consociational practice, Ta'if institutionalized a basic mutual veto among all sects. Consequently, the Ta'if Accord, and later the preamble of the constitution, proscribes any authority or policy that negates the "covenant of mutual coexistence" among all Lebanese sects.[24] What this loose constitutional proviso amounts to is veto power by each of the country's eighteen sects over any policy that any sect may deem threatening to its political prerogatives, cultural identity, or foreign relations.

The Ta'if Accord advanced a new formula to negotiate alternative cultural visions of the nation among different Muslim and Christian segments of the population. Lebanon was thus declared a country with "an Arab identity and belonging,"[25] a slippery and vague formulation that glides over rather than reconciles what continue to be deep cultural divisions among different segments of the population. Indeed, by way of confessional and communal practices, many parts of the country continue to inhabit separate worlds. More concretely, the postwar pact shifted the balance of executive power away from the Maronite president, placing it instead in the council of ministers in its collective capacity. This council, a grand coalition of sects, became the real custodian of executive authority. This naturally empowered the Sunni premier's office, establishing the council of ministers as an institution independent from the once all-powerful presidency.[26]

Presidential prerogatives were consequently constrained in the new decision-making mechanisms stipulated in Ta'if. Section 5 of Article 65 of the constitution declares that decisions in the council of ministers should be taken in a consociational manner, but failing that, by a majority vote of the ministers attending the cabinet session. "Basic topics," however—which include constitutional amendments, declaring a state of emergency, decisions on war and peace, international treaties, the state budget, long-term development plans, appointments to the top echelons of the public sector, redesigning the state's administrative boundaries, dismissing parliament and ministers, electoral laws, citizenship laws, and personal status (family) laws—all require the approval of two-thirds of the total number of ministers in the council.[27] This two-thirds vote amounts to another mutual veto over important decisions in the council of ministers. Moreover, the president can only postpone decisions taken in the council of ministers by a two-thirds majority for a maximum period of one month, after which he is obliged to publish them in the official gazette.[28]

Yet although the Ta'if Accord stripped the Maronite presidency of much of its prewar executive authority, it nevertheless retained for it a crucial role in executive power-sharing. Henceforth, formation of the council of ministers became the privilege of a three-way partnership involving the Maronite president, the Sunni premier, and the Shi'a speaker of parliament. Presidential consent is a precondition for its formation; otherwise the president will not sign the decree forming the council of ministers.[29] Given the aforementioned two-thirds super majority proviso for the council of ministers' decisions, presidents in the post-Syria era have consequently attempted to control the votes of at least one-third plus one of the total number of ministers.

Other constitutional amendments adopted by the Ta'if Accord also recalibrated the postwar balance of sectarian power. By strengthening parliamentary oversight over the executive, and making it almost impossible for the council of ministers to dissolve parliament, Ta'if increased the powers of the Shi'a speaker of parliament vis-à-vis both the council of ministers and the legislative assembly. The speaker is elected for a four-year term, equal to parliament's tenure, and is subject to a very difficult two-thirds vote of confidence, albeit only at the end of the second year of his tenure.[30] The speaker may ignore bills sent to parliament by the council of ministers, and is under no obligation to convene parliament outside constitutionally prescribed regular sessions. These prerogatives allow the Shi'a speaker to play a decisive role in the selection of the Sunni premier and the election of the Maronite president.

Ta'if applied the principle of equal confessional division of public offices. The prewar 6:5 quota in parliament in favor of Christians was replaced by a 5:5 one. Parliamentary seats were redistributed proportionally among the sects in the different electoral districts, as shown in Table 12.2. However, and given their postwar demographic weight, as demonstrated in Table 12.1, Maronites are overrepresented in parliament, and also in the council of ministers, where the number of portfolios they receive is equal to that of the Shi'a and Sunnis. Moreover, the distribution of all public posts is governed by delicate sectarian calculations. Although Maronites continue to occupy important positions in the public sector, Muslim sects captured important positions in the postwar civil and military bureaucracy. In fact, the postwar sectarian quota is far more sophisticated than the prewar one. Recruitment to the public sector is part of a complex ensemble protecting the political, economic, and security prerogatives of sectarian elites, while lubricating their clientelist networks.

Technologies of Sectarianization

Although anchored on this institutional architecture, the reproduction of sectarianism in Lebanon is the result of a far more complex material and

Table 12.2: Sectarian Distribution of Parliamentary Seats in 2009 Elections[31]

Electoral District	Seats/District	Number Of Seats Per Sect
Mount Lebanon (6 Districts)	35	
Northern Metn	8	4 Maronite, 2 Greek Orthodox, 1 Greek Catholic, 1 Armenian Orthodox
Shuf	8	3 Maronite, 2 Druze, 2 Sunni, 1 Greek Catholic
Ba'abda	6	3 Maronite, 2 Shi'a, 1 Druze
'Alay	5	2 Druze, 2 Maronite, 1 Greek Orthodox
Jbayl	3	2 Maronite, 1 Shi'a
Kiserwan	5	5 Maronite
North (1 District)	28	
'Akkar	7	3 Sunni, 1 Maronite, 2 Greek Orthodox, 1 'Alawi
Minieh–Dennieh	3	3 Sunni
Bshari	2	2 Maronite
Tripoli	8	5 Sunni, 1 Maronite, 1 Greek Orthodox, 1 'Alawi
Zgharta	3	3 Maronite
Batroun	2	2 Maronite
al-Koura	3	3 Greek Orthodox
Beirut (3 Districts)	19	
Beirut 1 Achrafieh–Rmeil–Saifi	5	1 Maronite, 1 Greek Orthodox, 1 Greek Catholic, 1 Armenian Orthodox, 1 Armenian Catholic
Beirut 2 Bachoura–Medawar–Port	4	2 Armenian Orthodox, 1 Sunni, 1 Shi'a
Beirut 3 Mazra'a–Msaytbé–'Ain el-Mraysé–Mina al-Hosn–Ras Beirut–Zqaq el-Blat	10	1 Greek Orthodox, 1 Evangelical, 1 Minorities (Christian), 1 Druze, 5 Sunni, 1 Shi'a
Beqa' (3 Districts)	23	
Ba'albak–Hermel	10	6 Shi'a, 2 Sunni, 1 Maronite, 1 Greek Catholic
Zahlé	7	2 Greek Catholic, 1 Sunni, 1 Maronite, 1 Shi'a, 1 Armenian Orthodox, 1 Greek Orthodox
Western Beqa'–Rashaya	6	2 Sunni, 1 Maronite, 1 Greek Orthodox, 1 Shi'a, 1 Druze
South (1 District)	23	
Sidon	2	2 Sunni

al-Zahrani	3	2 Shi'a, 1 Greek Catholic
Jezzine	3	2 Maronite, 1 Greek Catholic
Tyre	4	4 Shi'a
Nabatiyé	3	3 Shi'a
Bint Jbayl	3	3 Shi'a
Hasbaya–Marje'youn	5	2 Shi'a, 1 Sunni, 1 Druze, 1 Greek Orthodox

symbolic process that involves a whole array of technologies of social reproduction, material domination, and national imagination;[32] the sectarianization of public policies, the provision of social welfare, and the distribution of public expenditures;[33] and sectarian elite strategies sabotaging cross-sectarian or anti-sectarian civil society organizations promoting alternatives to sectarian identities and forms of political mobilization.[34]

The political economy of sectarianism in Lebanon is undergirded by a highly regressive tax system, sectarianized fiscal policies that impoverish the lower and middle classes while enriching an increasingly integrated sectarian and economic postwar elite and protecting their commercial, financial, and tertiary rentier profits. The overlapping alliance between members of the sectarian elite and the country's commercial–financial oligarchy manipulates "sectarianism to uphold class."[35] Sectarianism is deployed to camouflage wide income disparities among regions but also within sects, and to obfuscate debates about the country's political economy.[36] Sectarianism also serves as a country-wide patronage system that enables an otherwise discordant alliance of political and economic elites to maintain their control over the economy; perpetuates a lopsided economic model privileging investment in the tertiary sector at the expense of the productive sectors; protects existing business cartels; and impedes the emergence of a trans-sectarian working-class consciousness and concomitant interest-based rather than identity-based political affiliations.[37] Whether in dividing the state apparatus into elite-recognized sectarian fiefdoms, exposing state finances and the country's natural resources to the predatory neopatrimonial appetites of sectarian elites, protecting corrupt clients and institutions, perpetuating regional and sectoral economic disparities, politicizing everything—from the judiciary and the state's oversight agencies to public-sector appointments, sports activities and university campuses[38]—or sanctioning different forms of violence (especially against women and the voiceless), sectarianism is often invoked as a fig-leaf to normalize a type of everyday lawlessness that, in turn, impedes the emergence of any semblance of rule of law and transparent and accountable institutions.

The complex ensemble of institutional, clientelist, and discursive practices collectively sustains the political economy and ideological hegemony of Lebanon's sectarian system.[39] The disciplinary tentacles of this system reach deep into Lebanese society, and operate to produce and reproduce sectarian identities, loyalties, and forms of political mobilization. These practices ultimately manufacture disciplined sectarian subjects who embrace what are otherwise very modern and historically constructed sectarian identities. It is a complex ensemble that stretches over substantial areas of everyday life, demarcating the parameters of the possible, preventing the emergence of any semblance of rule of law or accountability, and is always ready to undermine challenges and alternatives to the sectarian system.

The violence of the sectarian system is profound and pervasive, if not always discernible or material. Its disciplinary logic denies Lebanese their existence as citizens with inalienable political and social rights, reducing them instead to unequal members of state-recognized sectarian communities. Sectarian elites, often in alliance with their clerical counterparts, deploy an array of practices that collectively aim at reproducing sectarian identities. Matters related to family law in its broadest sense are relegated to sectarian courts, an arrangement that produces sectarian subjects beleaguered by clientelist and kinship loyalties.

The same calculations shape citizenship laws, a state-sponsored sectarian welfare system, and educational policies. Postwar neoliberal state retrenchment compels the economically underprivileged to seek sectarian patronage for a range of social services. Large swathes of associational life are regulated and absorbed by a postwar neoliberal governance model. Civil society organizations are sectarianized, co-opted, or intimidated to prevent them from producing alternatives to sectarianism.[40]

Lebanon's postwar mediascape is a site for reciprocal demonization, deployed to construct the postwar sectarian "other." Not only do the privately owned visual media reflect postwar sectarian sentiments, they also create and fuel them in destructive ways.[41] Even the state's coercive institutions are divided into sectarian fiefdoms, with security and military promotions and appointments driven largely by clientelist sectarian calculations, at devastating cost to military morale, professionalism, and preparedness.[42]

The result of all these practices is a distorted incentive structure that devalues merit as a prerequisite for personal success and for access to public or private institutions, while the absence of rule of law and accountability allows innumerable forms of criminality—domestic violence (especially against women), petty crime, theft of public assets and lands, and sectarian vigilantism—to pass with impunity. Resisting this disciplinary ensemble invites both political-economic and symbolic forms of punishment: Lebanese who refuse to abide by the rules of the sectarian system are not only excluded from its material and political rewards, but may even find themselves denied proper burial rites.

Resisting the Logic of Sectarianism

But as Michel Foucault, James Tully, Antonio Gramsci, and Edward Said remind us, where there is disciplinary power, there is invariably resistance to this power.[43] Thus the sectarianization of identities and politics is resisted by women, workers, teachers, public-sector employees, students, civil society organizations and activists, and coalitions of NGOs that aim at undermining the sectarian system's hegemony in the long struggle toward piecemeal reform. The tireless efforts of these actors to introduce an optional civil personal status law, to criminalize all forms of domestic violence (especially those targeting women), to pass laws enabling women to grant citizenship to their children and foreign spouses, to defend the socioeconomic rights of the underprivileged and voiceless, to expose the lopsided social costs of the sectarian and economic elite's neoliberal policies, and to promulgate a new electoral law that opens up possibilities for new modes of political mobilization beyond sectarianism—and many more everyday acts of resistance—are small battles in a larger and inescapably protracted Gramscian "war of position" that may slowly chip away at the sectarian system's political economy and ideological hegemony.[44]

One such example of resistance to the sectarian system's disciplinary power transpired in the summer of 2015, when protests initiated by You Stink and other activists against a mounting garbage crisis and the government's infamous corruption and dysfunction, exploded in street demonstrations.[45] In typical clientelist sectarian fashion, the garbage crisis commenced when disagreements over commissions and profit shares among members of the sectarian elite surfaced. The public soon discovered that the cost of garbage collection in Lebanon far outstrips that of any other country in the region. Much like other sectors of the Lebanese economy—especially electricity, telecommunications, customs and port facilities, T-bills, stone quarries, maritime properties, and government contracts—garbage collection and waste management are primarily tools to siphon off state resources into the sectarian elite's ever-growing coffers. To be sure, other postwar sectors have had a far more damaging effect on the economy and public debt. However, the symbolic indignity of this particular episode underlined the insouciance of a postwar sectarian elite bent on deploying the state's public finances and the country's resources to serve their private fortunes and those of their business partners without any regard for people's wellbeing, the country's esthetic capital, or environmental health.[46]

Demonstrations organized by You Stink in August 2015 soon attracted other civil society groups and ordinary citizens fed up with the dysfunction and corruption of the sectarian political system and the country's dire economic conditions. A massive rally organized in Martyrs' Square in Beirut on August 29, 2015 attracted Lebanese from different sects, classes, ages, and regions. It assumed the air of an anti-sectarian carnival of national conviviality, with people determined to creatively express their national, rather than sectarian, affiliations.[47] You Stink activists followed their words with deeds, entering the Environment Ministry on September 1, 2015 and organizing a peaceful sit-in to demand the minister's resignation.[48]

Using the democratic logic of accountability—a foreign concept in the lexicon of Lebanon's institutionally entrenched and clientelist sectarian system—the activists contended that since the environment minister had failed to resolve the garbage crisis, he should tender his resignation. Not so by the logic of the sectarian system, however. The Interior Ministry's riot police stormed the building and evicted the protesters. Having placed the country on political pause for years waiting for the fog of the region's geopolitical battles to clear, the sectarian elite converged to condemn You Stink's bravado and reassert their power. A mix of coercion, benign neglect, and attrition ultimately deflated the garbage protests. Unorganized and spontaneous, and lacking a unified strategy for structural change, the protestors soon began squabbling among themselves over how to prioritize their demands and whether to resolve the emergency garbage crisis or challenge the sectarian system per se. A very resilient sectarian system had once again contained and sabotaged challenges to its political economy and ideological hegemony.

Sectarianization and Popular Uprisings

Backing up a decade, the sectarianization of Lebanese politics intensified after the assassination of Rafiq al-Hariri on February 14, 2005 and Syria's concomitant withdrawal from the country on April 26.[49] The fracture of Lebanese politics into two main cross-confessional blocs—the March 14 coalition[50] and the March 8 coalition[51]—and the attempt to represent this division as a cross-sectarian political–ideological one involving disagreements over different visions of Lebanon's domestic and foreign politics, could not hide the intense confrontation between the country's mainly Sunni and Shi'a sectarian elite over control of the post-Syria Lebanese state.[52] Maronite-dominated Lebanon, which gave way during Syria's occupation of the country (1990–2005) to a Muslim-dominated one, was now locked in a fierce power struggle among Sunni and Shi'a political and religious identity entrepreneurs. Multiple and successive crises consumed this contest over post-Syria Lebanon: the reorganization of the state's administrative posts and security institutions; the consociational modalities of cabinet decisions, but especially the Shi'a sectarian elite's insistence on a veto power over decisions pertaining to Hezbollah's security details; its national identity; and the future of Hezbollah's weapons arsenal, and the state's defensive policy vis-à-vis Israel; the by-laws of the Special Tribunal for Lebanon (STL) pertaining to the Hariri assassination; the true interpretation of UNSCR 1701 of August 11, 2006, which ended the war that summer between Israel and Hezbollah; the constitutional provisos pertaining to presidential elections; and Hezbollah's clandestine but sophisticated telecommunications infrastructure in the country.[53]

Transpiring in the shadow of an assassination campaign targeting members of the March 14 coalition and their allies, these contests resulted in the paralysis and atrophy of state institutions and the remilitarization of society along sectarian lines. They also elevated Sunni-Shi'a sectarian animosities to new heights, exploding on more than one occasion in the form of bloody clashes. Saudi-financed Sunni Salafi groups in Tripoli and Sidon were permitted operational space by pro-March 14 security agencies, while the Future Movement mobilized the Sunni religious establishment, intentionally underscoring the sectarian nature of the conflict, to balance against Hezbollah's political and military capabilities.[54] These tensions ultimately exploded in a military assault by the

Amal Movement and Hezbollah against the Future Movement's security infrastructure and media institutions in West Beirut on May 8, 2008. The Qatari-negotiated May 21, 2008 Doha Accord ended Hezbollah's violent takeover of West Beirut and paved the way for the election of army commander Michel Suleiman as a consensus president (2008–2014), and the organization of fresh parliamentary elections. It did nothing to end the contest over post-Syria Lebanon, however.

Table 12.3: Main Political Parties by Sectarian Affiliation

Party	Sectarian Affiliation
Hezbollah	Shiʻa
Amal	Shiʻa
Free Patriotic Movement	Maronite
Future Movement	Sunni
Progressive Socialist Party	Druze
Lebanese Forces	Maronite
Phalange Party	Maronite
Marada Movement	Maronite
Syrian Social Nationalist Party (SSNP)	secular but mainly Greek Orthodox
Armenian Revolutionary Federation/ Tashnag	Armenian
Lebanese Communist Party	secular and cross-sectarian

In fact, the aforementioned domestic confrontation overlapped with a wider regional geopolitical contest unleashed immediately after the US invasion and occupation of Iraq, pitting Iran and Syria against the USA and Saudi Arabia, one in which sectarianism was deployed for otherwise strictly balance-of-power ends.[55] The USA, supported by the March 14 coalition, sought to inherit Syria's once omnipotent role in Lebanon. Saudi Arabia also deployed Lebanon in its own regional contests with Iran and Syria. Riyadh calibrated its politics in Lebanon to serve its geopolitical struggle to balance or roll back Iran's growing regional power. The popular uprisings of the Arab Spring intensified this geopolitical confrontation, but especially between Riyadh and Tehran, allowing it to travel into new theaters, namely Syria and Yemen.[56] More specifically, the sectarianization of the overlapping domestic, regional, international "struggle over Syria" had a substantial spill-over effect on Lebanon, further exacerbating Sunni-Shiʻa sectarian tensions.[57]

Hezbollah's military intervention in Syria in support of the Assad regime was governed by strictly geopolitical calculations aimed at protecting its own strategic interests and those of its ideological and material patron, Iran.[58] Consequently, and at the risk of inflaming sectarian tensions even more, Hezbollah publicly declared its support for what was otherwise regarded across the region as a minority 'Alawi authoritarian regime defending its parochial sectarian interests against the democratic aspirations of a Sunni majority in Syria. Hezbollah's direct military involvement in Syria initially started in the form of strategic consultations with the Syrian regime on a range of nonconventional military tactics and the deployment of elite military units to defend the Sayyida Zaynab shrine in southern Damascus.[59] This intervention, and its impact on sectarian tensions in Lebanon and across the region, changed substantially with Hezbollah's public military participation in the Qusayr battles in April 2013: the party's offensive operation over the territory of an Arab country against Sunni armed groups.[60] Although the Qusayr battle resulted in intense and widespread resentment of Hezbollah across the region and beyond, the party was undeterred, viewing the struggle for Syria as a matter of geopolitical life or death. Consequently, it later expanded its military operations to cover most of the Syrian battlefield.[61]

Hezbollah's geopolitical justifications did nothing to contain the sectarian hornet's nest that exploded in the organization's face. Its political and symbolic capital, among Islamist movements in Lebanon and beyond, accumulated through decades of resistance, its instrumental role in liberating Lebanese lands from Israeli occupation, confronting the latter during the 2006 war, and then serving as a deterrent against future military operations, evaporated swiftly. Ignoring their own proxy roles in the service of Saudi Arabia's own regional objectives in Syria and Lebanon, Hezbollah's domestic opponents—especially the Future Movement—claimed that the party's military intervention in Syria proved that the main utility of its weapons arsenal is to protect Iran's geopolitical interests rather than Lebanon's security from Israeli aggression. In their inexorable quest to demonize the party, March 14 and Riyadh labeled Hezbollah's intervention in Syria a Shi'a "invasion" orchestrated by Iran to shore up a beleaguered 'Alawi regime in Damascus and protect Tehran's strategic interests. The Future Movement, at Saudi Arabia's behest, then publicly voiced its opposition to the party's one-time magic formula embodied in the slogan "al-jaysh, al-sha'b, al-moqawama," which represents the organic alliance between the Lebanese Armed Forces (LAF), the people, and the resistance, justifying the latter's weapons arsenal, and serving as a deterrent against any future Israeli attack.[62]

Hezbollah's military intervention in Syria ultimately brought upon it and the Shi'a community the ire of Sunni public opinion in Lebanon and the wider region. Moreover, the hardening of Salafi sentiments against the party supplied transnational Salafi-jihadi groups with new sanctuaries in Lebanon and fresh recruits, making it logistically easier to target Hezbollah's cadres and community in Beirut's southern suburbs with a wave of suicide terrorist attacks. Hezbollah's intervention in Syria was also used instrumentally by Sunni religious preachers to mobilize Salafi-jihadis from across the world for the war in Syria.[63] Led by Saudi Arabia, the GCC later designated Hezbollah a terrorist organization and began expelling Lebanese nationals considered affiliated with the party in a bid to turn Shi'a public opinion in Lebanon against the party. Saudi Arabia also accused Hezbollah of sending military advisors to aid Yemen's Houthi rebels in their war against Riyadh's local allies, and training sleeper cells across the Gulf countries.[64]

The spillover effects of the region's sectarianized geopolitical contests also affected Lebanon's Christian communities, which came to feel increasingly targeted by the region's rabid sectarianization, ISIS's sectarian (targeting other Muslims) and religious (targeting non-Muslims) cleansing in Syria and Iraq, and demographic pressures from the influx of overwhelmingly Muslim Syrian refugees. Already sidelined by the Sunni-Shi'a contest over post-Syria Lebanon, the country's Christian sectarian elite demanded institutional reforms that would give them greater control over their socioeconomic affairs and political representation. One such demand is broad political and administrative decentralization, intended to give Christian communities greater autonomy in the management of their political, economic, and developmental affairs rather than the current non-territorial cultural autonomy they enjoy according to the corporate power-sharing arrangement.[65]

The so-called Orthodox (electoral) Law is another. Blessed by the Maronite church and supported initially by all Christian parties, the Orthodox Law was born out of Christian disenchantment with their political underrepresentation in the postwar political order. This is especially so in parliament, where some Christian parties claim that "only 34 of the 64 seats reserved for Christians ultimately go to candidates that

231

represent Christian interests because in these electoral constituencies the Christian population is insufficient to elect Christian candidates."[66] The proposed Orthodox Law consequently called for the adoption of a proportional representation (PR) list system whereby the current twenty-six electoral districts are gathered in one single national district, but where the predetermined sectarian quota of parliamentary seats is retained as in the current electoral system: "To ensure that Christians, not other sects, are selecting Christian candidates, the Orthodox Law stipulates that instead of a common electoral roll, individuals will be allowed only to vote for candidates who belong to the same [sect]."[67] Voting consequently takes place between "11 different sect-based electoral contests, with MPs elected by PR rather than the current majoritarian system and multiple mixed districts."[68] These kinds of proposed institutional reforms are a reflection of deep Christian disenchantment with the postwar power-sharing arrangement, and its failure—at least in its present corporate consociational form—to achieve inter-sectarian and cross-confessional peace and coexistence.

Conclusion

Lebanon's sectarian political system has reached a dead end, and is currently undergoing two kinds of internal crises. The first is an intra-systemic crisis, manifested in the failure of the sectarian elite to agree on the organization of political power in post-Syria Lebanon. At the core of this crisis is the outdated corporate power-sharing arrangement anchoring the postwar political order. A majority of Christians and their political elite feel underrepresented politically and socioeconomically, demand greater control over their own local affairs, and have voiced demands for the renegotiation of the postwar sectarian balance of power. The second crisis is an anti-sectarian one, the peaceful demand by different civil society groups and activists for a complete overhaul of the sectarian system and its political and economic foundations. The former crisis signals the need to recalibrate the postwar power-sharing arrangement in a manner amenable to the demands of the country's Christian communities; the latter seeks an exit from the politics of sectarianism altogether.

It would be wrong to underestimate the durability of the sectarian system's political economy and ideological hegemony, however. Too many people continue to benefit from its neopatrimonial and clientelist networks tied directly to the sectarian elite. The complex ensemble of institutional, clientelist, and discursive practices operating to reproduce sectarianism distorts incentive structures and sabotages attempts to organize cross-sectarian forms of political mobilization. Moreover, sectarian elites possess substantial material, legal, and paralegal coercive capabilities. Their ideological hegemony, although not immune to challenge, is strong, cemented by a network of corporatist institutions deployed to produce disciplined and docile sectarian subjects.

Be that as it may, sectarian elites appreciate, perhaps more than anyone else, the threat that cross-sectarian and anti-sectarian groups pose to the dominant modes of political and ideological mobilization. Protests, such as the summer 2015 You Stink revolt, serve to demystify the clientelist core of the sectarian system, one devoid of any semblance of accountability. They expose the everyday violence it practices against Lebanese citizens across sectarian, class, or regional divides. Moreover, such protests trigger new fault lines within Lebanese society beyond sectarianism. They demonstrate that sectarian identities are not timeless, the byproduct of some immutable Lebanese essence, but are, rather, historically constructed and reproduced continuously through a set of institutional, clientelist, and discursive elite and non-elite practices that obviate the emergence of cross-sectarian alternatives. Consequently, there is nothing inevitable about sectarianism in Lebanon, just as there is nothing inevitable about the current sectarian wave spreading its poison across the wider region. Hence the violent manner with which sectarian identity entrepreneurs react to civil society activists engaged in peaceful protests, unleashing against them the full force of their legal and paralegal coercive machinery.

Paradoxically, even members of the sectarian elite seem alarmed by the level of corruption and criminality the country has reached as a result of the sectarianized domestic–external struggles over post-Syria Lebanon. Whether it is the garbage crisis fiasco and its catastrophic consequences on public health and the country's environment, illegal internet companies operating beyond the reach of the law, the import of expired food products, criminal gangs enslaving female prostitutes, the spread of all kinds of everyday violence with perpetrators often eluding punishment, the whimsical application of the law, or the callous disregard for anything related to public order and space: the perpetrators of all of these pathologies are protected by the clientelist networks of a stubborn sectarian system permeating every nook and cranny of public institutions. No less an establishment figure than Walid Jumblatt has voiced his astonishment at "the extensive level of corruption permeating state and administrative institutions" and the protection organized criminal rackets receive from public officials and members of the sectarian elite.[69]

Perhaps it is high time Lebanon's sectarian elites start thinking of alternatives to the postwar political economic pact that has brought nothing but perpetual instability, political deadlock, and socioeconomic misery to large segments of the population. There is dire need for the kind of institutional and political economic reforms—a new PR electoral law, decentralization measures, a civil marriage law, the progressive taxation of non-productive rentier profits[70]—that may open up spaces for the emergence of new political dynamics beyond sectarianism. The country's sectarian elites must agree to coexist alongside cross- and anti-sectarian groups, thus allowing the emergence of forms of political contestation along ideological rather than solely sectarian fault lines.

This, in turn, could shore up the system's representativeness and legitimacy, and hence stability. After all, the 2015 summer demonstrations—but also other types of resistance to the sectarian system's clientelist logic and ideological hegemony, such as the Beirut Madinati (Beirut my City) campaign launched by a group of non-sectarian activists to contest the May 2016 municipal elections in Beirut[71]—demonstrate that not all Lebanese are sectarian or willing to surrender to the complex ensemble of practices reproducing sectarianism. They may be swimming against the regional current of sectarianized geopolitical contests and identity mobilization, but their struggles are testimony to the will of many to imagine and practice new cross-sectarian or anti-sectarian modes of politics and coexistence.

SECTARIANISM, AUTHORITARIANISM, AND OPPOSITION IN KUWAIT

Madeleine Wells[1]

The June 26, 2015 bombing of a Shiʻa mosque in Kuwait that killed twenty-seven people and wounded 227 more was an unprecedented event that raised major questions about the past—and the future—of Sunni-Shiʻa relations in the country. But rather than instigating the sectarian maelstrom that ISIS intended, the bombing reinvigorated social unity and intensified government protection over Shiʻa citizens, who comprise around 30 per cent of the Kuwaiti population. The attack also came at an important historical juncture for sectarian relations in Kuwait and the Gulf. As the Middle East has become increasingly fragmented by sectarian politics, Kuwait has been drawn into a contentious Saudi-led coalition to fight a seemingly sectarian battle in Yemen, and tensions between Saudi Arabia and Iran are at an all-time high.

Kuwait is an interesting case because it has had a relatively sanguine history of sectarian relations, making it a regional outlier when compared to the more punitive treatment of Shiʻa by Saudi Arabia and Bahrain. Kuwait's relative inclusion of its Shiʻa population—including a small faction with clear links to Iranian clerical figures—stands out both in terms of theoretical expectations and historical evidence about how regimes should treat minorities with perceived links to outside powers.[2] In this context, the post-2003 period of regime-Shi'a relations is particularly puzzling. After Saddam Hussein was removed from power in Iraq in 2003 the perceived threat of Iran began to grow, particularly vis-à-vis regional Sunni hegemon Saudi Arabia, yet, as this regional power competition ramped up after 2003, and sectarian rhetoric increased among Kuwaiti MPs and independent media, leading figures in the ruling Al Sabah regime, including the crown prince and prime minister, exhibited an unprecedented increase in their accommodation and co-optation of the Shi'a minority, compared to Kuwait's neighbors—and its own history.[3]

What explains the unique shape of regime-Shi'a relations since the 2000s, and how does this answer help us to understand what drives sectarian politics in Kuwait? The answer, in short, is that a slew of highly co-optative Kuwaiti approaches to the Shi'a in the 2000s are best explained by the regime's increasing authoritarianism and strategic balancing of internal oppositional forces, rather than by other variables such as international threats from Iran. The Kuwaiti government is more focused on internal domestic challenges relating to regime survival, specifically the ongoing reformist demands of a vociferous tribal-Islamist-youth opposition that crystalized during the Arab Spring. Without understanding this domestic oppositional context, it is impossible to understand the unique shape of regime-Shi'a relations in Kuwait.

This chapter focuses on major changes in government policy toward the Shi'a since the early 2000s, particularly the intensification of a policy of co-optation. For the purposes of this chapter, I define co-optation as the purposeful movement of members of a non-core[4] group or a peripheral political or identity group into a political alliance with certain members of the core political identity group. Co-optation entails neutralizing a group's political power. It is more politically inclusive than simple accommodation[5] (in which groups gain respect from government institutions), as groups may derive legitimate political goods from it, even if it is short of true political inclusion and integration.[6]

This chapter proceeds as follows. First, I give the background to Kuwaiti institutions and regime-Shi'a relations. Next, I focus on the 1990s and the rise of a new Shi'a opposition. Here, as a traditionally apolitical Shi'a community lost ground to a pro-Iranian branch of Shi'a politicians allied with a new cross-sectarian opposition party in 1999, the regime endeavored to create a new class of Shi'a "clients" in order to reassert control over the community and shore up the group as a bulwark against the opposition.[7] Shaykh Sabah al-Ahmed al-Jaber (henceforth to be called Sabah al-Ahmed), who became emir of Kuwait in 2006, was an important executor of this strategy to re-cultivate ties with Shi'a notables. Starting in 2001, Sabah al-Ahmed (then minister of foreign affairs) began to position himself for a succession battle, and used mosques and Shi'a political grievances as one way to cultivate support for his political ambitions. Next, I show how in 2008 a commemoration of former Lebanese Hezbollah leader 'Imad Mughniyya was utilized by the regime as an opportunity to bring the Shi'a opposition back into its lane as traditional regime supporters in order to counterbalance a growing tribal-Islamist opposition coalition. I conclude by looking at recent authoritarian Kuwaiti policies against politically vociferous Shi'a and Sunnis alike as part and parcel of a larger strategy of regime survival vis-à-vis the opposition.

Kuwaiti Institutions, the Dynamic of Semi-Authoritarianism, and Regime Balancing

At the crux of the explanation I advance in this chapter is Kuwait's semi-authoritarian political structure and the type of dynamic it engenders.[8] As Kuwait is a semi-constitutional monarchy, its highly mobilized body politic can vote in free and fair parliamentary elections. The Kuwaiti parliament is unique in the Gulf for having the power to remove confidence in individual ministers and override the emir's veto via majority vote. Michael Herb argues that it is the unique power of the parliament to hold an "interpellation" (*istijwab*) of individual ministers—basically to remove confidence in individual ministers or effectively the prime minister—that sets the Kuwaiti parliament apart from the rest of the Gulf legislative bodies.[9] While no minister has actually lost a vote of confidence, several have resigned prior to the vote in anticipation of defeat.[10] Additionally, parliament has the power to approve or disapprove the emir's choice for crown prince. This important function of parliament makes leadership succession a crucial moment for the dynamic of alliances and interests within parliament itself.

At the same time, parliamentarians' choices are ultimately limited by an appointed cabinet that serves at the discretion of the emir, such that the cabinet is "not an extension of the parliament but rather is a fusion of the executive and the legislature."[11] The prime minister (typically the crown prince) chooses the cabinet, leads the government, and manages the parliament. Ministries of Defense, Foreign Affairs, Interior, and Oil are generally given to members of the Al Sabah family. Nevertheless, the relative degree of openness in Kuwaiti institutions means that the extent to which the opposition organizes has an impact on regime calculations. The shape of the political opposition and the threat it poses to the ruler are variables of primary importance in how any social groups, Sunni or Shiʻa, are treated by their ruler. That is to say, for the Al Sabah regime, *Realpolitik* is far more important than identity politics. Wielding power, and whatever instruments are necessary to reach the end of regime maintenance, are primary objectives that supersede primordial affinity toward a specific ideology, ethnicity, sect, or identity group.

A Legacy of Shiʻa Co-optation

With a few exceptions, Kuwaiti Shiʻa have equal access to the large coterie of welfare benefits offered by their rentier state.[12] Likewise, Kuwaiti Shiʻa generally express effusive feelings of loyalty toward their government and feel central to the state's history and its quest for survival. Rather than being mostly excluded from political life, Kuwaiti Shiʻa have often been accommodated and co-opted by their government. A brief history of the Shiʻa in Kuwait prior to the case study period will highlight the Al Sabah regime's high level of internal preoccupation with the political opposition throughout its history, while also demonstrating a penchant to co-opt various non-core groups to use as a bulwark against its opponents.

Pre-oil Kuwait was characterized by something of a grand bargain between the Al Sabah regime and merchant oligarchy of both sects. Among these merchants, the Shiʻa played a formative role in supporting the ruler both economically and politically from the turn of the nineteenth century and until the mid-1970s. Since 1938, when the Al Sabah regime faced its first real oppositional threat in the form of an assembly movement led by reformist Arab nationalists, the Shiʻa have been seen as a political force useful as a bulwark against Arab nationalist opposition. Throughout this time leaders of the Shiʻa community, threatened by their overall exclusion from the Sunni-leaning Arab nationalist movement and by the anti-Persian rhetoric of the assembly, allied with the Al

Sabah regime for protection. This alliance was ad hoc and happened to serve both the non-core group and the leadership's goals at the time. It lasted until 1976. Since the initial threat of the 1938 assembly, Kuwaiti policy toward non-core groups has been defined by the regime's preoccupation with oppositional political threats.[13]

After Kuwait's independence in 1961, despite their disproportionately low level of political representation, the Shi'a themselves—led by their traditionally privileged merchant elite—were rather unconcerned with Kuwaiti politics, until the 1970s. At that time, however, international and regional trends brought Shi'a clerical exiles from Iraq to Kuwait. The presence of these clerics, leaders of the al-Da'wa and Shirazi trends, catalyzed a local split over sources of religious authority and the politicization of a group of middle-class youth who wanted more than the traditionally co-opted merchant elite could offer them in political life.[14] By 1975 the *shabaab* (youth) affiliated with the al-Da'wa trend had become more involved in university and national politics. The *shabaab* mobilized for more Shi'a political participation, which resulted in the Shi'a winning the highest number of parliamentary seats ever, ten, and this led to the regime's appointment of the first ever Shi'a cabinet minister. In 1976 the Kuwaiti regime unconstitutionally shut down the parliament, largely due to fear of the opposition and additionally, according to archival evidence, due to fear of the nascent Shi'a political mobilization.[15] After this time a commitment to resume participatory politics led many Shi'a youth to move from their typical political demands, which were narrowly related to securing resources for their confessional group, to support a more basic political reform agenda for the entire country.

This overlapped with the Iranian revolution and the Iran-Iraq war of the 1980s, leading the Kuwaiti regime to fear the Shi'a for the first time as an *oppositional* threat on a political level. Indeed, by 1979 the Shi'a had allied with Sunni liberals in an attempt to bring back the dissolved parliament of 1976, in the first ever manifestation of an informal cross-sectarian alliance. Interestingly, policies toward the Shi'a in the 1980s were initially co-optative and nonviolent. However, the Kuwait regime, feeling threatened by the specter of Iran exporting its revolution, began to support its erstwhile enemy, Iraq, in the Iran-Iraq war and more violently exclude those Shi'a who demonstrated against the alliance with Iraq. By the end of the 1980s, as the perceived Iranian threat receded, the traditionally good relations between the Shi'a merchants and the Al Sabah regime had been significantly damaged. Kuwait's Shi'a could not find public-sector jobs in security or international affairs, or get mosque permits, and could certainly not hope to move toward further accommodation with the regime as a minority with autonomous religious institutions of their own. The 1990–1991 invasion and occupation of Kuwait by Iraq gave Kuwaiti Shi'a an opportunity to reassert their loyalty to the nation, and offered a possibility of rapprochement. That said, the system was slow to change in the 1990s; the Shi'a continued to be relatively disadvantaged as a religious non-core group and remained without a separate mosque endowment, *shari'a* courts, or educational accommodation.

The Post-Liberation Elections and the Rise of Sunni Islamist Opposition in the 1990s

The key to understanding post-liberation policies toward Kuwait's Shi'a is recognizing that a new grouping of opposition began to emerge in the 1990s. It was at this time that old regime elites were replaced in the assembly by an increasingly politically mobilized group of Sunni Islamists emanating from tribal districts. This truly unforeseen consequence of decades of balancing against Arab nationalists, liberals, and Shi'a put the regime—via its new recommitment to parliamentary politics—in the difficult position of needing to keep the system "open" to allow constituents to blow off steam, but also responding to a formidable domestic threat by a new identity group, largely of tribal origin, which had once been strategically neutralized and co-opted but was now flexing its political muscles.

The 1992 elections, the first since 1985, which came in the aftermath of the end of Iraq's occupation of Kuwait, resulted in thirty-one seats—more than half of the representatives of the sixty-person *majlis* (assembly or parliament)—in opposition to the government and the loss of multiple old elite allies of the ruling regime. The opposition was fairly homogeneous and increasingly Sunni Islamist, with tribes tending to support Sunni Islamist policies due to their resonance over shared conservative values.

1999: The Rise of an Institutionalized, Cross-Cutting Shi'a Opposition as a Threat

The Popular Action Bloc (PAB) was created in 1999 after Sunni politician Ahmed al-Sadoun lost his long-time role as speaker of the house in parliament.[16] This movement's formation is an important benchmark by which to understand the precursors to Shi'a co-optation in the 2000s, for it was the first time since the 1980s that the Shi'a posed a formal oppositional threat alongside Sunnis in parliament. Identity cross-cutting (read: cross-sectarian) issue-based coalitions are one of the most threatening forms of opposition faced by semi-authoritarian regimes. Laurence Louer describes how "issue-based coalitions" such as those that form between Shi'a Islamists and secular or "liberal" activists in Bahrain are more threatening than identity-based coalitions, because they signal "the ability of activists from competing ideologies to overcome their difference in order to promote a common political platform focusing on the demand for democratic reforms."[17]

The PAB immediately focused on populist issues such as housing, wages, and political reform. Their first move in parliament in 1999 was to interrogate the minister of housing. Between 1999 and 2008 the PAB was responsible for seven out of twenty-two interrogations in parliament, gaining a reputation as a formidable populist force. The new opposition movement cut across previously segmented Kuwaiti political identities in every way. The movement was not only a liberal-tribal alliance, but also an Islamist Sunni-Shi'a alliance.[18]

The Shi'a in the PAB, all members of the Islamic National Alliance (al-Tahaluf al-Islami al-Watani), are of particular interest, given splits within the Kuwaiti Shi'a community about participating in reformist politics since the 1970s and the climate of political and violent exclusion of the Shi'a in the 1980s. After the failure of a front intended to unite the entire Shi'a body politic after the 1991 Gulf war, al-Tahaluf emerged in 1998, and was ideologically and openly pro-Iran.[19] The alliance comprised old-school al-Da'wa-inspired Shi'a activists who managed to win seats in the assembly in 1981 in spite of gerrymandering.[20] These supporters, despite having their origins in the politically contentious Da'wa trend, were never put in jail or arrested despite their beliefs;[21] they claim they were more focused on change *within* the system, focusing on an interest to "re-establish the balance between the ruling family and the elected assembly."[22] Rather than referring to Hezbollah in Lebanon, or its incarnation in Kuwait, this moniker simply refers to the fact that the supporters were originally Da'wa-inspired members of the *khat al-Imam* line, that is, they followed the ideology of Ayatollah Khomeini in Iran to the extent that they thought religious jurists should lead the community.

241

They could, in some sense, initially be considered a loyal opposition, thus posing a minimal threat. However, al-Tahaluf's strategic location in the issue-based PAB constituted a configuration of opposition that remained a thorn in the regime's side compared to the vast majority of Shi'a, who remained disengaged from substantive political issues.

2003 as an Opportunity to Begin to Bring the Shi'a out of Opposition

As mentioned, a history of contentious relations between the National Assembly and the government significantly pre-dated the 2003 US invasion of Iraq, which intensified the level of sectarianism within Kuwait. In addition to rising Sunni Islamist opposition in the late 1990s, which led to dissolving parliament in 1999, Kuwaiti politics also began to split after September 11, 2001, when some Kuwaitis (mostly tribes [badu] and Sunni Islamists) began to decry US policies in the region, while others (generally urbanites, or liberals [hadhar], and most Shi'a) stayed pro-American and pushed for more liberalizing agendas.[23] While Kuwaiti respondents of multiple demographic backgrounds uniformly favored the US decision in 2003 to invade Iraq, what they—uniquely among Iraq's neighbors—call *tahrir al-Iraq* (the liberation of Iraq), they split in the aftermath of the invasion over issues such as the long-term US presence in the region.[24] At the same time that this anti-Americanism flared, there was a rising Sunni perception that liberation[25] of the Shi'a majority was a US "handover to Shiite Iran."[26] In some sense, this rise in Iranian influence was tangible at least in terms of the increase in communication and religious travel of Shi'a in the region. The fall of Saddam Hussein opened doors to transnational links among Shi'a, including interpersonal links to family long behind the "iron curtain" of Saddam's rule, as well as religious links to clerics (such as Ayatollah al-Sistani) and the possibility to travel to Shi'a shrines that had previously been off limits.

This Kuwaiti perception of heightened Iranian influence and threat was echoed, or perhaps inspired, at the regional level by (1) a popular rhetoric (started by the king of Jordan) about the rise of a "Shi'a crescent" and (2) rising Saudi-Iranian tensions as the two states moved to rebalance in a region now devoid of their usual third competitor for power, Saddam Hussein. Lastly, the increasing sectarian infighting in Iraq led to allegations by Sunni hardliners in Kuwait that the Kuwaiti government and the international community were not doing enough to protect Sunnis and tribes from Shi'a attacks abroad (i.e. in Iraq). Sunni mobilization and clerical fury was particularly heightened around the 2004 battle of Fallujah.[27] In the midst of such a regional and popular frenzy, the Kuwaiti government downplayed the identity ramifications of the invasion in an effort to pacify rising sectarianism at the societal level. Messages from the emir emphasized national unity and peace. This rising sectarianism in society, coupled with the rise of oppositional momentum in Kuwait, explains the re-co-optation of Shi'a Islamists in the following years.

Institutional Co-optation in Ministries: Rewarding Non-Oppositional Shi'a, Liberals, and Women

In light of the increasing links among Shi'a across the region, and the perception of many Sunni Arabs that Iraq and Iran were increasingly supportive of Gulf Shi'a, the literature on ethnic bargaining would expect Kuwaiti Shi'a to interpret regional developments as signals that they had increasing bargaining leverage against the state, and to radicalize their claims. Indeed, an initial push for greater cultural accommodation of Shi'a by the state was partially successful—and the level of inclusion of Shi'a rose following 2003. The trend toward Shi'a inclusion is most clearly visible at the institutional level in the uptick in the number of Shi'a appointed to cabinet-level positions in Kuwaiti governments following 2003.

During the 1990s through 2003 there was a consistent appointment of one Shi'a minister per cabinet (with the exception of two ministers in 1992, following the liberation of Kuwait). This major increase in the numbers of Shi'a leading Kuwaiti ministries marked a substantial change from co-optation of Shi'a in the past. While the new positions the Shi'a gained never had "sovereign"[28] or national security relevance, leadership of a ministry gives political influence and increases access these members have to potential policy benefits for their constituents.[29] For example, the appointment of Shi'a Massouma al-Mubarak in 2003, 2006, and 2007 to the Ministries of Planning and Administrative Development (both 2006 and 2007) and Ministry of Health (in 2007) might be considered substantive co-optation. Al-Mubarak also had the distinction of being appointed Kuwait's first female minister in 2003.[30] Again, as per my argument, such strategic appointments say more about instrumentally balancing the numbers and identities in the opposition for the end of maintaining power than they do about primordial proclivities toward the identities in politics themselves.

Table 13.1: Variation in Shi'a Appointment to Cabinet Positions in Kuwait, 1961–2011[31]

Year of Majlis	Number of Shi'a Heads of Ministries
1961–1975	0
1975–1976	1
1976–1991	0
1992–1993	2
1994–2002	1
2003–2011	2

Mosques as "Pork": Religious Co-optation in the 2000s

In addition to strategic government appointments, rich rentier states such as Kuwait interact with sectarian groups through the distribution of clientelist or "pork-barrel" spending on public religious goods. Such spending is co-optative whether it occurs in democratic or semi-authoritarian politics—the basic explicit or implicit terms are that the politician trades benefits to constituents for their political support. In Kuwait, the Shi'a have often invoked the constitution to suggest that it is incumbent upon the state to provide them with religious public goods such as religious buildings and courts, as it does for the Sunnis.[32] One respondent estimated that despite the fact that the Shi'a form around one-third of the population, there are currently over 1,200 Sunni mosques in Kuwait, while there are about forty Shi'a mosques in total.[33] From 1984 to 2003 there were no new Shi'a mosques built, while the number of Sunni mosques continued to increase steadily. This suggests that the halt in mosque permitting correlated with perceived Shi'a threats in private spaces after the Iranian revolution. Although several new mosques were rumored to have been permitted as of 2000, none had been built by 2003, after which the number of permits and mosques began to increase.

There are also potential political implications of full religious public good provision, as buildings that increase the spaces for worship for non-core groups may have organizational consequences. Policies that accommodate non-core religious groups in this realm may initially be apolitical, but can function simultaneously as locations where non-core groups can mobilize politically outside the watch of the state. As such, given the rising importance of transnational Shi'a links after 2003, the history of violence in the 1980s, and a perceived rising Iranian threat, one would expect the Kuwaiti government to continue to curb access to such unmonitored religious spaces. Instead, in 2004 a separate Shi'a mosque authority, the Ja'fari Awqaf, was established to regulate Shi'a mosques and endowments. The government began to increase the number of mosque permits while turning a blind eye to other unlicensed Shi'a prayer spaces. The government also allowed for more public Shi'a religious rituals, and 'Ashura demonstrations were allowed for the first time in 2004.[34] Shi'a media outlets also began to receive more permits to open.[35] Additionally, the government approved Shi'a requests for a separate Shi'a supreme court in 2003.[36]

I argue, however, that the easing of restrictions on Shi'a religious spaces in 2003 must be seen as a co-optative strategy chosen by the regime in light of domestic oppositional politics, that is, the particular rise of Sunni Islamist opposition at the same time. In July 2003, Kuwaitis went to vote in their first election since 1975 without the shadow of Saddam Hussein next door in Iraq. To the surprise of liberals, who had expected major gains over Islamists, the vote yielded another large Islamist opposition in parliament (twenty-one Islamists won seats, five of whom were Shi'a) although the regime retained twenty-six pro-government seats.[37]

In one instance of a Shi'a mosque permit being granted, it was only with prime minister Sabah al-Ahmed's personal intervention that the permit made it past municipal council infighting and to the National Assembly for approval. The Behbehani family, one of the oldest merchant families to settle in Kuwait from Iran, spent fifteen years getting its mosque approved and built in a majority-Sunni area of al-Qurain.[38] When I asked about the role of the prime minister in this process, one member of the family did not refer to his family's historical importance as merchants or their relations with the ruler; rather, he answered the following as though it were completely obvious: "The Salafis and *Ikhwan* [Muslim Brothers] are against the Shi'a, and the emir has to balance those factions."[39]

The Rise of the Kuwaiti Opposition and the Co-optation of al-Tahaluf

2006 Parliamentary Elections and the Growing Opposition in Assembly

The 2006 parliamentary elections were characterized by major fragmentation in the fabric of Kuwaiti politics, and perhaps the most threatening National Assembly opposition Kuwait had ever experienced. Ideologically polarized blocs cohered on the common issue of political reform. For example, Islamist groups such as the Islamic Constitutional Movement (ICM—the Kuwaiti variant of the Muslim Brotherhood) supported both hardline Shi'a and liberal candidates whose platforms were pro-reform. This mobilization for reform went beyond just the PAB—it suggested that new alliances were moving away from narrow tribal and personalist interests in the political sphere and toward a broader engagement in cross-sectarian, issue-based politics.

One top issue in the 2006 parliamentary elections was a motion submitted by twenty-nine MPs to reduce the number of districts from twenty-five (with two votes each) to five, ostensibly to reduce vote-buying and corruption in the electoral process. The Shi'a were split on this idea. The apolitical Shiraziyyin bloc wanted to keep the same districting because they wanted to ally with moderate Sunnis. The measure passed, with the support of both al-Tahaluf and the opposition, but it resulted in the election of an even more contentious and sectarian 2008 parliament, in which Sunni Islamists and tribes secured twenty-four out of fifty seats. Four Shi'a were elected to parliament, three from al-Tahaluf and only one Shirazi. By this point, the role of the Sunni tribes as the main opposition allied with Salafis had solidified. The largely tribal *badu* used anti-Shi'ism and sectarianism as "a card to discredit the royalty, especially the more liberal-leaning prime minister, and a tactic to win over the *hadhar* Sunnis."[40] Tribal Sunni opposition to the government was based on the complaint that the Kuwaiti government was not helping Sunnis in Iraq, was not independent enough from the USA, and was leaning toward Iran.

In regime politics, 2006 was also a noteworthy year. After Emir Jaber al-Ahmed passed away, Crown Prince Sa'ad al-Salem al-Sabah inherited the crown. But, due to his ill health, the normal rules of rotation were trumped. Parliament intervened in the succession crisis, forcibly impeaching the crown prince after only six days and installing Sabah al-Ahmed, another member of the Al Jaber branch. The new emir, in turn, chose his nephew, the now-infamous Nasser al-Mohammed, as his prime minister, and his brother as crown prince. The dismissal of the Al Salim branches for emir and prime minister also led other branches of the family that had never held the position of emir to begin to jockey for power.[41] These schisms began to play out to a certain extent in parliament, especially after 2008, when elements of the opposition to the regime from parliament and the royal family publicly criticized the emir and the prime minister for having pro-Shi'a policies.

Indeed, certain machinations of the regime throughout the 2000s were designed to foster "the emergence of new Shi'a merchants as notable intermediaries between the Al Sabah and the Shi'a masses" to supplant the loss of community power by the apolitical Shiraziyyin.[42] The regime also cultivated elites as supporters for various factions of the royal family, who often played out their schisms in parliament; this will be discussed further below.

Thus, while the increasing accommodation and co-optation of the Shi'a was a partial side-effect of intra-regime schisms and the proclivities of the emir and prime minister, there is little evidence that they specifically aimed to impact sectarian policies. Overwhelming support from this chapter and the rest of Kuwaiti history suggests that the dominant strategy of Al Sabah leaders over time has been to keep themselves in power via balancing the political opposition they face in parliament. Sabah al-Ahmed and Nasser al-Mohammed targeted the Shi'a with co-optative policies first and foremost to balance the opposition, as a way to bring hardline Shi'a back in as a bulwark to a rising tribal-Islamist oppositional threat they faced. Their intentions were to solidify Shi'a support for their rule and depoliticize a reformist Shi'a group that had long been a thorn in their side. And, who better to balance tribal-Sunni opposition than the predominantly *hadhar* Shi'a contingent, who needed protection from sectarianism in society and politics? A different formation of opposition, perhaps one that was more liberal or more homogeneous, might have led to a more exclusionary policy toward the oppositional Shi'a instead.

Mughniyya Demonstration

In 2008 a *ta'bin* (public commemoration) held in honor of Lebanese Hezbollah leader 'Imad Mughniyya provided the regime with a crucial opportunity to neutralize the remaining stronghold of Shi'a opposition.

Mughniyya, a prominent military commander, was assassinated by a car bomb in Damascus on February 12, 2008, as he marked the twenty-ninth anniversary of the Iranian revolution.[43] The response to the assassination reverberated all the way to the district of Maydan Hawali in Kuwait City, where two Shi'a MPs affiliated with al-Tahaluf—Adnan 'Abd-al-Samad and Ahmed Lari—led Kuwaiti Shi'a and foreigners in a public commemoration in honor of Mughniyya. Given the rising level of sec- tarianism and opposition since the 2003 invasion of Iraq, commemorat- ing Mughniyya was seen as tantamount to assaulting national unity and reopening the sectarian wounds of the 1980s. During that decade Mughniyya had been blamed for attempting to assassinate the emir and hijacking a Kuwaiti airplane in 1988,[44] and was linked to a series of bombings at the US Embassy in Kuwait in 1983.[45] Moreover, the Mughniyya commemoration was out of the norm for Shi'a conduct in the Kuwaiti public realm, which had been relatively uncontroversial since the sectarian rapprochement after the liberation from Iraq in the 1990s. Indeed, even though the al-Tahaluf bloc was pro-Iran, it had always played by Kuwaiti political norms and within proscribed red lines. This episode pushed those limits.

The *ta'bin* also provoked a harsh reaction from Sunnis. The Shi'a lead- ers of the commemoration were sanctioned by their Sunni peers in the *majlis* and were expelled from the cross-sectarian PAB.[46] One tribal Salafi MP encouraged the government to strip 'Abd-al-Samad of his citizenship and ban al-Tahaluf.[47] But 'Abd-al-Samad and Lari, two experienced politicians who were well aware of the taboo against Shi'a gatherings and the history of Kuwaiti hatred for Mughniyya, initially refused to apologize, and denied Mughniyya's link to the 1980s attacks.[48] In an attempt to calm the public, which firmly placed him on the side of the Shi'a, Prime Minister Mohammed also publicly cast doubt on Mughniyya's links to the attacks. In response, four Kuwaiti public lawyers filed suits against the Shi'a MPs and others, accusing them of links to Hezbollah. The leaders and a number of participants were detained by Amn al-Dawla (the National Security Bureau) and were charged with participating in the commemoration, belonging to political parties (which are technically illegal), working to change the system of government, and undermining the prestige of the state.[49]

How should the government have responded to this provocation? While the social response to the commemoration made sense within domestic and regional dynamics of spiraling sectarianism, the regime response suggests that domestic politics were a more pressing threat to the Al Sabah regime than the nearby rising power of Iran. First, it does not seem that the Kuwaiti regime perceived a threat from the rise of Iran as much as other Gulf powers did. The change in the regional balance of power after 2003 may have made for a more unstable alliance with Iran, but Iran wasn't perceived as an enemy or an existential threat the way it had been in the 1980s. It is plausible that the Kuwaiti regime's threat perception from Iran was mitigated by the fact that they no longer faced a threat from Saddam Hussein and they had preexisting good relations with Iran when Iran balanced Iraq for them in the previous decade.

In this respect, the Kuwaiti regime bucked the trend of its Gulf neighbors. It lightly reprimanded these Shi'a dissidents and chose to co-opt them instead. The policies the Al Sabah regime deployed were those of nominal co-optation and fit squarely within the co-optative norms of Kuwaiti history. Only one month later, the two MPs in question were cleared of wrongdoing.[50] All seven charged with weakening national unity were acquitted, and their cases were dismissed by October. The MPs quietly returned to the newly constituted parliament in May 2008, where hardline Shi'a Islamists made major electoral gains, increasing their representation from one to five MPs (due partially to districting changes as well). Four of the elected Shi'a were linked with al-Tahaluf. Adnan 'Abd-al-Samad was nominated to head the budget committee, giving him among the highest financial powers in parliament, and Ahmed Lari continued to represent the First District.

The regime clearly offered a policy of co-optation to its erstwhile political enemies. Fadhal Safar Ali Safar, whose previous political experience was limited to his election to the 2005 municipal council, was appointed by the government as an unelected minister of state for public works and municipal affairs—serving in the same cabinet as the interior minister who had detained him only a few months earlier.[51] Safar's appointment to government marked the first time that a "pro-Iran" al-Tahaluf deputy was appointed minister. At the same time, the regime allowed the reopening of the Social and Cultural Society, the original bastion of the Daw'a Shi'a from the 1970s that had been shut down in the late 1980s following a decade of violence and bad sectarian relations.

Rivka Azoulay explains that "for the first time since 1976 with the birth of a Shi'a opposition in Kuwait, the Shi'a were represented in the

Parliament by pro-government members and constituted a pillar of support for the government."[52] After the Mughniyya commemoration and its reintegration into parliament, al-Tahaluf did indeed change its political orientation despite a long history of opposition. To the uniform shock of my respondents and other Kuwaitis, the group became voting allies of the Kuwaiti government. They aligned themselves with Prime Minister Mohammed, who faced significant opposition in parliament at that time for charges of corruption and allegedly being too close to Iran, and was eventually forced out of office in 2011, a process described in more depth below. His resignation was a crucial moment for both Kuwaiti politics and Middle Eastern politics in general in which the opposition essentially forced regime change. After their experience with the *ta'bin*, Sunnis and Shi'a of other political blocs henceforth described al-Tahaluf as no longer motivated by the politics of opposition and reform, but rather by protecting its confessional group's relative position.[53] The regime thereby succeeded in splitting the ranks of the opposition.

Oppositional Balancing and Intra-Regime Schisms, not the International System

It is helpful to explore counterfactuals in this case as another way of seeing the extent to which domestic politics drove decision-making. One possibility is that the regime could have boldly and publicly used al-Tahaluf's transgression as a way to reassert its damaged Sunni credentials. This could have had a net positive effect for the Al Sabah regime, given that it faced an increasingly contentious and Salafi-affiliated opposition movement. Just next door in Bahrain, the Al Khalifa regime, while officially attempting to co-opt the biggest Shi'a political organization into its reopened assembly, had written a secret report in 2004 aimed at nothing short of remaking the demographic and thus oppositional balance in Bahrain through mass conversion, naturalization of Sunni foreigners, and a systematic media disinformation campaign to spread sectarianism and bring the Sunni opposition back to the side of the regime.[54] Kuwait's response, in contrast, was in keeping with the more inclusionary legacy of Shi'a-regime relations in the country. Tensions within the Al Sabah regime and the commitment of the emir and prime minister to a politics of balancing a particular architecture of opposition were also important factors.

In a sense, the strength and shape of the Kuwaiti opposition after 2003 cannot be disentangled from intra-regime schisms. Rivka Azoulay points specifically to machinations of the regime throughout the 2000s which were designed to foster "the emergence of new Shi'a merchants as notable intermediaries between the Al Sabah and the Shi'a masses" to supplant the loss of community power by the apolitical Shiraziyyin.[55]

These machinations were not limited to creating new elites, but about cultivating elite supporters for various factions of the royal family. The 2000s often saw branches of the ruling family playing out their schisms in parliament, particularly Prime Minister Mohammed's personal contention with Shaykh Ahmed al-Fahd, who had been passed over for prime minister in 2006. As Azoulay and Beaugrand explain, "with the government incapable of placating tribal constituencies, Sheikh Nasir resorted to the Shiites ... by allying himself to the Shiites, he also tried to support factions hostile to Sheikh Ahmad al-Fahd."[56] One participant in the commemoration for Mughniyya with whom I spoke also suggested that the position of the Shi'a got better after 2003 because of intra-ruling-family conflict. He was frank, however, in understanding that he had been used by the regime as part of this battle within the Al Sabah family, emphasizing, "Sabah al-Ahmed centralized more power than Jaber."[57]

In conclusion, while there is evidence that the increasing accommodation and co-optation of the Shi'a was a partial side-effect of intra-regime schisms and the proclivities of the emir and prime minister, Al Sabah leaders have, throughout Kuwaiti history, stayed in power by successfully balancing and co-opting their political opposition.

Life After (Re)Co-Optation: A New Bulwark for the Al Sabah Regime

The explanation advanced in this chapter about why the Shi'a experienced accommodation and co-optation after 2003 is based on where they, as a sectarian group, were located vis-à-vis the rest of the opposition. The regime's obsession with the growing tribal-Islamist opposition drove their decision-making toward the Shi'a in politics. This all-consuming fear of the opposition was more immediately threatening to the Kuwaiti regime than the regional events, such as the empowerment of Iran, which coincided with the 2003 US invasion and occupation of Iraq.

The May 2008 elections, only a few months after the Mughniyya commemoration, also demonstrate how the recently co-opted pro-Iranian Shi'a played into the opposition's narrative. As mentioned, the level of sectarianism in Kuwaiti society increased sharply after 2003. Elections were fractured, not only for sectarian reasons but because of a recent redistricting. Also as mentioned, Shiʻa quietist deputies from the Shirazi branch opposed the measure, hoping that the existing districts would allow them to ally with moderate Sunnis against their Shiʻa al-Tahaluf rivals, who supported redistricting along with the government.[58] The redistricting from 2006, which had inadvertently further fragmented Kuwaiti politics, led previous Sunni pro-regime elements to turn furiously against the measure. In the past, when there were only two deputies per electoral district, the Shiʻa had a majority in only two constituencies. In May 2008 the new system allowed each district to elect ten deputies, giving the Shiʻa more voting opportunities.[59] In an unforeseen triumph for the regime, redistricting inadvertently gave the Shiʻa Islamists five seats in the assembly, despite the recent controversy. This was a rather advantageous turnout for the regime, considering that those five seats had previously been oppositional and represented the most serious threat to the regime—a threat that was both large numerically and cross-sectarian. Additionally, the more moderate Hadas Islamist movement (the Kuwaiti branch of the Muslim Brotherhood) lost three seats. Lastly, the Sunni tribes further mobilized with the Salafis to gain ten out of fifty seats, double their previous number in parliament.[60] The new parliament was characterized by more criticism of the prime minister and cabinet by Salafi tribal MPs for not being Sunni enough in their foreign or domestic policy. In particular, the Salafis were upset with the government for accommodating the Shiʻa after the Iraq invasion through establishing the Jaʻafari Awqaf, new mosques, and a Shiʻa school.[61] In November 2008 three tribal Salafi deputies attempted to force the prime minister's resignation. He was defended by Shiʻa MPs. The early 2009 elections—the third set of elections held since 2006—brought about an even more fractured parliament, the most sectarian in Kuwaiti history.

After 2011: A More Authoritarian Turn[62]

Although the Shiʻa were neutralized as opposition, others were not. By 2010 the Kuwaiti parliament had once again become dysfunctional, and infighting was used by the minister of the interior to justify a ban on public gatherings and restrict media freedom in order to stop rising sectarianism.[63] Kuwait's iteration of the Arab Spring peaked on the night of November 16, 2011, when a number of demonstrators and opposition

MPs stormed the National Assembly and called for Prime Minister Nasser al-Mohammed al-Sabah to step down.[64] Nasser al-Mohammed resigned as prime minister in November 2011, and Kuwait's February 2012 elections installed a strong opposition with a Sunni Islamist majority.

A new and highly sectarian Sunni Islamist bloc formed, and pressed for legislation to make *shari'a* the source of all law and block new Christian churches. Sunni Islamist politicians also sought to reverse the establishment of the Ja'fari Awqaf, a move that could have further enflamed sectarian tensions. The emir pushed back against these plans and dissolved the National Assembly in June, reinstating the previous, pro-government, parliament. The December 2012 elections were boycotted by tribal, Islamist, and youth opposition after the emir decreed that citizens would only have one vote in the election, rather than the previous four to which they were accustomed. Having the opportunity to vote for several representatives per region, rather than one, was a feature of the previous voting system that had long allowed for voters to construct informal alliances prior to voting in the absence of the allowance of official parties.[65] The higher vote per district system had previously privileged government-supporting tribes, who started to become more oppositional in the 1990s. Critics, however, say that it facilitated corruption and vote-buying by allowing tribal leaders to pressure their kin to vote within the same clan. The boycott in turn led the Shi'a to win seventeen seats in parliament, their highest number ever, almost proportionate to their demographic numbers. Elections were held again in 2013, and this time ten Shi'a won seats, taking the number back to the same as the 1975 parliament, which had an all-time high of ten Shi'a MPs.

Regional Criminalization of Dissent

Yet, despite the high number of Shi'a in the Kuwaiti parliament following the Arab Spring—a group largely comprising those who supported the regime—a slew of persecutions of Kuwaiti Shi'a for speaking out against the sectarian policies of Kuwait's Gulf Cooperation Council (GCC) neighbors since 2013 has called into question—at least superficially—Kuwait's conciliatory treatment of the group. For example, the prominent Kuwaiti Shi'a lawyer and former member of parliament Khaled al-Shatti was arrested on April 2, 2015 for posting tweets critical of the Saudi-led Arab coalition's fight against the Houthis in Yemen.

Al-Shatti, who was released on bail April 6, 2015, was charged with challenging the emir, demoralizing Kuwaiti soldiers, offending the kingdom of Saudi Arabia, and threatening Saudi relations with Kuwait. Al-Shatti's Twitter protest is not the only evidence of discord against Kuwait's foreign policy, its treatment of Shi'a, and its increasing alignment in a professedly Sunni Gulf coalition against Iran. In the summer of 2015 seven out of ten Shi'a parliamentarians also initially criticized the Kuwaiti air force's participation in Saudi Arabia's Operation Decisive Storm in Yemen on the grounds that it violates Kuwait's constitutional prohibition on offensive war. Additionally, on January 13, 2016 Kuwait's Shi'a MPs boycotted parliament after the government sentenced more than twenty Shi'a to death for belonging to an Iranian-linked cell.[66]

The Kuwaiti regime's harsh response to Khaled al-Shatti and the Iran-linked cell seemed to mark a shift in Shi'a-regime relations. But did it? What had changed since the regime's careful re-co-optation of the Shi'a in the past decade that would lead Kuwait to join with its Arab allies in potentially controversial and sectarian causes at home and abroad that could rock the boat with its Shi'a allies at home?

The answer is that Kuwait, along with many of its neighbors, became more repressive in the aftermath of the region-wide and domestic uprisings that started in late 2010. Ruling elites are still reeling from the cross-class Islamist-tribal-youth coalition that has only intensified its demands for political reform since the Arab Spring. Intra-family factionalism and allegations of coup plotting have also fueled the anxiety of the Kuwaiti regime. To deal with this situation, the Kuwaiti government has revived some unique ways of stemming the ongoing opposition movement that go back to its policies in the 1980s. In 2014 the cabinet announced an "iron fist policy," which promised "a decisive and firm confrontation with whatever could undermine the state, its institutions and constitution." As a result, more than thirty people were deported and stripped of their citizenship for supposedly undermining the country's security.[67]

In addition to other major round-ups, at least eighteen people were reportedly arrested at an anti-government protest on March 23, 2015, including regional human rights defender Nawaf al-Hendal, who had addressed the UN Human Rights Council only three days earlier. Hendal has since been released, but his case has been referred to Kuwait's Criminal Court. Under current laws, questioning or "undermining" the emir is punishable with a five-year prison sentence, and quoting the emir without permission is a criminal offense. For example, in June 2015 Rana al-Sa'adoun, a founding member of rights group the National Committee for Monitoring Violations, was sentenced to three years in jail for posting a speech by opposition leader Musallam al-Barak on YouTube.[68] Kuwaiti policies have also increasingly targeted the stateless, also known as *bidun*, responding to their efforts to claim citizenship with violence and, after the June 26, 2015 mosque bombing, rhetorically depicting them as potential extremists.[69] After that attack, the government stopped issuing Article 17 passports,[70] a special class of passports for Kuwaitis with no citizenship that allows them to travel, albeit under certain conditions, the only means for eligible stateless residents to leave the country.[71] This change in policy collectively punished the group for the crimes of a few.

More importantly, it has become clear that there is not only a red line for Kuwaitis criticizing the emir, but a taboo on criticizing Kuwait's regional allies as well. Several other Kuwaitis who have criticized the Saudi regime or involved themselves in public domestic opposition campaigns have been targeted. Shatti was joined by Shi'a writer and academic Salah al-Fadhli, who was also arrested for speaking out about the war in Yemen. Another Shi'a MP, Abdulhameed Dashti[72], was sentenced in absentia to six years in prison with hard labor for insulting Bahrain and Saudi Arabia—three years for each country. Former Sunni MP Mubarak al-Duweileh[73] was been sentenced to two years in prison for insulting the United Arab Emirates. Kuwait is not out of the norm for suddenly prosecuting regional dissent—Bahrainis criticizing the Saudi campaign in Yemen were immediately arrested, too.

In this context, regional policy diffusion from Saudi Arabia has played an important role in guiding Kuwaiti politics in terms of how to respond to opposition politics. The regional criminalization of dissent has been facilitated by the GCC's Security Pact, which the Kuwaiti parliament has long opposed ratifying, though it has nevertheless impacted internal political norms. The pact has given legal means for the persecuting of opposition forces all over the Gulf, ostensibly on security terms. As Madawi Al-Rasheed explains:

> Meant to enhance security for economic development and stability of GCC countries, the pact has now turned into creating cross-border controls, evacuating the Arab Gulf of dissent and eliminating safe havens for dissidents of one country in another one.[74]

The Kuwaiti crackdown on Sunni and Shi'a dissent alike reveals that, if anything, the regime does share a strong threat perception with the rest of the GCC, but that it perceives its biggest transnational threat as not necessarily from Iran but from the diffusion of democratic movements that may uproot its allied Gulf regimes. In this context, regime-Shiʻa relations in Kuwait still have more to do with how formidable the domestic opposition is than any single other factor. Recent incidents of regime-Shiʻa tension are not evidence of sectarianism, but rather a reentrenchment of authoritarianism, in direct response to popular mobilization inspired by Arab Spring uprisings.

Conclusion

In this chapter I have argued that even as Iran's regional influence increased in the Middle East after 2003, the Kuwaiti government was far more concerned with the proximate threat that a new configuration of domestic political opposition posed to regime security. Kuwaiti government policies toward the Shiʻa, with the exception of those during the 1980s—when the perceived external threat was paramount—must be seen as a part and parcel of the contentious *pas-de-deux* between the ruling Al Sabah family and domestic oppositional forces over the years. Specifically, the rise of the tribal-Sunni Islamist opposition movement has led the Kuwaiti regime to placate and accommodate the Shiʻa in a counterbalancing maneuver in order to stay in power and compensate for its crisis of legitimacy. The Kuwaiti regime in the 2000s was primarily concerned with the Shiʻa inasmuch as they could become a political bulwark against a threatening new tribal-Sunni Islamist and youth opposition, rather than in terms of the political implications of their identity or links to Iran. These alleged links have become the subject of public scrutiny given the recent rise in Saudi-Iranian tensions, but the crackdown on Shiʻa and Sunni dissenters alike suggests that sectarianism must be seen within the context of fear of the opposition and regime survival strategies.

The findings of the Kuwaiti case suggest some tentative conclusions about the sectarianization process. First, understanding the lack of regime-led sectarianism in Kuwait has important implications for our understanding of where sectarianism comes from. The first and most obvious lesson is that, contrary to the new conventional wisdom, Sunni-Shiʻa tensions are not ancient or deep-seated. Regimes can decide to heighten or to downplay them as they need to strategically. The Kuwaiti regime has no anti-Shiʻa policy; it has an anti-opposition policy.

The Kuwaiti case may also shed some light on the impact of democratization in the region. On a superficial level, we might see Kuwait as more inclusive because it is more democratic and open than its Gulf neighbors. This would be wrong. Kuwaiti leaders did not co-opt the Shi'a out of some deep normative commitment to democracy or inclusion, but rather to thwart the opposition. The presence of some democratic institutions in a country simply means that there are more opportunities for opposition to form. But the particular shape and threat of opposition can vary from country to country. Bahrain is a good comparison. It has the most similar institutions to Kuwait and a lively civil society as well, yet its government has chosen exclusionary sectarian policies toward the Shi'a since the 1980s—largely, I would argue, because of the demographic-political reality that in Bahrain the Shi'a are a majority ruled by a Sunni minority regime.

Finally, the extent to which we view sectarianism through a transnational prism distorts rather than helps our analysis of the phenomenon. Viewing policies toward the Shi'a in a way that overemphasizes their transnational links may obscure the regime's stability concerns that stem from popular demands for democratic rights. As such, policymakers should first understand sectarianism in its domestic institutional context and how it relates to regime security concerns. Perhaps in understanding how and why sectarianism is deployed as a strategy of political rule, and how it relates to authoritarianism, policymakers can find solutions to de-escalate state-led sectarianism, too.

14

CONCLUSION

PEACEBUILDING IN SECTARIANIZED CONFLICTS: FINDINGS AND IMPLICATIONS FOR THEORY AND PRACTICE

Timothy D. Sisk

It is a common assertion in the scholarly literature on ethnic and religious conflict—including sectarian strife—that such groups are, following Benedict Anderson, "imagined communities."[1] That is, sectarian identities are created, and evolve over time, as the outcome of mobilization by elites who in turn provide a narrative about the nature and boundaries of the group. Those elites are followed, in turn, by "masses" with attachments and loyalties, by followers who develop "mental models" of identity-group relations, and alternately those who are deemed infidels or outsiders.[2] In sum, there is no fixed or "primordial" impetus to group formation and maintenance that informs "ancient hatreds." Just as group differentiation—such as sectarian framing of the other—is constructed, or invented, it can also be reconstructed and reinvented over time away from essentialist perspectives to more pragmatic ones.[3]

The scholarship in this volume affirms an essentially constructivist perspective on sectarianism in the modern Middle East. Sectarian or intra-religious differences have become a warrant for violence in Bahrain, Iraq, Pakistan, Syria, and Yemen particularly, and in each of these cases contributors to this volume point to the manipulation of identity by elites (especially by authoritarian political elites) and show how, over time, such violence leads to a sectarianized society. A deeper understanding of how sectarian group identity has taken shape in these countries and throughout the region, and how difference along sectarian lines is maintained socially over time, is essential to identifying and understanding the conditions under which measures can be taken to monitor, manage, reduce, and resolve sectarian strife through peacebuilding.[4]

Above all, the contributors to this book reaffirm much of the wider literature that suggests that while group identity can be salutary, as custom, culture, and intra-group caring are critical human traits—and there is nothing inherently violent about a sectarian perspective or about any particular religion or belief—sectarianism can also be the badge or basis for violence. The conditions under which violence erupts in the name of sectarian beliefs depend heavily on the ways in which religious elites have justified or catalyzed conflict along religious—including intra-religious or sectarian—lines, and how they have provided warrant for attacks on others.[5] At the same time, as we see in the contemporary Middle East, violence that emerges along sectarianized lines typically does so as a combination of religious mobilization and manipulation by political elites, social dislocation and discrimination, and external influence during troubled transitions from authoritarian rule. Some observers of global conflict trends have suggested that violence fueled by such tensions has interrupted the diminution in conflict globally—a global trend since the early 1990s: many of the new "onsets" of civil war in recent years have occurred in the Middle East,[6] including in Iraq, Libya, Syria, and Yemen—each precipitating significant, long-term humanitarian crises. According to a 2014 Pew Research Center report, social conflicts with ethno-religious dimensions are more prevalent now than they were earlier in the 2000s.[7]

Navigating beyond Sectarianization

The contributors to this volume also observe a fundamental paradox that emerges in understanding how sectarianization has gripped the region in recent years and the consequently difficult pathway forward for constructing a less violent, more tolerant political reality in the region that transcends, or at least nonviolently manages, the differences. Because sectarianism has been so carefully and consistently constructed to fit modern regional, national, and local political realities in an uncertain region, it appears to be exceedingly ill-advised to introduce highly majoritarian (or majority-rule oriented) democracy in such contexts. The ensuing ethnic mobilization—as elites fan the flames of sectarian division as an electoral strategy—may lead to further and additional cycles of violence: a point long appreciated by observers of ethnic conflict and democratization more broadly, and as Matthiesen demonstrates in this volume.[8] This paradox is especially acute for those such as UN envoys or personnel who are directly or indirectly mediating in ongoing sectarianized conflicts in the region (e.g. Iraq, Lebanon, Libya, Syria, Yemen). In other countries, moreover, hybrid (partial democracy) or closed authoritarian regimes continue to face social unrest from aggrieved sectarian and other minorities, and have in turn earned condemnation from global human rights groups (Bahrain, Kuwait, Turkey, Saudi Arabia).[9] In such contexts, the outcome of mediation by the UN often entails democratic transitions as a way to provide an exit from civil war or authoritarianism, as a strategic approach to building peace through new institutions and rules of the game through which to, ideally, nonviolently manage sectarian conflict through inclusive, democratic governance.[10]

Precisely because sectarianism is a socially constructed and historically contingent phenomenon in the Middle East, there should be identifiable ways to take measure to deliberately deconstruct and attenuate sectarian conflict through peacebuilding and inclusive or less competition-focused democratization and state-building. Today, there continues to be a sharp debate internationally on whether such an aim is realistically possible in the most conflict-affected contexts such as Iraq and Syria, after so much violence along sectarian lines, and where the political economy of state-building has resulted in new and deep patronage networks that essentially mirror identity segments in society. In both Iraq and Syria there are those who would abandon the Sykes-Picot arrangement of states in the region as inherited a century ago and instead "partition" these existing states into more identity-based territorial units (or, as sometimes described, "Balkanization").[11]

A seeming majority of views in the international community, however, is that partition doesn't solve the problem of "living together" or coexistence—it merely rearranges the positions of majorities and minorities. Equally, there is the reality that global powers such as the USA, Russia, and France oppose partition in cases of existing states, even as a two-state solution remains the stated principal outcome preference of these actors in the Israeli–Palestinian conflict.

Such a situation leaves important actors seeking to build peace in the region, such as the UN, with a long-term challenge of promoting regional stability, enhancing social cohesion and inclusive governance at the national level, and beginning to address the root causes of sectarian conflict. Today, the UN has in the field special political missions in key countries affected by sectarianized conflicts—including large special political missions (teams of civilians) in Iraq and Lebanon—as well as UN resident representatives in country offices in both conflict-affected countries in the region (such as the UNDP's Programme of Assistance to the Palestinian People, PAPP) and in those where regional conflict is closely felt (as in Jordan). While the UN is but a partner in the broader efforts to build peace in the sectarianized Middle East, it is perhaps the most important one in terms of working at regional, national, and local levels to develop, design, and, with partners, implement an integrated, concerted effort to address the myriad and interrelated sectarianized conflicts that autocracy, uneven and insufficient development, the interference/interventions of foreign powers, interrelated wars, and troubled transitions have all left in their wake.

In this concluding chapter I have three principal aims. First, I step back from the immediate, close-up analysis of the Middle East to define contemporary approaches to peacebuilding in identity-based conflict, to explore essential perspectives on peacebuilding, to identify institutions and models of ameliorating identity-based conflict through power-sharing, and to present common practices through which, in other cases, societies have sought to transcend religious difference, including sectarian difference, both in spirit and through specific processes and practices.

Second, I present five findings from across the chapters in this volume and draw out the common understandings among them and their implications for peacebuilding. Third, I present the implications of the work of the authors in this volume in findings designed to speak to potential peacebuilders—typically civil society organizations and individuals within countries, but also outsiders such as the UN, regional organizations and regional mediators, international development partners, and transnational civil society organizations seeking to build peace in a sectarianized region.

Finally, returning to the analysis of Nader Hashemi and Danny Postel in their introductory chapter to this volume, I outline several principal conditions for de-sectarianization: elites committed to an inclusive political settlement; cross-cutting civil society and economic relationships; confessionally balanced public policy and natural resources wealth-sharing agreements; regional stability and evolution of regional organizations; and a continued and indeed expanded UN and regional organization role dedicated to fostering social cohesion.

Peacebuilding in Sectarianized Conflicts: Perspectives, Institutions, Practices

In their introduction, Hashemi and Postel rightly place the challenging question of sectarianized conflict within the social-science literature on understanding conflict more broadly (particularly ethnic conflict and the related issues of nationalism, religious nationalism, and indigeneity) and other forms of identity-related social organization that can, at specific times and typically through a mix of structural factors and precipitating events, erupt into violence. The research has shown that often such conflicts evolve into "protracted social conflicts" in which groups that formerly resided together find it impossible to share a common destiny or "live together."[12] The critical factor is often violence along ethnic lines, which features the pernicious quality of the perpetrators determining the boundaries of the community and in which victims are identified as outsiders, infidels, or enemies. When communities in conflict must "live together" as a consequence of the history of state formation, such "deeply divided societies" typically seek balances between group solidarity and national identity, among territory and space, shared or inclusive symbols, and centralization and local autonomy in governance structures.

Before addressing the question of whether sectarian (or other forms of identity) conflicts can be de-escalated, or otherwise transformed such that socially organized and intergroup conflict no long occurs along sectarian lines, it is important to underscore the importance of perspectives of interdependence in identity-group relations. Research and scholarship have shown that armed conflict, and social violence once it begins, can sharply separate communities as individuals retreat into the security of co-communal relations. That is, the greater the degree of violence along communal lines, the greater the expected social pressures are for separation, rather than integration, or at a minimum for power-sharing and group autonomy versus any centralization of power or promise of moderation and inclusivity by dominant groups. That is, when conflict occurs along sectarian lines, physical separation and the development of within-group networks frequently result.

The literature on identity-based conflict such as sectarianism, and the various institutional and practical dimensions of peacebuilding in such contexts, has accelerated since the end of the Cold War.[13] The principal debates in this literature revolve around the conditions under which violence and conflict occur, patterns and processes within war, peace agreements and, after conflict, how groups can conceivably live together. Particularly, this literature focuses on the political dimensions of peacebuilding, especially the varieties of institutional arrangements than can facilitate inclusive governance and minority protections together with the practices of dialogue and problem-solving through which the character and processes of living together can be defined.

Particularly poignant in this literature is the institutional debate over whether power-sharing along confessional lines (consociationalism) leads to more sustainable peaceful outcomes than institutional arrangements that eschew identity-based or confessional representation. Perhaps in no country has this debate been stronger than in Lebanon, where confessional representation and consociational governance has been the system in place since the 1943 National Pact; although subsequent pacts such as the 1989 Ta'if Accord or the 2008 Doha Accord adjusted the consociational formula in Lebanon, the consociational power-sharing system has been claimed to be transitional even though it is now fully entrenched in political, economic, social, and geographic aspects of national life. Despite calls to reform the Lebanese system to make it more of a "citizen's state," institutionalized representation of identity at the center of the Lebanese state continues to perpetuate identity politics and frustrate socioeconomic development.[14] Yet there remains a deep-seated resistance to sectarian politics and economic life in Lebanon, together with hope that institutional changes such as electoral law reform and territorial decentralization may be a way to loosen the grip of sectarian elites. Until there is reform of political institutions, it appears that the widespread grassroots efforts to transcend sectarianism in Lebanon are "invariably limited."[15]

CONCLUSION

Absent such institutional change, peacebuilding in sectarianized con-
flicts relies on process-related options at the regional, national, and local
levels. Such practices typically focus on people-to-people interactions and
relationships, and can take any number of forms. As well, the term
peacebuilding is quite elastic, and many development projects as such
can be considered indirect contributions to creating the social conditions
for peace.

The research on peacebuilding processes in religious or sectarian dis-
putes consistently reports that such processes must be broadly inclusive,
should include not only organized religious leaders but also lay and civil
society groups, and should be substantively focused on ways to reconsider
and reinterpret religious canon and practice to be more tolerant and inclu-
sive.[16] More broadly, peacebuilding practice has led to an understanding
that stand-alone or "one-shot" dialogue processes are rarely successful, and
that countries that have experienced protracted social conflict need to
design a complex system of national, sub-national, and highly local institu-
tions for conflict monitoring, constructive dialogue, and crisis management
through so-called "architectures" for peace that create overlapping and
reinforcing informal and formal institutions for conciliation.

Understanding Sectarianization: Patterns and Paradoxes

The New Year 2016 execution of Shaykh Nimr al-Nimr, a prominent
Shi'a cleric put to death with forty-six others by Saudi Arabia, further
inflamed already widespread and deep-seated sectarian tensions through-
out the Middle East.[17] Al-Nimr was an outspoken cleric who called for
greater Shi'a rights in the Sunni-majority Saudi kingdom, serving as a
voice for the marginalized. As a religious leader, he could be viewed as a
communal mobilizer, as an "entrepreneur" of conflict, or as a champion
of religious minority rights under an authoritarian regime. Others would
suggest that the execution really wasn't about sectarianism as such—
although it clearly inflamed sectarian tendencies across the region—but
had more to do with the intricacies of regional power politics in the wake
of the Iran nuclear deal.[18]

In any case, the seismic effects of al-Nimr's execution deepened the
fracture in Saudi-Iranian relations, fueled local-level street violence in
Lebanon, emboldened extremist voices on all sides, and further
entrenched sectarian fault lines in the region. Local-level popular atti-

tudes often reflect a yearning for a non-sectarian future, sometimes with a nostalgic romanticism for earlier pan-Arabist aspirations. Today, although there are myriad sects and forms of religious identity in the Middle East, the overarching intra-Islamic Shi'a–Sunni divide is a "master cleavage" that overshadows issues such as the Kurdish question, the rights of minorities, or even the enduring Israeli–Palestinian conflict.

The first principal finding of this volume is that the current period of sectarianism is the result of a conjuncture of external and internal historical processes that:

- have roots in the Ottoman period
- reflect a failed century of "nation building" in the region and
- were exacerbated by the deep social dislocation and insecurity that have gripped the region since the 2003 US invasion and occupation of Iraq.

This book's editors and contributors argue that sectarianism is a "constructed" social phenomenon, related to historical social structures and patterns of mobilization, often in turbulent transitions from one regime to another. As such, the evolution of sectarianism in the modern Middle East is a deep-seated, dynamic, and continuously evolving process which, given its exacerbation in the 2000s, has threatened the fundamental order of sovereignty on which the region was built in the post-Ottoman period.

Ussama Makdisi offers a forceful challenge to the widespread view that the Shi'a–Sunni conflict derives from ancient, primordial hatreds.[19] His call to consider modern sectarianism as a product of *modern* struggles over nationalism and citizenship echoes the work of David Little, who has distinguished between forms of religious nationalism, their relationship to issues of interpretation of divine texts, and what fundamentalism may mean for the nature of the state and, often, the plight of minorities. Makdisi observes that the diverse and locally tolerant system of Ottoman rule was replaced over time with modern, Western imperial notions of a secular and citizenship-oriented state, yet such multi-religious entities have been unable to survive.[20]

Adam Gaiser takes constructivism further to evaluate the narratives of discourse within Islamic history, focusing on the "dynamic and conscious process of adaptation, maintenance, and manipulation of certain types of narrative identities." It would be erroneous, in his view, to equate Western notions of sect (derived as they are from the Catholic–Protestant divide, and further delineated in careful taxonomies according to belief) with Islamic ones; rather, Gaiser contends, it is not enough to evaluate the dynamics of conflict in terms of sect-related belief alone—we must take into account the confluence of economic, social, political, and geographic rationale for the justification of violence against others. Sectarianism is the language deployed, for example, by Salafi jihadists who target and kill those they perceive as threatening—representing them as "refusers" who follow different paths within Islam and "reject" Sunni traditions (*rafidha*, literally "rejectionists," is a pejorative word for Shi'a). He argues for newer models of understanding the dynamics of sectarianism in the region that focus on the process and maintenance of sect identity through discourse, markers, and processes of identity-formation.

Fanar Haddad echoes the view that the current manifestation of sectarian conflict in Iraq is the "product of the emergence of modern hatreds, and that sectarianism in Iraq (*ta'ifiyya*) is the result of political mobilization and state capture." The sectarianization of Iraqi society is "a tool with which regimes and conservative social elements can exclude perceived threats." In his view, the dynamic was more of a conflict between the Ba'athist state and the Shi'a than the Sunni-Shi'a divide as such. In addition to economic and social deprivation, the Shi'a (who were more religiously institutionalized) were politically excluded, which in turn led to "Shi'a-centric issues" and mobilization and, in the post-2003 era, the rise of Shi'a political movements. Echoing the conclusions of other authors in this volume, Haddad sees "no end in sight" to the politicization of identity in Iraq due to deep distrust among the population and a "mismanagement of communal plurality" by the post-Saddam state.

The second finding is that sectarian violence begets more sectarian violence; there are few mechanisms to control increasing fear, spiraling events, and instigations designed to invoke sectarian responses. Violence can be strategically pursued to target enemies and to exacerbate sectarian differences within otherwise coexisting groups. The issue of sectarianism in Syria is strongly debated, in terms of the role of the Assad regime in sectarianizing the conflict, the metamorphosis of the "Arab Spring" uprising into a mostly sectarian struggle, and whether/how a non-sectarian order can be created in the aftermath of the Syrian bloodbath, which has led in many locations to de facto separation of the population and to Kurdish autonomous regions.

Paulo Gabriel Hilu Pinto argues that the Assad regime turned to the language of sectarianism—in labeling protestors Salafi extremists, al-

Qaeda, or Muslim Brothers—and framing its crackdown on nonviolent, cross-confessional demonstrations as "anti-terrorism" operations against Sunni zealots. This in turn provoked a greater Sunni symbolism in the protests, such that the anti-regime uprising "gradually became more invested with Sunni meanings, deepening the tension between inclusive and sectarian understandings of religious nationalism." Combined with the regime's use of sectarian militias, targeted repression, and "selective distribution of violence" to punish sub-groups of protestors, sectarianization in Syria became, in Pinto's view, "a self-fulfilling prophecy."

The third finding of this volume is that sectarianism has become institutionalized in politics and engrained in patterns of political clientelism and regional economic and religious networks. Efforts to create cross-sectarian or "de-sectarianized" political, economic, or civil society structures face steep barriers, despite an apparent consensus among the people of the region that favors a tolerant, inclusive identity. The evolution of the Syrian conflict, combined with the emergence of ISIS, has further exacerbated already rigid networks and eroded the willingness to cooperate politically across social divisions or regional divides. Yezid Sayigh shows in his chapter why sectarianism alone cannot explain regional or national turmoil. In his view, "state policies that privilege certain communities or marginalize others—whether in terms of political access, social welfare, or economic opportunity—generate anti-systemic counter forces," particularly in the region's urban areas.

These dynamics intersect strongly in the case of regional alliances, and no more poignantly than in the wars in Syria and Yemen. The fourth major finding of this book is that regional and international power rivalries and interventions have exacerbated and, indeed, shaped sectarian differences in the region. Bassel F. Salloukh argues that ahistorical (primordialist or essentialist) thinking about sectarianism—even if it is at odds with historical fact—among those who are pursuing a regional geopolitical contest has fueled the sectarianization process. He contends that the aforementioned al-Nimr execution was not driven by sectarian logic, but instead a complicated international and regional landscape and foreign-policy agenda. Like others, however, he laments that although such sectarian differences have been inflamed by outsiders and wars of position for regional hegemony, at the local level they "take on a life of their own." He rightly notes that this is clear in the facts-on-the-ground presence of Kurdish autonomous regions, which will go against any claim for multi- or non-confessional governance well into the future.

Eskandar Sadeghi-Boroujerdi, too, claims that it is a gross oversimplification to state that Iran stokes sectarianism for some grand religious purpose (such as establishing, or restoring, a Shi'a/Persian "empire" into the twenty-first century). In his view, Iran's policy of backing Shi'a co-sectarians in Lebanon, Iraq, Syria, or Yemen should be viewed in *Realpolitik* terms: as that of a "regional middle power" whose foreign policy has been "shaped in the context of the systemic insecurity of a regional system penetrated by hegemonic Great Powers." He argues that it is the "nested and interlocking series of security dilemmas" in the region that have shaped conflicts along sectarian lines, a drama in which Iran's leadership has been a major protagonist.

A fifth set of findings relates to the nature of continued "hybrid" or autocratic regimes in the region and how they have pursued violence against minorities as a cover for their own feeble and/or corrupt rule. Bahrain stands out in the Arab Spring uprisings as a case in which the state relied on Sunni rhetoric and sectarianized security networks as a way to stave off demands for reform from social groups that cut across identity lines. Toby Matthiesen argues that the Bahraini regime employed "all means at its disposal, including the media, the security forces, and even vigilante groups, to scare the Sunnis with the specter of a Shi'a takeover and to portray the uprising as led by Shi'a radicals that wanted to establish an Iranian-style Islamic republic." Regime manipulation of sectarian differences had the effect of mobilizing support for the state against the protestors. Ironically, however, in strengthening the sectarian nature of opposition to the regime, it undermined security in the long run by alienating this critical element (the majority) of the population. Autocratic responses to demands for democracy, by playing the sectarian card, thus ultimately reinforce polarized regional relations and maintain ruling elites in power, but at a vital cost to regional and local tensions that portend greater insecurity in the long run.

The Saudi regime has used similar methods, as Madawi Al-Rasheed shows in her chapter. Indeed, this context is directly and intricately related to Bahrain. She argues that sectarian rhetoric is instrumental to such ruling elites, who are more loyal to clan ties than sects as such, and that "political maneuvering requires the regime to play on the fears of both the minority Shi'as and the majority Sunnis rather than assume a fixed sectarian identity." "The survival of the Al Saud clan," she argues, "rather than the protection of an almighty Sunni world, remains the most sacred project."

Kuwait's long history of more amicable relations across the Sunni-Shi'a divide requires explanation in a region beset by enmity between the two communities. In response to pressures for change in the Arab Spring environment, the Kuwaiti elite opted, as Madeline Wells shows, for a co-optation strategy aimed at "regime balancing" within its relatively more open or semi-democratic political institutions. She concludes that "Kuwaiti leaders did not co-opt the Shi'a out of some deep normative commitment to democracy or inclusion, but rather to balance its opposition." Regime stability concerns trumped an ostensible regional alliance with other Sunnis in facing a perceived Shi'a threat.

Quite differently, in Yemen, Stacey Philbrick Yadav explores the failure of the putative transition to democracy, which included features of power-sharing, electoral processes, and a widely trumpeted "National Dialogue" process, but which fell victim to the recurrence of sectarian strife. She argues that the Yemeni transition was ill-conceived by both internal and external forces, such that "structural features of Yemen's transitional process played a significant role in amplifying the sectarian framing of Islah–Houthi tensions" through its institutional misrepresentation of these social forces and the naming, particularly, of those subject to global sanctions and anti-terror targeting. By labeling such actors "spoilers," international actors limited the degree of inclusion necessary for the transition to succeed and led to the framing of the conflict in sectarian terms. As a result, she concludes: "A Yemen polarized along sectarian lines is now a social fact with which postwar planners will have to contend, despite building resentment of the Houthis even among their own supporters."

Toward De-Sectarianization: What Role for Peacebuilders?

While the contributors to this volume reluctantly conclude that "sectarianism" is here to stay (at least for the foreseeable future), which may suggest there is little role for peacebuilders in the region, there is no shortage of comparative experience with intergroup conflict management or peacebuilding with direct application to a sectarianized Middle East.

Two of the most important comparative cases for understanding the transformation of violent sectarianized conflicts into more peaceful orders are Northern Ireland and Bosnia. In Northern Ireland, an extended process of negotiation over power-sharing, together with underlying changes in economic exclusion, social inequality, and policing for the Catholic community have brought a new era of peace following a conflict that lasted some twenty-seven years. For many years the sectarian (Protestant–Catholic) conflict in Northern Ireland was deemed intractable, yet a combination of institutional changes (with inclusive power-sharing along "community" lines) and social reforms in employment, housing, policing, and management of symbols and parades has brought a new sense of peace and possibilities for coexistence.[21] Moreover, religious leaders played a critical role in articulating the imperative of living together, and several protagonists in the conflict directly sought to de-escalate tensions and signal a willingness for coexistence and cooperation.[22]

Bosnia also holds considerable "lessons learned" for peacebuilding that can inform contexts such as Iraq, Syria, and Yemen, especially in terms of ways to pair transitional power-sharing with bottom-up "social cohesion" programming as an approach to managing tensions along identity lines. The Bosnian conflict involved both an inter-religious component (Christians—of two sectarian varieties—against Muslims) and intra-religious sectarianism (Croatian Catholics against Serbian Orthodox Christians), with an overlay of ethnic division (Croats against Serbs).[23] In Bosnia, power-sharing institutions—while enforced by the security presence of NATO—have been inclusive of the three principal communities in the country. While Bosnia has seen the persistence of ethnic politics in the two decades since the end of the war, there were initial signs in the first postwar decade of an emerging, cross-national sense of cohesion in the war-torn country emanating from economic interdependencies, civil society integration, and youth-oriented education programming.[24]

In both Northern Ireland and Bosnia, détente and cooperation among regional powers were critical to progress in reducing tensions at the local level—a factor with direct implications for the prospects of de-escalating sectarian conflicts in the Middle East today.

Other cases that could offer insights into conflict management across religious and sectarian lines are those found in Nigeria, India (Kashmir), Sri Lanka, and Myanmar. One of the essential findings from comparative analysis is that within-community work is equally as important as between-community work in sponsoring religious dialogues for peace (see note 16).

These and other cases point to ways in which outside actors or peace-builders have sought to address identity-based social cleavages through direct approaches such as mediation and support for dialogue, and through indirect approaches in which development assistance is deployed in a conflict-sensitive manner to foster social cohesion across identity lines. A new set of international agendas for peacebuilding informs research and policy reflection in the area of social cohesion, namely the so-called New Deal for Engagement in Fragile States put forward by the "G7+" (2011).[25] The social cohesion concept is also found throughout the network of peacebuilding organizations—from other international and intergovernmental organizations, to regional organizations, transnational NGOs, and traditional (OECD) bilateral assistance providers. Its focus is building peace across two dimensions: the vertical, in which there is a reorientation of relations between the citizen and the state (a "citizen's state"); and the horizontal, or improving the "quotidian" relationships at the social level of everyday life.

For Middle East peacebuilders there seems at the moment to be a logic and role for a UN-focused approach to "de-sectarianization" in the region. Because of the low level of institutionalization across the sectarian divide in the region (i.e. across the Saudi-Iranian divide) the UN is by default called on to monitor and mediate peace agreements. Also in part because of the already extensive role of the world body are UN "special political missions" and/or special envoys, which are deployed in Iraq, Lebanon, Syria, and Yemen (all critical cases in this volume). Also, the UNDP, an organization with extensive experience and arguably some success in helping mitigate violent conflict globally and in the region, is present in the countries of the region in ways no other single state or perhaps regional organization operates—often in partnership with the "state": its Regional Bureau for Arab States (RBAS) already serves as a key entity regionally for a coordinated response to the scourge of sectarianization and its related local conflicts.[26]

How could the critical explorations of sectarianism in this volume help inform ostensibly well-intentioned international peacebuilders, such as the UN, to better understand social dynamics in the contemporary, conflict-affected Middle East? In turn, how might these insights into the extent and nature of sectarianization lead to more informed UN policy-making in national contexts for developing a coherent, context-sensitive, and visionary approach to fostering social cohesion in sectarianized countries as a strategic approach to peacebuilding?

Findings from the literature on identity-related conflicts suggest that there are several ways that peacebuilders can act effectively to manage sectarian strife and to build social cohesion along identity-group divides. Peacebuilding first requires adequate and accurate monitoring of conflict contexts, particularly of religious and minority rights. Global transnational civil society groups such as Minority Rights Group International (http://minorityrights.org/) have played critical roles, as have traditional human rights organizations such as Human Rights Watch. Within the UN system, offices such as the Office of the Special Adviser on the Prevention of Genocide regularly monitor patterns of identity-based violence and atrocities and link that monitoring to intervention by special political missions and other diplomatic processes.

The UN's major mediation missions to create new political settlements and facilitate war-to-peace transitions through demilitarization of conflict settings have made by far the largest impact in the region. The literature is quite clear that absent a core or foundational political pact, societies suffer serious insecurities along identity lines, and violence often occurs in contexts where the absence of elites provides license for local-level violent action.[27] Mediation through the UN struggles, at times, between the challenge of bringing wars to an end (which may involve group-based guarantees, or consociationalism) versus achieving "non-confessional" outcomes in which power-sharing is ostensibly based on regional or economic factors, or on an individual, meritocratic basis. It is clear from the scholarship and practitioner reflection that UN mediation—while still focused on getting a comprehensive settlement—is but one step in the organization's broader role in facilitating often decades-long transitions from war to sustainable democracy in countries affected by conflict. Indeed, the current Special Representative of the Secretary General for Syria, Staffan de Mistura, articulated this challenge when he reported to the UN Security Council in July, 2015:

> Syrians overall emphasize their own vision for a united, sovereign, independent—they're very proud people—non-sectarian, multi-confessional, all-inclusive state with territorial integrity, preserved but reformed state institutions, such as the Ministries—as we have seen in Iraq that was the biggest problem we faced when suddenly many institutions disappeared in one moment of the change—including the political, security and judiciary sectors led by those who can inspire public confidence and trust.[28]

Beyond the mediation of state-of-the-art comprehensive peace agreements, the UN has, in the last two decades, played a significant role in managing or facilitating transitions, supporting interim regimes and transitional governments, facilitating electoral and constitution-making processes, and in the broader process of postwar state-building.[29] In this vein, it is often the UN country offices and the programming and projects that have as explicit or implicit aims the promotion of social cohesion. Major UNDP initiatives are already underway in Iraq and Yemen, yet it is clear that these efforts can only be effective in the most divisive contexts when there is a broader peace agreement. Research has shown that building social cohesion requires progress in extending the presence of an inclusive, resilient, and responsive state—especially at the local level. Moreover, at the horizontal level of social cohesion (across group divides), it appears that indirect approaches see more success than dialogue projects—especially when dialogue is not followed up with resource allocations.[30]

Conclusion

Hashemi and Postel begin this volume with the prescient insight that sectarianized politics in the contemporary Middle East is deeply shaped by the political context of authoritarianism. Clearly, authoritarian rule has failed to manage intergroup relations as identity entrepreneurs have manipulated the levers of state power and created the conditions for popular mobilization of sectarian resentment and animosity. On the other hand, democracy's ability to manage religious difference has been challenged, both conceptually and in practice, such that consociational or confessional power-sharing arrangements evolve as a matter of practice, with highly mixed results. Thus, a principal concern going forward will be the context-specific monitoring and evaluation of political institutions in each of the countries of the region to manage the eventual pressures for greater democratization in a manner that enhances inclusion, respect, and representation.

Comparative experience would suggest that progress at the regional level is a precondition for local peace and management of intergroup relations. The contributors to this volume rightly see that, at a minimum, geopolitical dynamics and regional rivalries that cut across the Saudi-Iranian regional rivalry are prerequisites for progress in reducing sectarian violence in the Middle East.[31] An ostensibly common aim is the defeat of ISIS, the most extreme of the sectarian groups, whose mass atrocities and spectacular brutality appear designed to invoke maximum fear among the "other."[32] Some have argued that only dialogue will provide the basis for regional peace. Seasoned UN policymaker Jean-Marie Guéhenno has argued that because extremism is deeply rooted in local conditions, we should be on guard against the fallacy of "quick fixes" and "double standards" (in support for Christian Yazidis, for example, but with relatively less apparent concern for Muslim lives), and above all to engage early on with those actors locally who may be willing to participate peacefully in politics; the tendency to lump all Islamic political actors in the same basket limits opportunities for engaging in dialogue even with those deemed by others as the most extreme.[33]

If there is hope for consigning sectarianism to the private realm of faith, or a broader movement toward a citizens' state in the Middle East, it is most likely to emerge in areas where civil society organizations have the ability to form and operate across identity-group lines. Leila Al-Shami, co-author of *Burning Country: Syrians in Revolution and War*, makes this point vis-à-vis Syria:

> It's important to point out that it was a cross-sectarian uprising. There was a lot of work being done at the cross-sectarian and cross-ethnic level, such as that of the Kurdish–Arab Fraternity Coordination Committee in Aleppo, and the active civil society organizations working in mixed communities like Al-Salamiyah, Yabroud, and elsewhere with very mixed sectarian populations. There are still such activities happening and it will be necessary to develop these organizations more in the post-conflict period.[34]

Evidence from other contexts would suggest that cross-cutting civil society is a critical factor in keeping identity-based differences from becoming politicized, from identity becoming the basis for access to resources from the state (to include fair policing), and ensuring progress in the elimination of group-based disparities. Such civil society efforts can emerge in the Middle East, as evidenced by the You Stink movement, a cross-sectarian protest against poor governance of sanitation in Beirut, which can also be seen as a form of resistance to sectarian, clientelistic politics in Lebanon.[35] Such formations, unfortunately, stand in sharp contrast to the broader sectarianism that has enveloped the region.

Peacebuilders wading into the complex waters of the sectarianized Middle East will thus need to understand much more carefully, in each context, how sectarianism is intricately related to other underlying social, economic, or geographic drivers of conflict and violence. They will need to have better instruments for monitoring how local conflicts are being articulated or waged in sectarian or ethnic terms and how inequality may overlap with identity; and they will require new tools for understanding mobilization along such lines through online content and methods of communication. Peacebuilding in the region will require a new configuration of political centralization and decentralization—in part in recognition of how conflict has shaped local realities—and particularly of how the question of Kurdish autonomy will be managed within the context of existing states.[36] And peacebuilding will further need to address the long-term goal of creating a citizen's state throughout the region, one in which some form of national identity transcends and supersedes the particularism of a sectarian or religious one.

NOTES

INTRODUCTION: THE SECTARIANIZATION THESIS

1. It is often suggested that Sunni-Shi'a differences resemble the division between Catholics and Protestants. The more accurate parallel in Christianity, however, is between Roman Catholicism and Eastern Orthodoxy. For background see Marshall Hodgson, "How Did the Early Shi'a Become Sectarian?" *Journal of the American Oriental Society* 75:1 (1955), 1–13; Seyyed Hossein Nasr, *Ideals and Realities of Islam*, revised edition (Chicago: ABC International Group, Inc., 2011), 141–174; Wilferd Madelung, *The Succession to Muhammad: A Study of the Early Caliphate* (Cambridge: Cambridge University Press, 1997); Mahmoud Ayoub, *The Crisis of Muslim History: Religion and Politics in Early Islam* (Oxford: Oneworld, 2003).

2. See comments by National Public Radio reporter Deborah Amos and former US government official Elliott Abrams (now a Senior Fellow with the Council on Foreign Relations) in the Foreign Policy Association documentary *The Great Divide: Sunni vs. Shi'a*, available at https://youtu.be/6MZeHeOwEXI. Both of them echo a thesis heard twenty years ago in the context of the Balkan wars: that a strong dictator kept control of "ancient hatreds," but with his death these forces have become unleashed. *New York Times* columnist Thomas Friedman observes that sectarian tensions in the Middle East had "long been managed by iron fists from above." But after longstanding dictators were toppled, "a horrifying war of all against all has exploded." See his column "Contain and Amplify," *New York Times*, May 27, 2015, available at http://www.nytimes.com/2015/05/27/opinion/thomas-friedman-contain-and-amplify.html.

3. "Statement by the President on Syria," August 31, 2013; "Remarks by the President and First Lady on the End of the War in Iraq," December 14, 2011; and "Remarks of President Barack Obama—State of the Union Address,"

January 12, 2016, available at www.whitehouse.gov. See Karla Adam, "Obama Ridiculed for Saying Conflicts in the Middle East 'Date Back Millennia' (Some Don't Date Back a Decade)," *Washington Post*, January 13, 2016, available at https://www.washingtonpost.com/news/worldviews/wp/2016/01/13/obama-ridiculed-for-saying-conflicts-in-the-middle-east-date-back-millennia-some-dont-date-back-a-decade/. Like his predecessor Bill Clinton, these arguments were advanced to deflect calls for intervention to stop mass atrocities in Bosnia/Syria. For background see Michael Sells, "Religion, History, and Genocide in Bosnia-Herzegovina," in G. Scott Davis (ed.), *Religion and Justice: The War over Bosnia* (New York: Routledge, 1997), pp. 23–43 and Michael Sells, "Christ Killer, Kremlin, Contagion," in Michael Sells and Emran Qureshi (eds.), *The New Crusades: Constructing the Muslim Enemy* (New York: Columbia University Press, 2003), pp. 366–371.

4. Ted Cruz, "How US can stop ISIS," CNN.com, September 10, 2014, available at http://www.cnn.com/2014/09/10/opinion/ted-cruz-how-us-can-stop-isis/.

5. Andy Borowitz, "Pressure on Obama to Quickly Resolve Centuries-Old Sunni–Shiite Conflict," *The New Yorker*, June 18, 2014, available at http://www.newyorker.com/humor/borowitz-report/pressure-on-obama-to-quickly-resolve-centuries-old-sunni-shiite-conflict.

6. "George Mitchell Talks to Tony Harris," Al Jazeera America, June 26, 2014, available at http://america.aljazeera.com/watch/shows/talk-to-al-jazeera/articles/2014/6/27/george-mitchell-talkstotonyharris.html.

7. James Arkin, "Palin: Let Allah Sort it Out," *Politico*, August 31, 2013, available at http://www.politico.com/story/2013/08/sarah-palin-let-allah-sort-it-out-096128.

8. Thomas Friedman, "Tell Me How This Ends Well," *New York Times*, April 1, 2015, available at http://www.nytimes.com/2015/04/01/opinion/thomas-friedman-tell-me-how-this-ends-well.html.

9. Jon Stewart, "Now That's What I Call Being Completing F**king Wrong about Iraq," *The Daily Show*, June 17, 2014; Bill Maher, *Real Time with Bill Maher*, June 13, 2014, available at http://www.realclearpolitics.com/video/2014/06/14/maher_the_sunnis_and_shiites_are_going_to_have_this_out_and_we_just_have_to_let_them.html. National security/terrorism expert Richard Clarke and MSNBC journalist Krystal Ball, also guests on this show, both invoked the "ancient sectarian hatreds" thesis. Bill O'Reilly, "O'Reilly: Sunni and Shiite Iraqis 'have fun' when they 'kill each other'," *Media Matters for America*, January 26, 2007, available at http://mediamatters.org/video/2007/01/26/oreilly-sunni-and-shiite-iraqis-have-fun-when-t/137855.

10. CNN documentary, *The Long Road to Hell: America in Iraq*, October 26, 2015, available at http://www.cnn.com/TRANSCRIPTS/1510/26/csr.01.html

11. Joshua Landis, comments at forum on "Sectarianization: ISIS, the Syrian Conflict and the Future of the Middle East," University of Denver, October 1, 2014, available at https://youtu.be/CQ-CaglfQms. See also Joshua Landis, "The Great Sorting Out: Ethnicity and the Future of the Levant," *Qifa Nabki*, December 18, 2013, available at https://qifanabki.com/2013/12/18/landis-ethnicity/ and "Joshua Landis on ISIS, Syria & the 'Great Sorting Out' in the Middle East," in the *Middle East Dialogues* series produced by the University of Denver's Center for Middle East Studies, available at https://youtu.be/_-roW5Y7vbw. In a similar vein, Bernard Lewis described the genocide in Bosnia as a case of "internecine chaos." See his *The Middle East: A Brief History of the Last 2,000 Years* (New York: Scribner, 1995), p. 387.

12. Shadi Hamid, "The End of Pluralism," *The Atlantic*, July 23, 2014, available at http://www.theatlantic.com/international/archive/2014/07/the-end-of-pluralism/374875/.

13. Vali Nasr, *The Shia Revival: How Conflicts within Islam Will Shape the Future* (New York: W.W. Norton, 2006), p. 82.

14. The original quote is: "War is not merely an act of policy but a true political instrument, a continuation of political intercourse, carried on with other means." See Carl von Clausewitz, *On War*, translated and edited by Michael Howard and Peter Paret (New York: Everyman's Library, 1993), pp. 98–99.

15. Ashutosh Varshney, "Ethnicity and Ethnic Conflict," in Carles Boix and Susan Stokes (eds.), *The Oxford Handbook of Comparative Politics* (New York: Oxford University Press, 2009), pp. 274–294.

16. Gilles Kepel, *Jihad: The Trail of Political Islam* (Cambridge, MA: Harvard University Press, 2002), pp. 23–135; Mohammed Ayoob, *The Many Faces of Political Islam* (Ann Arbor, MI: University of Michigan Press, 2007), pp. 1–22.

17. David Little, "Religion, Nationalism and Intolerance," in Timothy D. Sisk (ed.), *Between Terror and Tolerance: Religious Leaders, Conflict, and Peacemaking* (Washington, DC: Georgetown University Press, 2011), pp. 9–28.

18. Anthony D. Smith, *Nationalism and Modernism: A Critical Survey of Recent Theories of Nations and Nationalism* (New York: Routledge, 1998); Walker Connor, "Beyond Reason: The Nature of the Ethnonational Bond," *Ethnic and Racial Studies* 16 (July 1993), 373–389; David Lake and Donald Rothschild (eds.), *The International Spread of Ethnic Conflict: Fear, Diffusion, and Escalation* (Princeton: Princeton University Press, 1998), p. 5; and John F. Stack, Jr., "Ethnic Mobilization in World Politics: The Primordial Perspective," in John F. Stack, Jr. (ed.), *The Primordial Challenge: Ethnicity in the Contemporary World* (New York: Greenwood Press, 1986), pp. 1–2.

19. Alana Tiemessen, "From Genocide to Jihad: Islam and Ethnicity in Post-Genocide Rwanda," paper presented at the Annual Meeting of the Canadian Political Science Association, June 2–5, 2005, London, Canada.

20. David Laitin, *Hegemony and Culture: Politics and Religious Change among the Yoruba* (Chicago: University of Chicago Press, 1986); David Lake and Donald Rothchild, "Spreading Fear: The Genesis of Transnational Ethnic Conflict," in David Lake and Donald Rothchild (eds.), *The International Spread of Ethnic Conflict: Fear, Diffusion, and Escalation* (Princeton: Princeton University Press, 1998), p. 8; Paul Brass, *Ethnicity and Nationalism: Theory and Comparison* (London: Sage, 1991); Paul R. Brass, "Elite Groups, Symbol Manipulation and Ethnic Identity among the Muslims of South Asia," in David Taylor and Malcolm Yapp (eds.), *Political Identity in South Asia* (London: Curzon Press, 1979), pp. 35–77.

21. Benedict Anderson, *Imagined Communities: Reflections on the Origins and Spread of Nationalism* (New York: Verso, 1983); Crawford Young (ed.), *The Rising Tide of Cultural Pluralism: The Nation-State at Bay?* (Madison: University of Wisconsin Press, 1993). For a comparison and contrast between instrumentalism and constructivism see Varshney, "Ethnicity and Ethnic Conflict," pp. 285–288.

22. Lake and Rothchild (eds.), *The International Spread of Ethnic Conflict*, p. 6.

23. Vali Nasr, "International Politics, Domestic Imperatives, and Identity Mobilization: Sectarianism in Pakistan, 1979–1998," chapter 5 in this volume.

24. Ibid.

25. Pew Research Center, "Mapping the Global Muslim Population," October 7, 2009.

26. Joel Migdal, *Strong Societies and Weak States: State-society Relations and State Capabilities in the Third World* (Princeton: Princeton University Press, 1988), pp. 3–41.

27. Joel Migdal, "The State in Society: An Approach to Struggles for Domination," in Joel Migdal, Atul Kohli, and Vivienne Shue (eds.), *State Power and Social Forces: Domination and Transformation in the Third World* (Cambridge: Cambridge University Press, 1994), p. 9.

28. Migdal, *Strong Societies and Weak States*, pp. 206–237.

29. Nasr, "International Politics, Domestic Imperatives, and Identity Mobilization," chapter 5 in this volume.

30. Little, "Religion, Nationalism and Intolerance," p. 10.

31. Abdullah al-Arian, *Answering the Call: Popular Islamic Activism in Sadat's Egypt* (New York: Oxford University Press, 2014); Kepel, *Jihad*.

32. Khaled Abou El Fadl, *Reasoning with God: Reclaiming Shari'ah in the Modern Age* (Lanham, MD: Rowman & Littlefield, 2014), pp. 203–270.

33. S.V.R. Nasr, "The Rise of Sunni Militancy in Pakistan," *Modern Asian Studies* 34:1 (2000), 139–180.

34. Steve Coll, *Ghost Wars: The Secret History of the CIA, Afghanistan and Bin Laden, from the Soviet Invasion until September 10* (New York: Penguin Books, 2004);

Thomas Hegghammer, *Jihad in Saudi Arabia: Violence and Pan-Islamism since 1979* (Cambridge: Cambridge University Press, 2010), pp. 24–30.

35. Simon Mabon, *Saudi Arabia and Iran: Soft Power Rivalry in the Middle East* (New York: I.B. Tauris, 2013); Ben Hubbard and Mayy El Sheikh, "Wikileaks Show a Saudi Obsession with Iran," *New York Times*, July 16, 2015, available at http://www.nytimes.com/2015/07/17/world/middleeast/wikileaks-saudi-arabia-iran.html; Hugh Naylor, "The Seven Most Important Moments of the Saudi-Iranian Rivalry," *Washington Post*, January 4, 2016, available at https://www.washingtonpost.com/news/worldviews/wp/2016/01/04/the-most-important-moments-of-the-saudi-iranian-rivalry/; Rami G. Khouri, "The Saudi-Iranian Rivalry Threatens the Entire Middle East," *Al Jazeera America*, January 5, 2016, available at http://america.aljazeera.com/opinions/2016/1/the-saudi-iranian-rivalry-threatens-the-entire-middle-east.html.

36. A similar number of Iranian pilgrims died during the 2015 Hajj pilgrimage as a result of a stampede. This led to a further deterioration of Saudi-Iranian relations, but the difference between the two events is that the latter was an accident while the former was perceived as a deliberate massacre by the Saudi regime on Iranian pilgrims. See Rick Gladstone, "Death Toll from Hajj Stampede Reaches 2,411 in New Estimate," *New York Times*, December 10, 2016, available at http://www.nytimes.com/2015/12/11/world/middleeast/death-toll-from-hajj-stampede.html.

37. F. Gregory Gause III, *The International Relations of the Persian Gulf* (Cambridge: Cambridge University Press, 2010), pp. 130–134.

38. Shibley Telhami, "2008 Arab Public Opinion Poll," Survey of the Anwar Sadat Chair for Peace and Development at the University of Maryland (with Zogby International), available at http://www.brookings.edu/~/media/events/2008/4/14%20middle%20east/0414_middle_east_telhami.

39. Ian Black, "Fear of a Shia Full Moon," *The Guardian*, 27 January 2007, available at http://www.theguardian.com/world/2007/jan/26/worlddispatch.ianblack. The inclusion of Syria in this list might seem odd given that the majority of Syrians are Sunni. The ruling Assad family, however, comes from the minority/offshoot 'Alawi sect of Shi'a Islam. For background on the "Shi'a threat" debate see Augustus Richard Norton, "The Shiite 'Threat' Revisited," *Current History*, December 2007, 434–439.

40. On the significance of these events see Danny Postel, introductory remarks, panel discussion on *The People Reloaded: The Green Movement and the Struggle for Iran's Future* at Columbia University, February 25, 2011, available on C-SPAN2's Book TV at http://www.c-span.org/video/?298490-1/book-discussion-people-reloaded.

41. Reza Garmabadri, "The Sedition was the Foundation for the House Arrest not the Cause and the Reason," *Sobh-e Sadeq* 15: 680 (December 22, 2014), p. 6.

42. "Karroubi's Reaction to Ayatullah Jannati's Claims," *Fars News*, July 31, 2010, available at http://www.farsnews.com/newstext.php?nn=8905090301; "Shariatmadari: Due to Banking Difficulties Money from King Abdullah Did Not Reach the Leaders of Sedition," *Baztab*, January 4, 2013, available at http://baztab.net/fa/news/20743/.

43. This document was spurious: "Iran's State Media Launches Yet another Attack on UN Special Rapporteur," International Campaign for Human Rights in Iran, July 29, 2015, available at https://www.iranhumanrights.org/2015/07/judiciary-accusations-dr-shaheed/.

44. Fariba Sahraei, "Syria War: Afghans Sent by Iran to fight for Assad," BBC Persian, April 15, 2016, available at http://www.bbc.com/news/world-middle-east-36035095; "Parliamentary Motion: the Government Should Give Iranian Citizenship to the Families of Non-Iranian Martyrs," BBC Persian, May 2, 2016, available at http://www.bbc.com/persian/iran/2016/05/160502_l10_majlis_nationality.

45. See Mohamad Bazzi, "Lebanon and the Start of Iran and Saudi Arabia's Proxy War," *The New Yorker*, May 26, 2015, available at http://www.newyorker.com/news/news-desk/lebanon-and-the-start-of-iran-and-saudi-arabias-proxy-war

46. See Nader Hashemi and Danny Postel (eds.), *The Syria Dilemma* (Cambridge, MA: MIT Press, 2013).

47. Alexandra Siegel, "Does Twitter bridge the Sunni-Shiite divide or make it worse?" *The Monkey Cage (Washington Post* blog), January 7, 2016, available at https://www.washingtonpost.com/news/monkey-cage/wp/2016/01/07/does-twitter-bridge-the-sunni-shiite-divide-or-make-it-worse/. This builds on already polarized views as revealed in a 2015 Pew Research Poll. See Jacob Poushter, "The Middle East's Sectarian Divide on Views of Saudi Arabia, Iran," Pew Research Center, January 7, 2016, available at http://www.pewresearch.org/fact-tank/2016/01/07/the-middle-easts-sectarian-divide-on-views-of-saudi-arabia-iran/.

48. Tim Arango, "Turkey, which Sought Middle Ground, Enters Saudi-Iranian Dispute," *New York Times*, January 8, 2016, available at http://www.nytimes.com/2016/01/09/world/middleeast/turkey-iran-saudi-arabia.html.

49. Ussama Makdisi, *The Culture of Sectarianism: Community, History, and Violence in Nineteenth-Century Ottoman Lebanon* (Berkeley: University of California Press, 2000). See also "Sectarianism and Modernity: A Conversation with Historian Ussama Makdisi," in the *Middle East Dialogues* series produced by the University of Denver's Center for Middle East Studies, available at https://youtu.be/sMnq0T-O4Yo.

50. Vali Nasr, "International Politics, Domestic Imperatives, and Identity Mobilization: Sectarianism in Pakistan, 1979–1998," chapter 5 in this volume.

51. Fanar Haddad, *Sectarianism in Iraq: Antagonistic Visions of Unity* (London: Hurst, 2011).

52. Raymond Carver, *What we Talk about When we Talk about Love* (New York: Alfred A. Knopf, 1981).

53. See, for example, Bassel F. Salloukh, "The Sectarianization of Geopolitics in the Middle East" (chapter 2 in this volume) and his earlier article, "The Arab Uprisings and the Geopolitics of the Middle East," *The International Spectator* 48:2 (June 2013), 32–46. See also Toby Matthiesen, *Sectarian Gulf: Bahrain, Saudi Arabia, and the Arab Spring That Wasn't* (Stanford: Stanford University Press, 2013); and F. Gregory Gause III, *Beyond Sectarianism: The New Middle East Cold War*, Brookings Doha Center Analysis Paper, July 11, 2014, available at https://www.brookings.edu/wp-content/uploads/2016/06/English-PDF-1.pdf. Important exceptions include Toby Matthiesen, *The Other Saudis: Shiism, Dissent and Sectarianism* (Cambridge: Cambridge University Press, 2014); Fouad Ibrahim, *The Shi'is of Saudi Arabia* (London: Saqi, 2006); and Al-Rasheed's own earlier work, including *A History of Saudi Arabia*, 2nd ed. (Cambridge: Cambridge University Press, 2010).

54. Stacey Philbrick Yadav, *Islamists and the State: Legitimacy and Institutions in Yemen and Lebanon* (London: I.B. Tauris, 2013).

55. See the extraordinary Al Jazeera documentary *Bahrain: Shouting in the Dark*, available at http://www.aljazeera.com/programmes/2011/08/201184144547798162.html.

56. Toby Matthiesen, *Sectarian Gulf: Bahrain, Saudi Arabia, and the Arab Spring That Wasn't* (Stanford: Stanford University Press, 2013).

57. See Timothy D. Sisk, *Power Sharing and International Mediation in Ethnic Conflicts* (Washington, DC: United States Institute of Peace Press, 1996); "Peacemaking in Civil Wars: Obstacles, Options and Opportunities," in Ulrich Schneckener and Stefan Wolff (eds.), *Managing and Settling Ethnic Conflicts: Perspectives on Successes and Failures in Europe, Africa, and Asia* (New York: Palgrave Macmillan, 2004); "Political Violence and Peace Accords: Searching for the Silver Lining," in John Darby (ed.), *Violence and Reconstruction* (Notre Dame, IN: University of Notre Dame Press, 2006); *International Mediation in Civil Wars* (London: Routledge, 2009); and *Statebuilding: Consolidating Peace after Civil War* (Cambridge: Polity, 2013); Timothy D. Sisk (ed.), *Between Terror and Tolerance: Religious Leaders, Conflict, and Peacemaking* (Washington, DC: Georgetown University Press, 2011); Anna K. Jarstad and Timothy D. Sisk (eds.), *From War to Democracy: Dilemmas of Peacebuilding* (Cambridge: Cambridge University Press, 2008); Roland Paris and Timothy D. Sisk (eds.), *The Dilemmas of Statebuilding: Confronting the Contradictions of Postwar Peace Operations* (London: Routledge, 2009); David Chandler and Timothy D. Sisk (eds.), *The Routledge Handbook of International Statebuilding* (New York: Routledge, 2013).

58. United Nations Development Program, *Arab Development Report 2002: Creating*

Opportunities for Future Generations (New York: United Nations Development Program, 2002). All of the reports are available at: http://www.arab-hdr. org/. Also see David Gardner, "Autocracy is the Cause, Not the Cure, of the Middle East's Ills," *Financial Times*, May 5, 2015, available at https://next. ft.com/content/88625538-f27c-11e4–892a-00144feab7de.

59. See Jean-Pierre Filiu, *From Deep State to Islamic State: The Arab Counter-Revolution and its Jihadi Legacy* (London: Hurst, 2015).

60. F. Gregory Gause III, "The New Middle East Cold War," presentation at the symposium "US Foreign Policy after the Iran Nuclear Deal and the Changing Geopolitics of the Middle East," Josef Korbel School of International Studies, University of Denver, May 2, 2016, available at https://youtu.be/jUejRWBDbEE.

61. Jeff Colgan, "How Sectarianism Shapes Yemen's War," *The Monkey Cage* (*Washington Post* blog), April 13, 2015, available at https://www.washington-post.com/blogs/monkey-cage/wp/2015/04/13/how-sectarianism-shapes-yemens-war/; see also "Yemen's War and the Geopolitics of Sectarianism," in the *Middle East Dialogues* series produced by the University of Denver's Center for Middle East Studies, available at https://youtu.be/HIJ2kDRYZgk.

62. Zaid al-Ali, "The Only Way to Solve Iraq's Political Crisis," *New York Times*, May 5, 2016, available at http://www.nytimes.com/2016/05/06/opinion/the-only-way-to-solve-iraqs-political-crisis.html.

63. Madawi Al-Rasheed, "Sectarianism as Counter-Revolution," chapter 8 in this volume.

64. Peter Gay, *The Cultivation of Hatred*, volume III of his *The Bourgeois Experience: Victoria to Freud* (New York: W. W. Norton & Company, 1993).

1. THE PROBLEM OF SECTARIANISM IN THE MIDDLE EAST IN AN AGE OF WESTERN HEGEMONY

1. This chapter is based on a lecture I delivered at the University of Denver on April 30, 2015.

2. Sigmund Freud, *Civilization and its Discontents*, translated by James Strachey (New York: Norton, 2005), p. 104.

3. Jeremy Bowen, "Sharpening Sunni–Shia Schism Bodes Ill for the Middle East," BBC News, December 20, 2013, available at http://www.bbc.com/news/world-middle-east-25458755.

4. Karen Barkey, *Empire of Difference: The Ottomans in Comparative Perspective* (Cambridge: Cambridge University Press, 2008).

5. JJas Brant, "Memorandum on Reform in Turkey," in David Gillard, ed., *The Ottoman Empire in the Balkans, 1856–1875*, Part 1, Series B, Vol. 1 of *British Documents on Foreign Affairs: Reports and Papers from the Foreign Office Confidential Print*, Kenneth Bourne and D. Cameron Watts, general eds. (Frederick, MD: University Press of America, 1984), p. 8.

6. Carter Vaughn Findley, *Turkey, Islam, Nationalism, and Modernity: A History, 1789–2007* (New Haven: Yale University Press, 2010), pp. 174–175.

7. Lital Levy, "Partitioned Pasts: Arab Jewish Intellectuals and the Case of Esther Azhari Moyal (1873–1948)," in Dyala Hamzah (ed.), *The Making of the Arab Intellectual: Empire, Public Sphere and the Colonial Coordinates of Selfhood* (New York: Routledge, 2011), pp. 128–163.

8. In my forthcoming book, provisionally titled *Understanding Sectarianism*, to be published by the University of California Press.

9. Max Weiss, *In the Shadow of Sectarianism: Law, Shi'ism and the Making of Modern Lebanon* (Cambridge, MA: Harvard University Press, 2010).

10. Benjamin Thomas White, *The Emergence of Minorities in the Middle East: The Politics of Community in French Mandate Syria* (Edinburgh: Edinburgh University Press, 2011).

11. Laura Robson, *Colonialism and Christianity in Mandate Palestine* (Austin: University of Texas Press, 2011).

12. Samir Murqus, *al-Himaya wa al-'iqab: al-gharb wa al-mas'ala al-diniyya fi al-sharq al-awsat* (Cairo: Mirit lil-Nashr wa-al-Ma'lūmāt, 2000).

13. Fouad Ajami, *The Arab Predicament: Arab Political Thought and Practice since 1967* (Cambridge: Cambridge University Press, 1992), p. 3.

14. Orit Bashkin, *New Babylonians: A History of Jews in Modern Iraq* (Stanford: Stanford University Press, 2012).

2. THE SECTARIANIZATION OF GEOPOLITICS IN THE MIDDLE EAST

1. For a debunking see Benjamin Denison and Jasmin Mujanović, "Syria isn't Bosnia. And no, the Problem isn't 'Ancient Hatreds'," *The Monkey Cage* (*Washington Post* blog), November 17, 2015, available at https://www.washingtonpost.com/news/monkey-cage/wp/2015/11/17/syria-isnt-bosnia-and-no-the-problem-isnt-ancient-hatreds/.

2. Quoted in Karla Adam, "Obama Ridiculed for Saying Conflicts in the Middle East 'Date Back Millennia' (Some Don't Date Back a Decade.)," *Washington Post*, January 13, 2016, available at https://www.washingtonpost.com/news/worldviews/wp/2016/01/13/obama-ridiculed-for-saying-conflicts-in-the-middle-east-date-back-millennia-some-dont-date-back-a-decade/.

3. Sami Zubaida, "Reading History Backwards," *Middle East Report* (Middle East Research and Information Project) 160 (September/October 1989), pp. 39–41, available at http://www.merip.org/mer/mer160/reading-history-backwards.

4. Edward W. Said, *Orientalism* (London: Penguin, 2003 [1979]), p. 325.

5. Toby Matthiesen, "The World's Most Misunderstood Martyr," *Foreign Policy*, January 8, 2016, available at http://foreignpolicy.com/2016/01/08/the-worlds-most-misunderstood-martyr/.

6. Marc Lynch, "Why Saudi Arabia Escalated the Middle East's Sectarian Conflict," *The Monkey Cage* (*Washington Post* blog), January 8, 2016, available at https://www.washingtonpost.com/news/monkey-cage/wp/2016/01/04/why-saudi-arabia-escalated-the-middle-easts-sectarian-conflict/.

7. See Rex Brynen, Pete W. Moore, Bassel F. Salloukh, and Marie-Joëlle Zahar, *Beyond the Arab Spring: Authoritarianism and Democratization in the Arab World* (Boulder: Lynne Rienner, 2012).

8. I have made this argument earlier in Bassel F. Salloukh, "The Arab Uprisings and the Geopolitics of the Middle East," *The International Spectator* 48:2 (June 2013): 32–46. See also the excellent analysis in F. Gregory Gause, III, *Beyond Sectarianism: The New Middle East Cold War*. Brookings Doha Center Analysis Paper no. 11, July 2014, available at http://www.brookings.edu/~/media/research/files/papers/2014/07/22%20beyond%20sectarianism%20cold%20war%20gause/english%20pdf.pdf.

9. See Andrew Flibbert, "The Consequences of Forced State Failure in Iraq," *Political Science Quarterly* 128:1 (2013): 67–95; Toby Dodge, "Can Iraq Be Saved?" *Survival* 56:5 (October–November 2014): 7–20; and Christopher Phillips, "Sectarianism and Conflict in Syria," *Third World Quarterly* 36:2 (February 2015): 357–376.

10. See Bassel F. Salloukh, "Overlapping Contests and Middle East International Relations: The Return of the Weak Arab State," Project on Middle East Political Science (POMEPS), August 12, 2015, available at http://pomeps.org/2015/08/12/overlapping-contests-and-middle-east-international-relations-the-return-of-the-weak-arab-state/.

11. See, for example, F. Gregory Gause, III, "Balancing What? Threat Perception and Alliance Choice in the Gulf," *Security Studies* 13:2 (2003/04): 273–305; Michael C. Barnett, *Dialogues in Arab Politics: Negotiations in Regional Order* (New York: Columbia University Press, 1998); Malcolm H. Kerr, *The Arab Cold War: Gamal 'Abd al-Nasir and his Rivals, 1958–1970*, 3rd ed. (New York: Oxford University Press, 1971); Rex Brynen, "Palestine and the Arab State System: Permeability, State Consolidation and the *Intifada*," *Canadian Journal of Political Science* 24:3 (September 1991): 595–621; F. Gregory Gause, III, "Sovereignty, Statecraft and Stability in the Middle East," *Journal of International Affairs* 45:2 (Winter 1992): 441–469; and Steven R. David, "Explaining Third World Alignment," *World Politics* 43:2 (January 1991): 233–256.

12. See Bassel F. Salloukh and Rex Brynen (eds.), *Persistent Permeability: Regionalism, Localism, and Globalization in the Middle East* (London: Ashgate Publishing Limited, 2004).

13. Gause, *Beyond Sectarianism*, p. 8.

14. See Jihad al-Zayn, "La khatar 'ala Lubnan yu'adel khatar infijar al-'ilaqaat al-Suriya al-Sa'udiya," *al-Nahar*, August 18, 2007.

15. See George W. Bush's "Forward Strategy of Freedom" speech of November 6, 2003, available at http://www.al-bab.com/arab/docs/reform/bush2003.htm.

16. See Martin Chulov, "ISIS: The Inside Story," *The Guardian*, December 11, 2014, available at http://www.theguardian.com/world/2014/dec/11/-sp-isis-the-inside-story.

17. For a general overview see F. Gregory Gause, III, *The International Relations of the Persian Gulf* (Cambridge: Cambridge University Press, 2009).

18. See Abdel Rahman al-Rashed, "Hamas: ima Iran aw al-'Arab?", *al-Sharq al-Awsat*, January 19, 2009.

19. See King Abdullah's comments to the *Washington Post*, December 8, 2004, available at http://www.kingabdullah.jo/index.php/en_US/news/view/id/2751/videoDisplay/1.html.

20. See Juan Cole, "A 'Shiite Crescent'? The Regional Impact of the Iraq War," *Current History* 105 (January 2006): 20–26.

21. See F. Gregory Gause, III, "Saudi Arabia: Iraq, Iran, the Regional Power Balance, and the Sectarian Question," *Strategic Insights* 6:2 (March 2007): 1–8.

22. See "US Embassy Cables: Hillary Clinton Says Saudi Arabia 'A Critical Source of Terrorist Funding'," *The Guardian*, December 5, 2010, available at http://www.theguardian.com/world/us-embassy-cables-documents/242073; Patrick Cockburn, "Isis Consolidates," *London Review of Books*, August 21, 2014, available at http://www.lrb.co.uk/v36/n16/patrick-cockburn/isis-consolidates.

23. See Martin Chulov, "Qassem Suleimani: The Iranian General 'Secretly Running' Iraq," *The Guardian*, July 28, 2011, available at http://www.guardian.co.uk/world/2011/jul/28/qassem-suleimani-iran-iraq-influence; J.F. Burns and M.R. Gordon, "US Says Iran Helped Iraqis Kill Five GI's," *New York Times*, July 3, 2007, available at http://www.nytimes.com/2007/07/03/world/middleeast/03iraq.html.

24. See Wadood Hamad, "al-Bahth 'an hawiya 'Iraqiya," *al-Safir*, April 30, 2015.

25. Dodge, "Can Iraq Be Saved?" p. 16.

26. See the PBS Frontline documentary *The Rise of ISIS*, October 28, 2014, available at http://www.pbs.org/wgbh/pages/frontline/rise-of-isis/.

27. See Nussaibah Younis, "A Cross-Sectarian Vision for Defeating the Islamic State in Iraq," Carnegie Middle East Center, July 6, 2015, available at http://carnegie-mec.org/2015/07/06/cross-sectarian-vision-for-defeating-islamic-state-in-iraq/icvn.

28. See Nqoula Nassif, "al-'Ilaqat al-Amerkiya-al-Sa'oudiya: talaqen 'ala talqin Suriya darsan," *al-Akhbar*, April 7, 2008.

29. See Bassel F. Salloukh, "Demystifying Syrian Foreign Policy under Bashar," in Fred H. Lawson (ed.), *Demystifying Syria* (London: Saqi Books, 2009), pp. 159–179.

30. See Jean 'Aziz, "I'lan Dimashq: ma lam yuktab fih akhtar," *al-Akhbar*, April 1, 2008.

31. See Mehran Kamrava, "Mediation and Qatari Foreign Policy," *Middle East Journal* 65:4 (Autumn 2011): 539–556; Mehran Kamrava, *Qatar: Small State, Big Politics* (Ithaca, NY: Cornell University Press, 2013); and Uzi Rabi, "Qatar's Relations with Israel: Challenging Arab and Gulf Norms," *Middle East Journal* 63:3 (Summer 2009): 443–459.

32. See Mustapha al-Labbad, "Qatar: ahlam kabira wa qudarat mahdouda," *al-Safir*, July 30 and August 6, 2012.

33. See Jamie Tarabay, "A (Temporary) Lifeline for Morsi," *The Atlantic*, April 11, 2013, available at http://www.theatlantic.com/international/archive/2013/04/a-temporary-lifeline-for-morsi/274904/.

34. See "Egypt Returns $2 Billion to Qatar in Sign of Growing Tensions," Reuters, September 19, 2013, available at http://www.reuters.com/article/us-egypt-qatar-deposits-idUSBRE98I0N020130919.

35. Dexter Filkins, "What Are Turkish Troops Doing in Northern Iraq?" *New Yorker*, December 9, 2015, available at http://www.newyorker.com/news/news-desk/what-are-turkish-troops-doing-in-northern-iraq.

36. See Constanze Letsch, "Syrian Conflict Brings Sectarian Tensions to Turkey's Tolerant Hatay Province," *The Guardian*, September 3, 2013, available at http://www.theguardian.com/world/2013/sep/03/syria-crisis-threatens-turkish-tolerance.

37. See Tim Arango, "Turkey, Which Sought Middle Ground, Enters Saudi-Iranian Dispute," *New York Times*, January 8, 2016, available at http://www.nytimes.com/2016/01/09/world/middleeast/turkey-iran-saudi-arabia.html?_r=0.

38. See Filkins, "What Are Turkish Troops Doing in Northern Iraq?"

39. Quoted in David Hearst, "Why Saudi Arabia is Taking a Risk by Backing the Egyptian Coup," *The Guardian*, August 20, 2013, available at http://www.theguardian.com/commentisfree/2013/aug/20/saudi-arabia-coup-egypt

40. Hearst, "Why Saudi Arabia is Taking a Risk."

41. See David D. Kirkpatrick, "Saudis Expand Regional Power as Others Falter," *New York Times*, January 25, 2015, available at http://www.nytimes.com/2015/01/26/world/middleeast/saudis-expand-regional-power-as-others-falter.html.

42. See F. Gregory Gause, III, *Saudi Arabia in the New Middle East*, Council on Foreign Relations Special Report no. 63 (New York: Council on Foreign Relations, December 2011), available at http://www.cfr.org/saudi-arabia/saudi-arabia-new-middle-east/p26663. The Saudi-owned daily newspaper *al-Sharq al-Awsat* and the satellite news channel Al Arabiya played an instrumental role in anti-Iranian and anti-Shi'a agitation.

43. See Toby Matthiesen, *Sectarian Gulf: Bahrain, Saudi Arabia, and the Arab Spring That Wasn't* (Stanford: Stanford University Press, 2013).

44. For the Saudi perspective see Abdel Rahman al-Rashed, "Awn wa Berri wa inqaz al-Asad," *al-Sharq al-Awsat*, November 17, 2011.

45. See Patrick Seale, *Asad of Syria: The Struggle for the Middle East* (Berkeley: University of California Press, 1988).

46. See Adam Entous, Nour Malas, and Margaret Coker, "A Veteran Saudi Power Player Works to Build Support to Topple Assad," *Wall Street Journal*, August 25, 2013, available at http://online.wsj.com/article/SB100014241 27887323423804579024452583045962.html.

47. Saudi Arabia also financed a Central Intelligence Agency (CIA) rebel training operation code-named Timber Sycamore in Syria. See Mark Mazzetti and Matt Apuzzo, "US Relies Heavily on Saudi Money to Support Syrian Rebels," *New York Times*, January 23, 2016, available at http://www.nytimes.com/2016/01/24/world/middleeast/us-relies-heavily-on-saudi-money-to-support-syrian-rebels.html.

48. See Yezid Sayigh, "Unifying Syria's Rebels: Saudi Arabia Joins the Fray," Carnegie Middle East Center, October 28, 2013, available at http://carnegie-mec.org/2013/10/28/unifying-syria-s-rebels-saudi-arabia-joins-fray/greh. Alloush was killed in late December 2015 in what is believed to be a Russian airstrike on Jaysh al-Islam's headquarters near Damascus.

49. See Humeyra Pamuk and Nick Tattersall, "Turkish Intelligence Helped Ship Arms to Syrian Islamist Rebel Areas," Reuters, May 21, 2015, available at http://www.reuters.com/article/us-mideast-crisis-turkey-arms-idUSKBN0 O61L220150521; Can Dündar, "I Revealed the Truth about President Erdoğan and Syria. For that, he had me Jailed," *The Guardian*, December 28, 2015, available at http://www.theguardian.com/commentisfree/2015/dec/28/truth-president-Erdoğan-jailed-turkey-regime-state-security-crime.

50. David Kenner, "Saudi Arabia's Shadow War," *Foreign Policy*, November 6, 2013, available at http://foreignpolicy.com/2013/11/06/saudi-arabias-shadow-war/.

51. See Farnaz Fassihi, Jay Solomon, and Sam Dagher, "Iranians Dial up Presence in Syria," *Wall Street Journal*, September 16, 2013, available at http://online.wsj.com/article/SB10001424127887323864604579067382861808 984.html.

52. Dexter Filkins, "The Shadow Commander," *New Yorker*, September 30, 2013, available at http://www.newyorker.com/magazine/2013/09/30/the-shadow-commander.

53. See Toby Matthiesen, "Syria: Inventing a Religious War," *New York Review of Books*, June 12, 2013, available at http://www.nybooks.com/blogs/nyrblog/2013/jun/12/syria-inventing-religious-war/.

54. Lynch, "Why Saudi Arabia Escalated the Middle East's Sectarian Conflict."

55. See Sam Dagher, "Syria's Alawite Force Turned Tide for Assad," *Wall Street Journal*, August 26, 2013, available at http://online.wsj.com/article/SB100 01424127887323997004578639903412487708.html.

56. See the PBS Frontline documentary *The Rise of ISIS*.

57. See Curtis Ryan, "Regional Responses to the Rise of ISIS," *Middle East Report* (Middle East Research and Information Project) 276 (Fall 2015), available at http://www.merip.org/mer/mer276/regional-responses-rise-isis.

58. See Robert F. Worth, "Yemen: The Houthi Enigma," NYR Blog, March 30, 2015, available at http://www.nybooks.com/blogs/nyrblog/2015/mar/30/yemen-houthi-enigma/.

59. See Amer Hassan, "Min Ali Saleh ila Tawakkol Karman," *al-Akhbar*, June 29, 2015.

60. See Abdel Rahman al-Rashed, "Waqf al-tahdid min Najran ila Jeddah," *al-Sharq al-Awsat*, April 22, 2015.

61. See Dan Murphy, "Reducing Yemen's Houthis to 'Iranian Proxies' is a Mistake," *Christian Science Monitor*, April 2, 2015, available at http://www.csmonitor.com/World/Security-Watch/Backchannels/2015/0402/Reducing-Yemen-s-Houthis-to-Iranian-proxies-is-a-mistake-video.

62. See Lynch, "Why Saudi Arabia Escalated the Middle East's Sectarian Conflict."

63. See "al-Hurub ila al-federaliya fi Lubnan ba'da Suriya wa-l-Iraq," *al-Safir*, May 12, 2015.

64. See Wafiq Qanso, "Gebran Bassil: musta'edun li-fart al-nizam," *al-Akhbar*, July 7, 2015.

65. See Nicolas Pelham, "ISIS and the Shia Revival in Iraq," *New York Review of Books*, June 4, 2015, available at http://www.nybooks.com/articles/archives/2015/jun/04/isis-shia-revival-iraq/.

66. See Younis, "A Cross-Sectarian Vision for Defeating the Islamic State in Iraq."

67. See Claire Shuker, "al-Mantaqa tursam min jadid … wa hadith 'an Suriya al-mufida," *al-Safir*, July 1, 2015.

68. See "al-Qusa al-kamila li-qarar al-tadakhul al-'askari al-Rusi fi Suriya," *al-Safir*, 20 October 2015.

69. See John R. Bolton, "To Defeat ISIS, Create a Sunni State," *New York Times*, November 24, 2015, available at http://www.nytimes.com/2015/11/25/opinion/john-bolton-to-defeat-isis-create-a-sunni-state.html.

70. For a comprehensive discussion see Bassel F. Salloukh, Rabie Barakat, Jinan S. al-Habbal, Lara W. Khattab, and Shoghig Mikaelian, *The Politics of Sectarianism in Postwar Lebanon* (London: Pluto Press, 2015).

71. See Bassel F. Salloukh, "The End of the Arab Affair," *The New Arab*, March

28, 2016, available at https://www.alaraby.co.uk/english/Comment/2016/3/28/The-end-of-the-Arab-affair.

72. Vali Nasr, "The War for Islam," *Foreign Policy*, January 22, 2016, available at http://foreignpolicy.com/2016/01/22/the-war-for-islam-sunni-shiite-iraq-syria/.

3. THE ARAB REGION AT A TIPPING POINT: WHY SECTARIANISM FAILS TO EXPLAIN THE TURMOIL

1. Malcolm Kerr, *The Arab Cold War: Gamal 'Abd al-Nasir and his Rivals, 1958–1970*, 3rd ed. (New York: Oxford University Press, 1971).
2. Elizabeth Monroe, *Britain's Moment in the Middle East* (London: Chatto & Windus, 1963).
3. Jeffrey Goldberg, "The Obama Doctrine," *The Atlantic* (April 2016), available at http://www.theatlantic.com/magazine/archive/2016/04/the-obama-doctrine/471525/.
4. Nazih Ayubi, *Over-stating the Arab State: Politics and Society in the Middle East* (New York: I.B. Tauris, 2009).
5. Mehran Kamrava (ed.), *Fragile Politics: Weak States in the Greater Middle East* (New York: Oxford University Press, 2016).
6. Adel Abdel Ghafar and Fraus Masri, "The Persistence of Poverty in the Arab World," *Al Jazeera* (English), February 28, 2016, available at http://www.aljazeera.com/indepth/opinion/2016/02/persistence-poverty-arab-world-160228072928685.html.
7. Bryan Turner, "Class, Generation and Islamism: Towards a Global Sociology of Political Islam," *British Journal of Sociology* 54:1 (March 2003): 139–147.
8. "Remarks by President Obama to the Australian Parliament," November 17, 2011, available at https://www.whitehouse.gov/the-press-office/2011/11/17/remarks-president-obama-australian-parliament/.
9. Goldberg, "The Obama Doctrine."
10. Gilbert Achcar, *The People Want: A Radical Exploration of the Arab Uprising*, translated by Geoffrey Michael Goshgarian (Berkeley: University of California Press, 2013).
11. Robin Wright, "Imagining a Remapped Middle East," *New York Times*, September 28, 2013, available at http://www.nytimes.com/2013/09/29/opinion/sunday/imagining-a-remapped-middle-east.html?pagewanted=all; F. Gregory Gause, III, "Is This the End of Sykes-Picot?" *The Monkey Cage* (*Washington Post* blog), May 20, 2014, available at https://www.washingtonpost.com/news/monkey-cage/wp/2014/05/20/is-this-the-end-of-sykes-picot/; "On GPS: Landis on a Syria Solution—Fareed goes 1-on-1 with Syria Expert Joshua Landis to Discuss an Innovative Solution to the Ongoing Syrian Crisis," *Fareed Zakaria GPS* (CNN), November 8, 2014, available at

http://www.cnn.com/videos/bestoftv/2014/11/08/exp-gps-landis-sot-syria.cnn; James Gelvin, "Don't Blame Sykes-Picot," Oxford University Press blog, February 7, 2015, available at http://blog.oup.com/2015/02/dont-blame-sykes-picot/.

4. A NARRATIVE IDENTITY APPROACH TO ISLAMIC SECTARIANISM

1. William H. Swatos Jr., "Weber or Troeltsch? Methodology, Syndrome and the Development of Church–Sect Theory," *Journal for the Scientific Study of Religion* 15:2 (1976), p. 131.

2. John A. Coleman, "Church–Sect Typology and Organizational Preca-riousness," *Sociological Analysis* 29:2 (1968), p. 55.

3. Max Weber, *Economy and Society: An Outline of Interpretive Sociology*, edited by Guenther Roth and Claus Wittich (New York: Bedminster Press, 1968), p. 1164.

4. *From Max Weber: Essays in Sociology*, edited and translated by Hans Heinrich Gerth and C. Wright Mills (Oxford: Oxford University Press, 1946), p. 314.

5. Weber, *Economy and Society*, pp. 1204–1205.

6. Weber, *Economy and Society*, p. 1208.

7. Swatos, "Weber or Troeltsch?" p. 133.

8. Ernst Troeltsch, *The Social Teachings of the Christian Churches*, translated by Olive Wyon (London: George Allen & Unwin Ltd., 1949), p. 331.

9. Swatos, "Weber or Troeltsch?" p. 134; Lorne L. Dawson, "Creating 'Cult' Typologies: Some Strategic Considerations," *Journal of Contemporary Religion* 12:3 (1997), p. 367; see also Helmut Richard Niebuhr, *The Social Sources of Denominationalism* (New York: H. Holt & Co., 1929).

10. Swatos, "Weber or Troeltsch?" pp. 134–135.

11. Howard Becker, *Systematic Sociology on the Basis of the Beziehungslehre and Gebildelehre of Leopold von Wiese* (New York: Wiley, 1932), pp. 114–118; Howard Becker, "Sacred and Secular Societies: Considered with Reference to Folk-State and Similar Classifications," *Social Forces* 28:4 (1950): 362–376; Swatos, "Weber or Troeltsch?" p. 135.

12. J. Milton Yinger, *Religion and the Struggle for Power: A Study in the Sociological Study of Religion*, Dissertations in Sociology (New York: Arno Press, 1980 [1946]), pp. 18–23; J. Milton Yinger, *Religion, Society and the Individual* (New York: Macmillan, 1957), pp. 142–145.

13. Benton Johnson, "On Church and Sect," *American Sociological Review* 28 (1963), p. 542; Rodney Stark and William Sims Bainbridge, *The Future of Religion: Secularization, Revival and Cult Formation* (Berkeley: University of California Press, 1986), p. 23.

14. Rodney Stark and William Sims Bainbridge, *A Theory of Religion* (New York: Peter Lang, 1987), p. 124.

15. Roland Robertson, *The Sociological Interpretation of Religion* (New York: Schocken, 1970), pp. 122–128; Paul M. Gustafson, "UO-US-PS-PO: A Restatement of Troeltsch's Church–Sect Typology," *Journal for the Scientific Study of Religion* 6 (1967): 64–68; Paul M. Gustafson, "Exegesis on the Gospel According to St. Max," *Sociological Analysis* 34:1 (1973): 12–25.

16. William H. Swatos, "Monopolism, Pluralism, Acceptance, and Rejection: An Integrated Model for Church–Sect Theory," *Review of Religious Research* 16:3 (1975): 174–185 (esp. Figure 1 on p. 177); see also Roy Wallis, "Scientology: Therapeutic Cult to Religious Sect," *Sociology* 9:1 (1975), p. 98.

17. Bryan Wilson, *Religious Sects: A Sociological Study* (New York: McGraw-Hill, 1970), pp. 36–40.

18. Wilson, *Religious Sects*, pp. 26–27.

19. Albert I. Baumgarten, *The Flourishing of Jewish Sects in the Maccabean Era: An Interpretation* (Leiden: Brill, 1997), p. 7.

20. John J. Collins, *Scriptures and Sectarianism: Essays on the Dead Sea Scrolls* (Tübingen: Mohr Siebeck, 2014), p. 177.

21. Michael Cook, "Weber and Islamic Sects," in Toby E. Huff and Wolfgang Schluchter (eds.), *Max Weber and Islam* (New Brunswick: Transaction, 1999), p. 276.

22. Cook, "Weber and Islamic Sects," p. 277.

23. Cook, "Weber and Islamic Sects," p. 278.

24. See Steven Judd, "Muslim Persecution of Heretics during the Marwānid Period (64–132/684–750)," *al-Masaq* 23:1 (2011): 3–14.

25. Such is the case with the early Kharijites and Ibadiyya, on whom see John Wilkinson, *Ibāḍism: Origins and Early Development in Oman* (Oxford: Oxford University Press, 2010), pp. 156–160.

26. The term *milla/milal* tended to denote, following the Qur'anic usage (2:14–15; 7:86–87; 14:16; 18:19–20), divisions among discrete religious traditions, such as between Jews, Christians, Zoroastrians, and Muslims.

27. Dawson, "Creating 'Cult' Typologies," p. 366.

28. Ussama Makdisi, *The Culture of Sectarianism: Community, History, and Violence in Nineteenth-Century Ottoman Lebanon* (Cambridge: Cambridge University Press, 2000), p. 6; see also Max Weiss, *In the Shadow of Sectarianism: Law, Shi'ism, and the Making of Modern Lebanon* (Cambridge, MA: Harvard University Press, 2010), p. 13.

29. Fanar Haddad, *Sectarianism in Iraq: Antagonistic Visions of Unity* (New York: Columbia University Press, 2011), p. 25.

30. See Haddad, *Sectarianism in Iraq*, p. 32.

31. Makdisi, *The Culture of Sectarianism*, pp. 6–7; Haddad, *Sectarianism in Iraq*, pp. 10–23.

32. See Weiss, *In the Shadow of Sectarianism*, pp. 13ff.; Jutta Jokiranta, *Social Identity*

and Sectarianism in the Qumran Movement (Leiden: Brill, 2013), pp. 77ff.; Lawrence Potter (ed.), *Sectarian Politics in the Persian Gulf* (London and New York: Hurst/ Oxford University Press, 2014), pp. 2–3; on the limits of the concept of "identity" see Rogers Brubaker and Frederick Cooper, "Beyond 'Identity'," *Theory and Society* 29 (2000): 1–47.

33. Margaret R. Somers, "The Narrative Constitution of Identity: A Relational and Network Approach," *Theory and Society* 23:5 (1994), pp. 613–614.
34. Somers, "The Narrative Constitution of Identity," pp. 613–614.
35. Somers, "The Narrative Constitution of Identity," p. 606.
36. See the criticism of Somers' approach in Brubaker and Cooper, "Beyond 'Identity'," pp. 11–12.
37. It is mainly for this reason that I find Somers' approach to narrative identity far more useful to the study of sectarianism than the notion of the "myth–symbol complex" (see Stuart J. Kaufman, *Modern Hatreds: The Symbolic Politics of Ethnic War* [Ithaca: Cornell University Press, 2001], p. 25; Haddad, *Sectarianism in Iraq*, p. 17). Though they are very similar to the idea of narrative identity (the myth–symbol complex is ultimately a kind of narrative), Kaufman tends to treat myth–symbol complexes as mostly static narratives that exert an almost irresistible influence over their (mostly passive) consumers. He does not adequately explain, for example, how "the existence, status and security of the groups" comes to depend on "the status of group symbols" (p. 25). Similarly, he tends to reserve agency for "leaders" who "manipulate ... symbols for dubious or selfish purposes," casting the followers of these leaders as simple dupes, or for mass movements in which the relation of group to symbol is obscure. The narrative identity approach, on the other hand, highlights how actors participate (both actively and passively) in the narratives of sect and school. Somers' approach thus comes closer (à la Talal Asad, "Idea of an Anthropology of Islam," *Qui Parle* 17, 2 [2009], p. 16) to treating people as participants in sectarianism as a discursive tradition.
38. Somers recognizes several dimensions of narrativity, notably what she calls "ontological narratives" and "public narratives" ("The Narrative Constitution of Identity," pp. 618–619). This sensitivity to the individual and collective aspects of narrativity mirrors in some ways the concerns of Brubaker and Cooper in specifying modes of identification/self-understanding and commonality, connectedness, and groupness (Brubaker and Cooper, "Beyond 'Identity'," pp. 14–21).
39. Abdulaziz Sachedina, *Islamic Messianism: The Idea of the Mahdi in Twelver Shi'ism* (Albany: State University of New York Press, 1981), p. 31.
40. Mia Bloom, "Understanding ISIS' Appeal," paper presented at the University of Denver, January 22, 2016, available at https://youtu.be/iEASsZiyB3I.
41. Bloom, "Understanding ISIS' Appeal."

42. Fanar Haddad, "The Language of Anti-Shiism," *Foreign Policy*, August 9, 2013, available at http://foreignpolicy.com/2013/08/09/the-language-of-anti-shiism/.

5. INTERNATIONAL POLITICS, DOMESTIC IMPERATIVES, AND IDENTITY MOBILIZATION: SECTARIANISM IN PAKISTAN, 1979–1998

1. Mobilization of identity refers to "the process by which … [a community defined in terms of identity] … becomes politicized on behalf of its collective interests and aspirations": Milton J. Esman, *Ethnic Politics* (Ithaca: Cornell University Press, 1994), p. 28.
2. Figures have been compiled from the *Herald* (Karachi), Sept. 1996, p. 78; the *Economist*, May 10, 1997, p. 34; the *International Herald Tribune*, Aug. 16–17, 1997, p. 1.
3. *Newsline* (Karachi), Oct. 1996, pp. 71–72.
4. Donald Horowitz, *Ethnic Groups in Conflict* (Berkeley: University of California Press, 1985).
5. See Esman, *Ethnic Politics*, pp. 10–12.
6. Timothy M. Frye, "Ethnicity, Sovereignty and Transitions from Non-Democratic Rule," *Journal of International Affairs* 45:2 (Winter 1992), p. 602; Anthony D. Smith, "The Ethnic Sources of Nationalism," *Survival* 35:1 (Spring 1993): 50–55.
7. Horowitz, *Ethnic Groups in Conflict*, pp. 105–35; Crawford Young, *The Politics of Cultural Pluralism* (Madison: University of Wisconsin Press, 1976).
8. Paul Brass, *Ethnicity and Nationalism: Theory and Comparison* (London: Sage, 1991), p. 8.
9. Charles F. Keyes, "The Dialectics of Ethnic Change," in Charles F. Keyes (ed.), *Ethnic Change* (Seattle: University of Washington Press, 1981), pp. 5–11.
10. See David Laitin, *Hegemony and Culture: Politics and Religious Change among the Yoruba* (Chicago: University of Chicago Press, 1986).
11. The rise of Muslim nationalism and Islamism in South Asia has been so explained. See Paul Brass, "Elite Groups, Symbol Manipulation and Ethnic Identity among the Muslims of South Asia," in David Taylor and Malcolm Yapp (eds.), *Political Identity in South Asia* (London: Curzon Press, 1979), pp. 35–77; S.V.R. Nasr, "Communalism and Fundamentalism: A Re-examination of the Origins of Islamic Fundamentalism," *Contention* 4:2 (Winter 1995): 121–39.
12. Horowitz, *Ethnic Groups in Conflict*, pp. 4–6; Raymond Taras and Rajat Ganguly, *Understanding Ethnic Conflict: The International Dimension* (New York: Longman, 1998).
13. Brass points to a role for the state in ethnic mobilization in India, but not a

deliberate one. He argues that the centralizing drive of the state in India since the 1970s has erased the boundaries between federal and local politics with the effect of making the political center more sensitive to ethnic politics: Brass, *Ethnicity and Nationalism*, pp. 111–112.

14. On state capabilities see Joel Migdal, *Strong Societies and Weak States: State-Society Relations and State Capabilities in the Third World* (Princeton: Princeton University Press, 1988); Michael Mann, "The Autonomous Power of the State: Its Origins, Mechanisms, and Results," *Archives Européennes de Sociologie* 25:2 (1984), pp. 189–90.

15. The term "state" underscores the institutional basis of Pakistan's politics and the continuity of its fundamental characteristics above and beyond changes in governments. See Hamza Alavi, "The State in Postcolonial Societies: Pakistan and Bangladesh," in Kathleen Gough and Hari P. Sharma (eds.), *Imperialism and Revolution in South Asia* (New York: Monthly Review Press, 1973), pp. 145–173.

16. Joel S. Migdal, "Introduction: Developing a State-in-Society Perspective," in Joel S. Migdal, Atul Kohli, and Vivienne Shue (eds.), *State Power and Social Forces: Domination and Transformation in the Third World* (Cambridge and New York: Cambridge University Press, 1994), p. 8.

17. Thomas Callaghy, "From Reshaping to Resizing a Failing State: The Case of Zaire/Congo," in Ian Lustick, Thomas Callaghy, and Brendan O'Leary (eds.), *Rightsizing the State: The Politics of Moving Borders* (New York: Oxford University Press, 2002).

18. Migdal, *Strong Societies*, pp. 26–27.

19. See Migdal, "Introduction."

20. See S.V.R. Nasr, "The Rise of Sunni Militancy in Pakistan: The Changing Role of Islamism and the Ulama in Society and Politics," *Modern Asian Studies* 34:1 (2000): 139–180. Muhammad Qasim Zaman, "Sectarianism in Pakistan: The Radicalization of Shi'i and Sunni Identities," *Modern Asian Studies* 32:3 (July 1998): 687–716.

21. See Charles Kennedy, "Islamization and Legal Reform in Pakistan, 1979–89," *Pacific Affairs* 63 (Spring 1990): 62–77; Mumtaz Ahmad, "Islam and the State: The Case of Pakistan," in Matthew Moen and L. Gustafson (eds.), *The Religious Challenge to the State* (Philadelphia: Temple University Press, 1992), pp. 230–240.

22. Zaman, "Sectarianism in Pakistan."

23. Interview with former foreign minister Agha Shahi.

24. Syed Mujawar Hussain Shah, *Religion and Politics in Pakistan (1972–88)* (Islamabad: Quaid-i-Azam University, 1996), pp. 261–262.

25. It is argued by many in Pakistan that the military uses the instability caused by sectarian violence to pressure elected governments. See Samina Ahmed,

"Centralization, Authoritarianism, and the Mismanagement of Ethnic Relations in Pakistan," in Michael E. Brown and Sumit Ganguly (eds.), *Government Policies and Ethnic Relations in Asia and the Pacific* (Cambridge, MA: MIT Press, 1997), pp. 107–127.

26. S. Jamal Malik, "Islamization in Pakistan 1977–1985: The Ulama and their Places of Learning," *Islamic Studies* 28:1 (Spring 1989): 5–28.

27. *Herald*, Aug. 1992, p. 67.

28. *Herald*, Sept. 1992, p. 34.

29. *Herald*, Aug. 1992, p. 66.

30. Mary Ann Weaver, "Children of Jihad," *The New Yorker*, June 12, 1995, p. 46.

31. *Dawn* (Karachi), Sept. 20, 1997.

32. *Dawn*, Jan. 16, 1998.

33. The Afghan war with the Soviet Union ended in 1989 with the withdrawal of the Soviet troops from Afghanistan. Thenceforth a civil war was waged for control of the country. The anti-Soviet Islamist forces and the Pakistani military continue to be involved in the struggle for power in Afghanistan. The alliances that oversaw the resistance to Soviet occupation are therefore still in place. While the nature of the Afghan war has changed over time, from an anti-Soviet war of independence in the 1980s to a civil war in the 1990s, the strategic alliances and their political ramifications for Pakistan have changed little. This chapter therefore does not distinguish between the various periods in that war.

34. See Marvin Weinbaum, *Pakistan and Afghanistan: Resistance and Reconstruction* (Boulder: Westview, 1994).

35. The escalation of tensions resulted from the abduction and murder of a number of Iranian diplomats and journalists by the Taliban in 1998. Iran has, moreover, accused the Taliban of advocating "ethnic cleansing" of Shi'a, openly characterizing the stand-off between the two countries as a sectarian conflict. See the comments of the Iranian Supreme Leader, Ayatollah Khamene'i, in *Hamshahri* (Tehran), Sept. 16, 1998.

36. *Far Eastern Economic Review*, March 9, 1995, p. 24.

37. *Herald*, December 1997, p. 64.

38. See Ikramul Haq, "Pak–Afghan Drug Trade in Historical Perspective," *Asian Survey* 36:10 (October 1996): 945–963.

39. Interviews with police officials in Karachi and Punjab.

40. See Theodore P. Wright, Jr., "Center–Periphery Relations and Ethnic Conflict in Pakistan: Sindhis, Muhajirs, and Punjabis," *Comparative Politics* 23:3 (April 1991): 299–312; Moonis Ahmar, "Ethnicity and State Power in Pakistan," *Asian Survey* 36:10 (October 1996): 1031–1048.

41. *Nawa-i Waqt* (Lahore), Aug. 24, 1997.

42. S.V.R. Nasr, "Democracy and the Crisis of Governability in Pakistan," *Asian Survey* 32:6 (June 1992): 521–537.

297

43. S.V.R. Nasr, "Pakistan: State, Agrarian Reform, and Islamization," *International Journal of Politics, Culture and Society* 10:2 (Winter 1996): 249–272.
44. *Herald,* June 1994, p. 29.
45. *Economist,* Jan. 28, 1996, p. 37.
46. Interviews, former minister of interior, General Nasirullah Babur.
47. *Herald,* June 1997, p. 53.
48. *Nawa-i Waqt,* Aug. 27, 31, 1997.
49. *Nawa-i Waqt,* Aug. 4, 1997.
50. Zaman, "Sectarianism in Pakistan."
51. *Economist,* May 10, 1997, p. 34.
52. Farida Shaheed, "The Pathan–Muhajir Conflict, 1985–6: A National Perspective," in Veena Das (ed.), *Mirrors of Violence: Communities, Riots and Survivors in South Asia* (Delhi: Oxford University Press, 1990), pp. 194–214.
53. *Herald,* Sept. 1996, p. 78.
54. *Dawn,* July 23, 1997.
55. Interviews with TJP leaders.
56. Interviews with Qazi Husain Ahmad, S. Faisal Imam, and Mawlana Abdul-Sattar Niazi, who sat on the council.
57. *Herald,* Oct. 1996, p. 53, June 1997, pp. 54–55.

6. SECTARIAN RELATIONS BEFORE "SECTARIANIZATION" IN PRE-2003 IRAQ

1. For the purposes of this chapter the term "sectarian relations" will refer solely to Sunni-Shi'a relations. Rather than being a definitional stance this merely reflects my research interests and the subject at hand.
2. The term "sectarianism" appears in quotation marks throughout, because the term has no definitive meaning. Until we are able to define "sectarianism," a more coherent way of addressing the issue would be to use the term "sectarian" followed by the appropriate suffix: sectarian hatred; sectarian unity; sectarian discrimination; and so forth.
3. For a more detailed discussion of the terminology and the impact it has had on our understanding of the subject see Fanar Haddad, "'Sectarianism' and its Discontents in the Study of the Middle East," *The Middle East Journal* (forthcoming, 2017).
4. Khalil F. Osman, *Sectarianism in Iraq: The Making of a Nation since 1920* (London: Routledge, 2015); Harith Hassan al-Qarawee, "Heightened Sectarianism in the Middle East: Causes, Dynamics and Consequences," Italian Institute for International Political Studies, Analysis no. 205, November 2013, 1–10, available at http://www.ispionline.it/sites/default/files/pubblicazioni/analysis_205_2013_0.pdf; 'Isam Nu'man, "Munaqashat," in 'Abd al-Ilah Bilqiz (ed.), *al-Ta'ifiyya wa-l-tasamuh wa-l-'adalah al-intiqaliyya: min al-fitna ila dawlat al-*

qanun (Beirut: Markaz Dirasat al-Wahda al-'Arabiyya, 2013); Farian Sabahi, "Iran, Iranian Media and Sunni Islam," in Brigitte Maréchal and Sami Zemni (eds.), *The Dynamics of Sunni–Shia Relationships: Doctrine, Transnationalism, Intellectuals and the Media* (London: Hurst, 2012).

5. Eric Davis, "Introduction: The Question of Sectarian Identities in Iraq," *International Journal of Contemporary Iraqi Studies* 4:3 (2010): 229–242; Ahmed Rasim al-Nifis, "al-Ta'ifiyya wa-l-'unsuriyya," in Oriental Affairs, *al-Mas'ala al-ta'ifiyya wa-l-'ithniyya: al-'Iraq namudhaj* (Beirut: Markaz Dirasat al-Mashriq al-'Arabi, Summer 2008); Mahdi al-Shar', "al-Mukawinat al-siyasiyya li-l-ta'ifiyya fi al-'Iraq," in Oriental Affairs, *al-Mas'ala al-ta'ifiyya wa-l-'ithniyya*; Tareq Ismael and Jacqueline Ismael, "The Sectarian State in Iraq and the New Political Class," *International Journal of Contemporary Iraqi Studies* 4:3 (2010): 339–356; Rashid al-Khayoon, *Dhid al-ta'ifiyya: al-'Iraq, jadal ma ba'd 2003* (Beirut: Madarik, 2011); Lawrence G. Potter, "Introduction," in Lawrence G. Potter (ed.), *Sectarian Politics in the Persian Gulf* (London: Hurst, 2013).

6. Suleiman Taqi al-Din, "al-Ta'ifiyya wa-l-madhabiyya wa atharahum al-siya-siyya," in Bilqiz (ed.), *al-Ta'ifiyya wa-l-tasamuh*; Elisheva Machlis, *Shi'i Sectarianism in the Middle East: Modernisation and the Quest for Islamic Universalism* (London: I.B. Tauris, 2014); Peter Sluglett, "The British, the Sunnis and the Shi'is: Social Hierarchies of Identity under the British Mandate," *International Journal of Contemporary Iraqi Studies* 4:3 (2010): 257–273. In Sluglett's view (p. 258, fn. 1) "sectarianism" refers to "a state of mind in which the religious or sectarian affiliation into which an individual was born … has come to dominate his or her other identities and in which he/she may join together with 'co-religion-ists' against members of 'other' religions or sects, usually in order to obtain, or deny, political representation or political rights."

7. One study defines *ta'ifiyya* in the following terms: "The word *ta'ifiyya* refers to a confessional order in which a system of proportional power sharing between different religious groups is instituted as in Lebanon": Brigitte Maréchal and Sami Zemni, "Introduction: Evaluating Contemporary Sunnite–Shiite Relations: Changing Identities, Political Projects, Interactions and Theological Discussions," in Maréchal and Zemni (eds.), *The Dynamics*, p. 253, fn. 4. Other works that adopt a similar approach include Orit Bashkin, "'Religious Hatred Shall Disappear from the Land'—Iraqi Jews as Ottoman Subjects, 1864–1913," *International Journal of Contemporary Iraqi Studies* 4:3 (2010): 305–323; Ahmed al-Zu'bi, "al-Ta'ifiyya wa-mushkilat bina' al-dawla fi-Lubnan," in al-Mesbar Center, *al-Ta'ifiyya: sahwat al-fitna al-na'ima* (Dubai: al-Mesbar Studies and Research Center, 2010), pp. 47–65.

8. Ussama Makdisi, *The Culture of Sectarianism: Community, History, and Violence in Nineteenth-Century Ottoman Lebanon* (Berkeley: University of California Press, 2000), p. 7.

9. 'Abd al-Ilah Bilqiz, "Muqadima" and "Munaqashat," in Bilqiz (ed.), *al-Ta'ifiyya wa-l-tasamuh*, pp. 9–18, 78–81; Taqi al-Din, "al-Ta'ifiyya wa-l-mad-habiyya," in Bilqiz (ed.), *al-Ta'ifiyya wa-l-tasamuh*; Farhad Ibrahim, *al-Ta'ifiyya wa-l-siyasa fi al-'alam al 'Arabi: namudhaj al-shi'a fi al-'Iraq* (Cairo: Madbouly, 1996), pp. 23–24; Fanar Haddad, *Sectarianism in Iraq: Antagonistic Visions of Unity* (London: Hurst, 2010), pp. 25–29; Max Weiss, *In the Shadow of Sectarianism: Law, Shi'ism and the Making of Modern Lebanon* (Cambridge, MA: Harvard University Press, 2010), pp. 11–15; Vali R. Nasr, "International Politics, Domestic Imperatives and Identity Mobilization: Sectarianism in Pakistan, 1979–1998," *Comparative Politics* 32:2 (2000): 171–190; Justin Gengler, "Understanding Sectarianism in the Persian Gulf," in Potter (ed.), *Sectarian Politics*.

10. Abbas Kadhim, "Efforts at Cross-Ethnic Cooperation: The 1920 Revolution and Sectarian Identities in Iraq," *International Journal of Contemporary Iraqi Studies* 4:3 (2010): 275–294; Muhammad al-Sadr, *al-Ta'ifiyya fi-Nadhar al-Islam* (Beirut: Matba'at al-Basa'ir, 2013); Antoine Dhaw, "Munaqashat," in Bilqiz (ed.), *al-Ta'ifiyya wa-l-tasamuh*; Roel Meijer and Joas Wagemakers, "The Struggle for Citizenship of the Shiites of Saudi Arabia," in Maréchal and Zemni (eds.), *The Dynamics*; Hassan bin Musa al-Saffar, *al-Ta'ifiyya bayn al-siyasa wa-l-din* (Casablanca: al-Markaz al-Thaqafi al-'Arabi, 2009).

11. This has been vividly demonstrated by the reactions to the conflict in Yemen in 2015. Despite the complex and local drivers behind the conflict, some commentators seem content to frame it as part of a broader sectarian, Sunni-Shi'a conflict. The most breathtaking example of this reductionist logic may be Thomas Friedman's assertion that "… the main issue [in Yemen] is the 7th century struggle over who is the rightful heir to the Prophet Muhammad— Shiites or Sunnis": Thomas Friedman, "Tell Me How This Ends Well," *New York Times*, April 1, 2015. This overlooks the fact that the Houthis are Zaydis whose views on succession to the Prophet are closer to mainstream Sunni than Twelver Shi'a Islam. For more nuanced analysis on the conflict in Yemen see Susanne Dahlgren and Anne-Linda Amira Augustin, "The Multiple Wars in Yemen," *Middle East Report* (Middle East Research and Information Project), available at http://www.merip.org/multiple-wars-yemen. June 18, 2015; International Crisis Group, *Yemen at War*, Briefing No. 45, Middle East & North Africa, 28 March 2015, available at https://www.crisisgroup.org/mid-dle-east-north-africa/gulf-and-arabian-peninsula/yemen/yemen-war. On how sectarian identity figures in popular perception of the conflict see, for example, Maria Abi-Habib and Sam Dagher, "Sunnis Cheer Saudi-Led Battle for Yemen," *Wall Street Journal*, March 27, 2015, available at http://www.wsj.com/articles/sunnis-cheer-saudi-led-battle-for-yemen-1427507176

12. Typically this would follow definitions such as "… sectarianism is defined as

feelings of narrow-minded prejudice, which often result in intolerance, discrimination and hatred towards people of other religious sects or ethnic groups": Kadhim, "Efforts at Cross-Ethnic Cooperation," p. 276.

13. Steve Garner, "A Moral Economy of Whiteness: Behaviours, Belonging and Britishness," *Ethnicities* 12:4 (2012), p. 451.

14. Hence the apparent paradox of highly sect-centric actors—sectarian entrepreneurs even—marrying members of the other sect: in such cases the prejudice harbored against the sectarian other is shaped by class prejudice or anti-religious bigotry leaving room for "good Shi'as" (as opposed to the "Shi'a hordes") and "good Sunnis" (as opposed to "Wahhabis").

15. A *takfiri* is a Muslim who makes a point of accusing other Muslims of apostasy.

16. Batatu has explored these intersections at some length. See Hanna Batatu, *The Old Social Classes and the Revolutionary Movements of Iraq: A Study of Iraq's Old Landed and Commercial Classes and of its Communists, Ba'thists, and Free Officers* (Princeton: Princeton University Press, 1978), pp. 44–50, 422–423, 1078–1079, 1132.

17. Marion Farouk-Sluglett and Peter Sluglett, "Some Reflections on the Sunni/ Shi'a Question in Iraq," *Bulletin of the British Society for Middle Eastern Studies* 5:2 (1978), p. 84. Needless to say that despite this, the *perception* that the regime relied on sectarian considerations often outweighed the fact that this was not necessarily the case.

18. See Ali al-Wardi, *Dirasa fi tabi'at al-mugtama' al-'Iraqi* (Baghdad: Matba'at al-'Ani, 1965), pp. 135–136; Batatu, *The Old Social Classes*, pp. 134–137.

19. For a broader discussion of the term *shrug* and how class and regional dynamics animate sectarian relations see Haddad, *Sectarianism in Iraq*, pp. 56–58, 101–102.

20. Hence it is misleading to take secularism as the antidote, much less the antonym, of "sectarianism." See Fanar Haddad, "Secular Sectarians," Middle East Institute, June 17, 2014, available at http://www.mei.edu/content/map/secular-sectarians.

21. For more on these themes see Milton J. Esman, *Ethnic Politics* (Ithaca, NY: Cornell University Press, 1994), pp. 3–5.

22. The obvious exception here is the nation-state that is based, or claims to be based, on religion; where religious identity becomes the marker for inclusion and legitimacy.

23. A Sunni politician summarized the point while reflecting on the impact of 2003: "… we awoke one day and suddenly discovered that we are all Sunnis." Quoted in International Crisis Group, *Make or Break: Iraq's Sunnis and the State*, Report No. 144, Middle East & North Africa, 14 August 2013, available at https://www.crisisgroup.org/middle-east-north-africa/gulf-and-arabian-

peninsula/iraq/make-or-break-iraq-s-sunnis-and-state, pp. 4–5. For a dis-
cussion of the emergence of Sunni identity in post-2003 Iraq see Fanar
Haddad, "A Sectarian Awakening: Reinventing Sunni Identity in Iraq After
2003," *Current Trends in Islamist Ideology* 17 (2014): 145–176.

24. As Azar Gat argues in his discussion of power relations and ethno-coding:
"One's own culture, especially a great and dominant one, appears transpar-
ent. Only the others are ethnic." See Azar Gat, *Nations: The Long History and
Deep Roots of Political Ethnicity and Nationalism* (Cambridge: Cambridge
University Press, 2013), p. 272.

25. Esman, *Ethnic Politics*, pp. 4–5.

26. See Guldem Baykal Buyuksarac, "Unheard Voices: State-Making and Popular
Participation in Post-Ottoman Iraq," *Ethnic and Racial Studies* 38:14 (2015):
2551–2568. Describing state–minority relations in Iraq, Buyuksarac argues
(p. 2560) that, since the Mandate, "… the state–minority relationship has
been locked in a loop of exclusionary politics and securitization."

27. Hamit Bozarslan, "Rethinking the Ba'thist Period," in Jordi Tejel et al. (eds.),
Writing the Modern History of Iraq: Historiographical and Political Challenges
(Singapore: World Scientific Publishing, 2012), p. 145.

28. The Nationality Law divided Iraqis into "original" and "non-original," "orig-
inal" meaning those who had been registered as Ottoman subjects. This fol-
lowed the precedent set by the first Iraqi constitution of 1921 and the Law
for the Election of the Constituent Assembly of 1922, both of which simi-
larly divided Iraqis into "original" and "non-original."

29. These targeted Kurds, Turkomans, and Assyrians in northern Iraq. See "Iraq:
Forcible Expulsion of Ethnic Minorities," Human Rights Watch 15:3 (March
2003), available at http://www.hrw.org/sites/default/files/reports/Kirkuk
0303.pdf and "Claims in Conflict: Reversing Ethnic Cleansing in Northern
Iraq," Human Rights Watch 16:4 (August 2004), available at http://www.
hrw. org/reports/2004/iraq0804/iraq0804.pdf.

30. *Shu'ubiyya* refers to an eighth-century movement that challenged the privi-
leged position of Arabs in the early Islamic empires, arguing that Islam does
not differentiate between believers on the basis of ethnicity. In the twentieth
century the term was revived by pan-Arabists to describe internal enemies
of the Arab world. It was most notably used to discredit Iraqi communists.
See Sami A. Hanna and George H. Gardner, "al-Shu'ubiyyah Up-Dated:
A Study of the 20th Century Revival of an Eighth Century Concept," *Middle
East Journal* 20:3 (Summer 1966): 335–351. *Taba'iyya* is commonly translated
as "dependency." In recent Iraqi history the term is shorthand for *taba'iyya
Iraniyya* meaning those who are of "Iranian dependency"—i.e. registered as
Persian rather than Ottoman subjects—as stipulated by the Nationality Law
of 1924. The charge of *taba'iyya* was used to justify the deportation of hun-

dreds of thousands of Shi'a. See Ali Babakhan, "The Deportation of Shi'as during the Iran-Iraq War: Causes and Consequences," in Faleh A. Jabar (ed.), *Ayatollahs, Sufis and Ideologues: State, Religion and Social Movements in Iraq* (London: Saqi, 2002).

31. This and the following section borrow from Fanar Haddad, "Shia-Centric State Building and Sunni Rejection in Post-2003 Iraq," Carnegie Endowment for International Peace, January 7, 2016, available at http://carnegieendowment.org/2016/01/07/shia-centric-state-building-and-sunni-rejection-in-post-2003-iraq/is5w.

32. Quoted in Elie Kedourie, "Anti-Shiism in Iraq under the Monarchy," *Middle Eastern Studies* 24:2 (April 1988), p. 253.

33. To illustrate, in 1985 Ofra Bengio lamented the fact that "The extent to which the regime has suppressed the [Shi'a] issue can be gathered from the fact that the term Shi'i itself has become almost taboo in the Iraqi media. This in itself poses tremendous difficulties for the analyst": Ofra Bengio, "Shi'is and Politics in Ba'thi Iraq," *Middle Eastern Studies* 21:1 (Jan 1985), p. 13, fn. 1.

34. Sa'dun Shakir speaking at a high-level party committee meeting in August 1987. Quoted in Amatzia Baram, *Saddam Husayn and Islam, 1968–2003: Ba'thi Iraq from Secularism to Faith* (Baltimore: Johns Hopkins University Press, 2014), p. 166.

35. Peter Sluglett, *Britain in Iraq: Contriving King and Country, 1914–1932* (New York: Columbia University Press, 2007), p. 224.

36. See Sluglett, *Britain in Iraq*, pp. 103–105. Batatu, *The Old Social Classes*, pp. 327–328.

37. For full text see Abdul Razzaq al-Hasani, *Tarikh al-wizarat al-'Iraqiyya*, 7th ed. (Baghdad: Dar al-Shu'oon al-Thaqafiyya al-'Ama, 1988), vol. 4, pp. 92–94.

38. Memorandum written by Faisal in March 1932 addressing Iraq's political elite in which he gave his personal assessment of the state of the country. The memorandum can be found in full in Salih Abd al-Razzaq, *Masharee' izalat al-tamyeez al-ta'ifi fi al-'Iraq: min mudhakarat Faisal ila majlis al-hukm, 1932–2003* (Beirut: al-Ma'arif, 2010), pp. 16–27.

39. Baram, *Saddam Husayn and Islam*, chapter 3.

40. This was by no means restricted to Sunni Arab Iraqis; however, given that the sect-centricity in question is Shi'a sect-centricity, suspicion was more likely to emanate from Sunni quarters in the same way that sympathy was more likely to emanate from Shi'a ones.

41. For the opposition-in-exile see Tareq Y. Ismael and Jacqueline S. Ismael, *Iraq in the Twenty-First Century: Regime Change and the Making of a Failed State* (New York: Routledge, 2015), pp. 84–89. For the changes in Shi'a political consciousness, particularly in the diaspora, see Ali Allawi, *The Occupation: Winning*

the War, Losing the Peace (London: Yale University Press, 2007), pp. 36–37, 50–51, 74–75, 137–138.

42. The principle was adopted at the Iraqi opposition conferences of Vienna in June 1992 and Salah al-Din in October 1992. See Allawi, *The Occupation*, p. 50; Ismael and Ismael, *Iraq*, pp. 86, 88. Hayder al-Khoei has argued that the idea of ethno-sectarian quotas dates even further back to 1987 when it was adopted in an opposition conference held in Tehran: Hayder al-Khoei, "The Construction of Ethno-Sectarian Politics in Post-War Iraq: 2003–05," master's thesis, International Studies and Diplomacy, School of Oriental and African Studies (SOAS), University of London, 2012, p. 12.

43. Haddad, *Sectarianism in Iraq*, chapters 4–6.

44. International Crisis Group, *The Next Iraqi War? Sectarianism and Civil Conflict*, Report No. 52, Middle East & North Africa, 27 February 2006, https://www.crisisgroup.org/middle-east-north-africa/gulf-and-arabian-peninsula/iraq/next-iraqi-war-sectarianism-and-civil-conflict, p. 29. The report adds: "Already in early 2004, a secular Shiite academic had told Crisis Group that at the end of the day, confronted with the choice to vote for a secular or an overtly Shiite party, he would vote for the latter out of 'Shiite solidarity'— to ensure the realisation of the Shiite majority's dream of ruling Iraq": p. 29, fn. 204.

45. For a more in-depth discussion of these dynamics see Fanar Haddad, "Sectarian Relations and Sunni Identity in Post-Civil War Iraq," in Potter (ed.), *Sectarian Politics*.

46. As Joel Rayburn put it, "When the long-contained Shi'a population began to emerge in 2003, many Sunnis simply could not believe their eyes": Joel Rayburn, *Iraq after America: Strongmen, Sectarians, Resistance* (Stanford: Hoover Institution Press, 2014), p. 130.

47. Though not a position universally subscribed to, the argument one commonly encounters amongst Sunni Arabs is that they constitute 42 per cent of the Iraqi population while the Shi'a account for 41 per cent; hence, according to this logic, alongside the mostly Sunni Kurdish north, Iraq is a Sunni-majority country. Many Sunni figures have publicly stated their rejection of any notion that they are a numerical minority: from religious leaders such as the late Harith al-Dhari (former general secretary of the Association of Muslim Scholars) to politicians such as Khalaf al-Ulayan, Muhsin Abd al-Hamid (former head of the Iraqi Islamic Party), and Osama al-Nujaifi to extremists such as Taha al-Dulaymi. In fact, as early as August 2003, Dulaymi was calling the idea that Sunnis are a minority a lie. See http://www.islam-memo.cc/2003/10/02/2626.html.

48. Harith Hasan al-Qarawee, presentation given at "National Reconciliation and Negotiation: The Path Forward in Iraq and Syria," Johns Hopkins

University, School of Advanced International Studies (SAIS), December 15, 2014, available at https://www.youtube.com/watch?v=Na5tfjOiB3M

49. It is interesting to speculate as to whether or not most Sunnis would have been willing to excuse all these changes and the Shi'a elites' sect-centricity had the latter succeeded in establishing a functioning state capable of delivering basic needs and providing security and hopes for a better future.

50. Initially there were two broad tendencies amongst Sunni Arabs: one that clung to the sect-averse political frames of reference of the pre-2003 world, and another that essentially tried to catch up with Shi'a in terms of building a politicized sectarian identity. Although this divergence still exists to some degree, the latter trend quickly gained ground, as evidenced by the December 2005 elections, in which the Sunni Islamist coalition, Tawafuq, secured the majority of Sunni seats. See Stephen Wicken, "Iraq's Sunnis in Crisis," Institute for the Study of War, May 2013, available at http://www.understandingwar.org/sites/default/files/Wicken-Sunni-In-Iraq.pdf, p. 36; International Crisis Group, "Make or Break," p. 5.

51. See Rayburn, *Iraq after America*, chapter 5; Shireen T. Hunter, "The Real Causes of Iraq's Problems," *LobeLog*, June 14, 2014, available at https://lobelog.com/2014-06-the-real-causes-of-iraqs-problems/.

52. The paradox of wanting a greater share of a system deemed illegitimate and the consequently ambivalent relationship with anti-state violence has led some Sunni politicians to collude with anti-state insurgents. See Benjamin Bahney, Patrick B. Johnston, and Patrick Ryan, "The Enemy You Know and the Ally You Don't," *Foreign Policy*, June 23, 2015, available at https://foreignpolicy.com/2015/06/23/the-enemy-you-know-and-the-ally-you-dont-arm-sunni-militias-iraq/.

53. These paradoxes of Iraqi Sunni identity are discussed in more detail in Haddad, "A Sectarian Awakening," pp. 153–165.

54. See Fanar Haddad, "Iraq: Atrocity as Political Capital," in Bridget Conley-Zilkic (ed.), *How Mass Atrocities End: Studies from Guatemala, Burundi, Indonesia, the Sudans, Bosnia-Herzegovina, and Iraq* (Cambridge: Cambridge University Press, 2016).

55. Mari Luomi, "Sectarian Identities or Geopolitics? The Regional Shia–Sunni Divide in the Middle East," Finnish Institute of International Affairs, Working Paper 56, 2008, available at http://www.fiia.fi/en/publication/4/sectarian_identities_or_geopolitics/.

56. Fanar Haddad, "Sunni–Shia Relations after the Iraq War," United States Institute of Peace (USIP), Peace Brief 160, November 2013, available at http://www.usip.org/sites/default/files/PB160.pdf.

57. This is more relevant to the Mashriq, where the uprisings were affected by varying degrees of sect-coding, most clearly seen in Bahrain and Syria. For

an interesting discussion of these dynamics see Heiko Wimmen, "Divisive Rule: Sectarianism and Power Maintenance in the Arab Spring: Bahrain, Iraq, Lebanon and Syria," German Institute for International and Security Affairs, Research Paper 4, March 2014, available at https://www.swp-berlin.org/fileadmin/contents/products/research_papers/2014_RP04_wmm.pdf.

58. This was mistaken for the Arabic, *idhrab al sayyida Aisha*—strike Aisha. For a collage of clips showing religious leaders from various parts of the Arab world warning of the evils of this toy see https://www.youtube.com/watch?v=-gto2qXk_gs. The video also includes footage of the issue being raised in the Egyptian House of Representatives and a rebuttal explaining what the toy actually says. Remarkably, videos are still uploaded warning Sunnis that the toy exhorts children to strike Aisha. For one such video uploaded as recently as August 2015 see https://www.youtube.com/watch?v=b08FTasF83s.

7. THE SHATTERED NATION: THE SECTARIANIZATION OF THE SYRIAN CONFLICT

1. This definition was inspired by Ussama Makdisi's analysis of the emergence of sectarianism in nineteenth-century Lebanon, in which he points out that "sectarianism refers to the deployment of religious heritage as a primary marker of modern political identity." See Ussama Makdisi, *The Culture of Sectarianism: Community, History, and Violence in Nineteenth-Century Ottoman Lebanon* (Berkeley: University of California Press, 2000), p. 7.

2. For a more complete account of the early events of the Syrian uprising see Paulo G. Pinto, "Syria," in Paul Amar and Vijay Prashad (eds.), *Dispatches from the Arab Spring: Understanding the New Middle East* (Minneapolis: University of Minnesota Press, 2013), pp. 204–242.

3. The Ba'ath Party took power in Syria through a *coup d'état* in 1963. In 1970 Hafez al-Assad took power in an "internal coup" and was sworn in as president of Syria the following year. After Hafez's death in 2000 his son Bashar succeeded him as president of Syria, a position which he still held in 2016.

4. On January 26, 2011, Hassan Ali Akleh, a young Kurdish man, poured gasoline over his body and set it on fire in Hassaka, in northeastern Syria. He was emulating the example of Muhammad Bouazizi, whose self-immolation unleashed the wave of protests that brought down Ben Ali's dictatorship in Tunisia.

5. "Protests' Shockwave Hits Syria and Djibouti," Al Arabiya News, February 18, 2011, available at https://www.alarabiya.net/articles/2011/02/18/138195.html.

6. "Interview with Syrian President Bashar al-Assad," *Wall Street Journal*, January

31, 2011, available at http://www.wsj.com/articles/SB1000142405274870 3833204576114712441122894.

7. Paulo G. Pinto, "'Oh Syria, God Protects You': Islam as Cultural Idiom under Bashar al-Asad," *Middle East Critique* 20:2 (2011), pp. 191–192.

8. The *dhikr* (evocation/remembering of God) is the main public ritual of Sufism, the mystical branch of Islam.

9. Jonathan Littell, *Syrian Notebooks: Inside the Homs Uprising* (London: Verso, 2015), pp. 37–38.

10. Aleppo: "25 March, Syrian Policemen Wear Civil Clothes [*sic*] Attack Protesters at Umayyad Mosque in Aleppo City," available at https://youtu.be/V3mh-StEuSA; Damascus: "A Protest at Umayyad Mosque in the Syrian Capital Damascus on Friday 18 March," available at https://youtu.be/aOyPDonA30A.

11. Pierre Nora defines the *lieux de memoire* as events, places, monuments, and symbols that are invested with the collective memory of a group. See Pierre Nora, "General Introduction: Between Memory and History," in Pierre Nora (ed.), *Realms of Memory: The Reconstruction of the French Past*, vol. 1 (New York: Columbia University Press, 1996), pp. 1–20.

12. SANA (Syrian Arab News Agency), "'Syria Will Remain Free'—President Bashar al-Assad Speech on January 10, 2012," available at https://syrian-freepress.wordpress.com/2012/01/10/syria-will-remain-free-president-bashar-al-assad-speech-on-january-10-2012-full-english-text/.

13. The Salafiyya is a reform movement in Islam that appeared in the nineteenth century, preaching a "return" to the sources of the Islamic tradition. In Syria the Salafiyya was met with fierce competition from the religious establishment, which was heavily influenced by Sufism, only gaining some ground in rural areas and middle-sized towns, mainly because of the labor migration of residents from these areas to Gulf countries and Saudi Arabia, where they were exposed to various forms of ultraconservative Wahhabi religiosity. See Arnaud Lenfant, "L'évolution du salafisme en Syrie au XXe siècle," in Bernard Rougier (ed.), *Qu'est-ce que le salafisme?* (Paris: PUF, 2008).

14. Lenfant, "L'évolution du salafisme en Syrie au XXe siècle," p. 171.

15. Lenfant, "L'évolution du salafisme en Syrie au XXe siècle," p. 169.

16. Lenfant, "L'évolution du salafisme en Syrie au XXe siècle," p. 173.

17. Littell, *Syrian Notebooks*, p. 55.

18. Al Jazeera, Syria Live Blog, April 22, 2011, available at http://blogs.aljazeera.net/live/middle-east/syria-live-blog-april-22.

19. Al Jazeera, Syria Live Blog, April 23, 2011, available at http://blogs.aljazeera.net/live/middle-east/syria-live-blog-april-23.

20. The 'Alawis are a branch of Shi'a Islam which developed an esoteric and, sometimes, allegorical understanding of Islamic doctrines and rituals. While

traditionally religious knowledge was secretive and reserved to the shaykhs, there has been a long process of convergence between the 'Alawis and Twelver Ja'fari Shi'ism, with the adoption of doctrinal and ritual traditions of the latter by the former. Many Sunni Muslims still see the 'Alawis as heretics, however. See Sabrina Mervin, "Quelques jalons pour une histoire du rapprochement (taqrîb) des Alaouites vers le chiisme," in Rainer Brunner, Monika Gronke, Jens Laut, and Ulrich Rebstock (eds.), *Islamstudien ohne Ende: Festschrift für Werner Ende* (Deutsche Morgenländische Gesellschaft, Ergon Verlag Würzburg, 2002) and Bruno Paoli, "Et maintenant, on va où?: les Alaouites à la croisée des destins," in François Burgat and Bruno Paoli (eds.), *Pas de printemps pour la Syrie: les clés pour comprendre les acteurs et les défis de la crise (2011–2013)* (Paris: La Découverte, 2013).

21. Littell, *Syrian Notebooks*, p. 51.
22. Littell, *Syrian Notebooks*, p. 48.
23. See Michel Seurat, "Les populations, l'état et la société," in André Raymond (ed.), *La Syrie d'aujourd'hui* (Paris: Éditions du CNRS, 1980) and Nikolaos Van Dam, *The Struggle for Power in Syria: Politics and Society under Asad and the Ba'th Party* (London: I.B. Tauris, 1996).
24. Umar Abd-Allah, *The Islamic Struggle in Syria* (Berkeley: Mizan Press, 1983), p. 109.
25. These documents are reproduced in Abd-Allah, *The Islamic Struggle in Syria*, pp. 201–267.
26. *The Manifesto of the Islamic Revolution in Syria*, in Abd-Allah, *The Islamic Struggle in Syria*, p. 211.
27. See the anti-'Alawi documents reproduced in Olivier Carré and Michel Seurat, *Les Frères musulmans (1928–1982)* (Paris: L'Harmattan, 1983), pp. 173–178.
28. The estimates of civilian casualties in the army attack on Hama vary between 5,000 and 30,000. See Abd-Allah, *The Islamic Struggle in Syria*, pp. 192–193; Van Dam, *The Struggle for Power in Syria*, p. 111.
29. At the same time, stories of Sunni violence against Shi'a and Christian civilians in Iraq produced a similar sense of victimization among religious minorities in Syria.
30. The concepts of saturation and precipitation were taken from Robert Weller's analysis of protest movements and revolts in China, in which he shows how the cultural idioms can become saturated by being invested with divergent social imaginaries, and how this leads to the precipitation of divergent social movements and political projects. See Robert Weller, *Resistance, Chaos and Control in China: Taiping Rebels, Taiwanese Ghosts and Tiananmen* (Seattle: University of Washington Press, 1994).
31. By cultural equivalence I mean the capacity of the protests to articulate the various political and social projects, expectations, and meanings being

invested in them in such a way that would resonate with those who took part in them.

32. Thomas Pierret. "Le parcours du combattant des opposants syriens," *Le monde*, April 7, 2011, available at http://www.lemonde.fr/idees/article/2011/04/06/le-parcours-du-combattant-des-opposants-syriens_1503828_3232.html.

33. See Pinto, "Syria," p. 221.

34. Some authors attribute the spread of these sectarian slogans in the early protests to regime agents who infiltrated the opposition. By 2012 anti-ʿAlawi slogans could be heard in protests in Homs. See Paoli, "Et maintenant, on va où?" p. 136.

35. Thomas Pierret, "Qui sont les oulémas contestataires en Syrie?" *Mediapart*, August 15, 2011, available at https://blogs.mediapart.fr/thomas-pierret/blog/150811/qui-sont-les-oulemas-contestataires-en-syrie.

36. Thomas Pierret, "Les oulémas: une hégémonie religieuse ébranlée par la révolution," in Burgat and Paoli (eds.), *Pas de printemps pour la Syrie*, p. 100.

37. "Syrian Sunni Cleric Threatens: 'We Shall Mince [the Alawites] in Meat Grinders'," available at https://youtu.be/Bwz8i3osHww.

38. After 2011 Shaykh ʿArʿur softened the sectarian tone of his discourse, focusing on the suffering of the victims of regime repression. See Pierret, "Les oulémas," pp. 104–105.

39. Pierret, "Les oulémas," p. 104.

40. ʿAbd al-Rahman al-Hajj, *al-Islam al-siyasi wa al-thawra fi Suriya*, Al-Jazeera Center for Studies, available at http://studies.aljazeera.net/ar/, pp. 7–8; Littell, *Syrian Notebooks*, p. 58.

41. "Syria Muslim Brotherhood Issues Post-Assad State-for-All Commitment Charter," Ikhwanweb, April 7, 2012, available at http://www.ikhwanweb.com/article.php?id=29851&ref=search.php.

42. Nebras Chehayed, "'Nos autels sont tachés de sang!': l'appel du Père Nebras Chehayed aux évêques de Syrie, 12 Juillet 2011," in Burgat and Paoli (eds.), *Pas de printemps pour la Syrie*, p. 44.

43. "Mother Agnes Mariam: Facts about the chemical attack in Damascus," available at https://youtu.be/95IAkNSU8yA.

44. Paoli, "Et maintenant, on va où?" p. 140.

45. Paoli, "Et maintenant, on va où?" pp. 130–131.

46. See Wendy Pearlman, "Understanding Fragmentation in the Syrian Revolt," Project on Middle East Political Science (POMEPS), February 12, 2014, available at http://pomeps.org/2014/02/12/understanding-fragmentation-in-the-syrian-revolt/.

47. Interview with a Syrian Brazilian who was in Latakiya until September 2011.

48. Data collected in interviews with ʿAlawi and Christian Syrian Brazilians who had family in Latakiya, Homs, and Tartus.

49. Basma Atassi, "Q&A: Syria's Daring Actress. Fadwa Soliman, an Alawite who Became an Icon in the Uprising against Bashar al-Assad, Speaks to Al Jazeera from Hiding," Al Jazeera English, November 23, 2011, available at http://www.aljazeera.com/indepth/features/2011/11/2011112314215792 4333.html.

50. François Burgat, "La stratégie al-Assad: diviser pour survivre," in Burgat and Paoli (eds.), *Pas de printemps pour la Syrie*, p. 27.

51. Human Rights Watch, "Syria: UN Inquiry Should Investigate Houla Killings. Survivors Describe Execution of Family Members," May 27, 2012, available at https://www.hrw.org/news/2012/05/27/syria-un-inquiry-should-investigate-houla-killings.

52. Nir Rosen, "Assad's Alawites: The Guardians of the Throne," Al Jazeera English, October 10, 2011, available at http://www.aljazeera.com/indepth/features/2011/10/20111010122434671982.html.

53. François Burgat and Romain Caillet, "Une guérilla 'islamiste'? Les composantes idéologiques de la résistance armée," in Burgat and Paolo (eds.), *Pas de printemps pour la Syria*, p. 61.

54. Burgat and Caillet, "Une guérilla 'islamiste'?" p. 64.

55. Littell, *Syrian Notebooks*, pp. 6–7.

56. Jean-Pierre Filiu, *Je vous écris d'Alep: au coeur de la Syrie en révolution* (Paris: Éditions Denoël, 2013), pp. 43–54.

57. Filiu, *Je vous écris d'Alep*, pp. 23–24.

58. Interview by telephone on December 12, 2012.

59. Cited in Burgat and Caillet, "Une guérilla 'islamiste'?" p. 79.

60. In pre-uprising Aleppo many shaykhs constructed and enacted the *shari'a* as forms of justice based on mediation of conflicts and fairness to the social persona of the people involved in them. See Paulo G. Pinto, "Ritual, Mysticism and Islamic Law in Contemporary Syrian Sufism," in Alfonso Carmona (ed.), *El Sufismo y las Normas del Islam* (Murcia: Editora Regional de Murcia, 2006), pp. 461–462.

61. Filiu, *Je vous écris d'Alep*, pp. 55–68.

62. Pierre-Jean Luizard, *Le piège Daech: l'État Islamique ou le retour de l'histoire* (Paris: La Découverte, 2015), pp. 149–152.

63. "al-Nusra Fighters Kill 20 Druze Villagers in Syria: Activists," Al Bawaba News, June 12, 2015, available at http://www.albawaba.com/news/al-nusra-fighters-kill-20-druze-villagers-syria-activists-706786.

64. Burgat, "La stratégie al-Assad: diviser pour survivre," p. 27; Luizard, *Le piège Daech*, pp. 15–151.

65. Richard Spencer, "Syrian al-Qaeda Group ISIS Expelled from Second City Aleppo: A Militant al-Qaeda Group has been Driven out of the Northern Syrian City of Aleppo by an Alliance of Other Rebels, According to

Activists," *The Telegraph*, January 9, 2014, available at http://www.telegraph.
co.uk/news/worldnews/middleeast/syria/10561857/Syrian-Al-Qaeda-
group-ISIS-expelled-from-second-city-Aleppo.html.
66. Filiu, *Je vous écris d'Alep*, pp. 90–91.
67. Filiu, *Je vous écris d'Alep*, p. 112.
68. Burgat and Caillet, "Une guérilla 'islamiste'?" pp. 81–82.

8. SECTARIANISM AS COUNTER-REVOLUTION: SAUDI RESPONSES
TO THE ARAB SPRING

1. This chapter draws on discussions with various Saudi activists since January
2011, statements by opposition groups and government agencies with respect
to the events in the Arab world and inside the country, a survey of local and
international media, and analysis of various Saudi internet web pages, includ-
ing Islamist and liberal discussion boards, Facebook, Twitter, and YouTube.
2. Madawi Al-Rasheed, *A History of Saudi Arabia*, 2nd ed. (Cambridge: Cambridge
University Press, 2010).
3. See F. Gregory Gause III, *Oil Monarchies: Domestic and Security Challenges in the
Arab Gulf Monarchies* (New York: Council on Foreign Relations Press, 1994);
Giacomo Luciani and Hazem Beblawi (eds.), *The Rentier State* (London: Croom
Helm, 1987).
4. For a review of the literature on the rentier state and its relevance to the Saudi
regime see Madawi Al-Rasheed, *Is it Always Good to be King?: Saudi Regime
Resilience after the 2011 Arab Popular Uprisings*, London: LSE Middle East Center
Working Paper 12, 2015.
5. Vali Nasr, *The Shia Revival: How Conflicts within Islam Will Shape the Future* (New
York: W.W. Norton, 2006).
6. Guido Steinberg, "The Shiites in the Eastern Province of Saudi Arabia (al-
Ahsa), 1913–1953," in Rainer Brunner and Werner Ende (eds.), *The Twelver
Shi'a in Modern Times: Religious Culture and Political History* (Leiden: Brill, 2001).
7. Toby Jones, "Embattled in Arabia: Shi'is and the Politics of Confrontation in
Saudi Arabia," Occasional Paper Series, Combating Terrorism Center at West
Point (June 3, 2009), available at http://goo.gl/JjxW3y.
8. International Crisis Group, *Popular Protests in North Africa and the Middle East
(III): The Bahrain Revolt*, Report no. 105, Middle East & North Africa, 6 April
2011, available at https://www.crisisgroup.org/middle-east-north-africa/gulf-
and-arabian-peninsula/bahrain/popular-protests-north-africa-and-middle-
east-iii-bahrain-revolt. Cortni Kerr and Toby Jones, "A Revolution Paused in
Bahrain," *Middle East Report* (Middle East Research and Information Project),
February 23, 2011, available at http://www.merip.org/mero/mero022311;
and Toby Matthiesen, *Sectarian Gulf: Bahrain, Saudi Arabia, and the Arab Spring
That Wasn't* (Stanford: Stanford University Press, 2013).

9. See Al-Rasheed, *A History of Saudi Arabia*; Fouad Ibrahim, *The Shi'is of Saudi Arabia* (London: Saqi, 2006); Toby Craig Jones, *Desert Kingdom: How Oil and Water Forged Modern Saudi Arabia* (Cambridge, MA: Harvard University Press, 2010); and Toby Matthiesen, *The Other Saudis: Shiism, Dissent and Sectarianism* (Cambridge: Cambridge University Press, 2014).

10. Robert Vitalis, *America's Kingdom: Mythmaking on the Saudi Oil Frontier* (Stanford: Stanford University Press, 2007).

11. Al-Rasheed, *A History of Saudi Arabia*; Ibrahim, *The Shi'is of Saudi Arabia*; Jones, *Desert Kingdom;* Matthiesen, *The Other Saudis*.

12. Madawi Al-Rasheed, "The Shi'a of Saudi Arabia: A Minority in Search of Cultural Authenticity," *British Journal of Middle Eastern Studies* 25: 1 (1998): 121–38.

13. Al-Rasheed, *A History of Saudi Arabia;* Stéphane Lacroix, *Awakening Islam: The Politics of Religious Dissent in Contemporary Saudi Arabia*, translated by George Holoch (Cambridge, MA: Harvard University Press, 2011).

14. Madawi Al-Rasheed, *Contesting the Saudi State: Islamic Voices from a New Generation* (Cambridge: Cambridge University Press, 2007).

15. The Saudi Day of Rage was advertised on many web pages. The Saudi authorities tried to block them, but activists would quickly set up alternative Facebook pages. One page that was still accessible on April 21, 2011 is http://www.facebook.com/Saudis.Revolution.

16. Information is based on communications and electronic messages between March and April 2011 with Fuad Ibrahim (Khalas Shi'a opposition), Saad al-Faqih (Movement for Islamic Reform in Arabia), Muhammad al-Masari (al-Tajdid), and Muhammad al-Mufarih (Islamic Ummah Party). In Saudi Arabia, communication with many activists who prefer to remain anonymous provided much of the assessment in this chapter. In addition, it was surprising that many Saudi students studying abroad on government scholarships are active net-citizens. Many students used their time abroad to escape internet censorship. Their various communications and email messages provided valuable insight on their dreams and aspirations.

17. Several web pages appeared and were claimed by the Free Youth Movement and National Youth Movement. See http://www.facebook.com/notes. php?id=130993796971053. The site has become a platform to follow up on the cases of political prisoners, while continuing to press for political reform. While it is very difficult to know who set up the page, I had confirmation from several Saudi activists, who drew my attention to their statements, that they had participated in posting opposition messages.

18. Muhammad al-Wadani called on the internet for the overthrow of the monarchy, using a YouTube posting. See http://www.youtube.com/user/Edr3aan#p/a/u/2/iOeqTN2bRa8. He posted this video before he was arrested on March 7. In this video he calls for *jum'at al-hashd* (the Friday of

Mobilization) to precede the Day of Rage on March 11, 2011. After his arrest his friends posted a video of the actual arrest, in which a civilian assisted by several other men surrounded al-Wadani and drove him away in a car. I received the video by email only an hour after his arrest.

19. MIRA endorsed the demonstrations on its web page. See http://www.islah. info/ index.php?/1684/. The newly founded Islamic Umma Party also supported the demonstration on their party web page. The party's communiqués were accessible at http://www. islamicommaparty.com/Portals/default/ in April–June 2011. In addition to consulting these internet-based sources of information, I relied on interviews and communication with activists affiliated with the two Islamist movements during April and June. My discussion with the spokesman of the Islamic Umma Party was conducted through Skype, as the spokesman was in hiding after the arrest of five founding members of the party.

20. As early as 2009, and following clashes between Shi'a pilgrims and Saudi authorities in Madina, a group called Khalas emerged to defend Shi'a rights for free worship and, more importantly, equality. The group adopted the name Khalas to distinguish themselves from the early Shi'a opposition groups who reconciled with the government in 1993 (Al-Rasheed, "The Shia of Saudi Arabia"). On the emergence of Khalas see Anees al-Qudaihi, "Saudi Arabia's Shia Press for Rights," BBC Arabic Service, March 24, 2009, available at http://news.bbc.co.uk/2/hi/7959531.stm. This new Shi'a opposition established its own website to post opinions and commentaries, regarded by the old Shi'a opposition inside Saudi Arabia as too radical. The group associated with Hasan al-Safar, a Shi'a scholar who returned to Saudi Arabia in 1994 after reconciling with the regime, remains loyal to the government— at least in its public statements. As such, al-Safar distances himself from Khalas and another Shi'a opposition group called Hizbullah al-Hijaz (see Toby Matthiesen, "Hizbullah al-Hijaz: A History of the Most Radical Saudi Shi'a Opposition Group," *Middle East Journal* 64: 2 (Spring 2010): 179–197). For more details on Khalas's opinions see http://www.moltaqaa.com/.

21. Evgeny Morozov, *The Net Delusion: How Not to Liberate the World* (London: Allen Lane, 2011).

22. Amnesty International, "Saudi Arabia: Repression in the Name of Security," December 1, 2011, available at https://www.amnesty.org/en/documents/ MDE23/016/2011/en/.

23. Human Rights Watch, "Saudi Arabia: Arrests for Peaceful Protest on the Rise," March 27, 2011, available at https://www.hrw.org/news/2011/03/27/ saudi-arabia-arrests-peaceful-protest-rise.

24. Salwa Ismail, "The Syrian Uprising: Imagining and Performing the Nation," *Studies in Ethnicity and Nationalism* 11:3 (2011): 538–549.

25. For the text of the *fatwa* see the official web page of the Saudi Ifta Council

at http://www.alifta.net/. The *fatwa* was later reported in the local Saudi press (see "Demonstrations are Forbidden," *al-Riyadh*, March 7, 2011).

26. Al-Rasheed, *Contesting the Saudi State*.

27. Personal communication with political activist who sent me a copy of the *fatwa* that he collected after Friday noon prayers on March 11, 2011 in Riyadh.

28. Two internet discussion boards clearly reflected attempts by intelligence services to infiltrate these sites as new members under pseudonyms joined to defend the regime and spread the message that demonstrations are forbidden in Islam (see al-Saha at http:// www.alsaha.com/ and the Saudi Liberal Network at http://humanf.org, which were both accessible on March 11, 2011).

29. In *al-Riyadh*, journalist Muhammad al-Mahfud posted several articles calling for the promotion of citizenship at the expense of divisive sectarianism (see http://www.rasid.com/artc.php?id=45168 and http://www.rasid.com/artc.php?id=44415). Abdul Rahman al-Rashid, the ex-editor of *al-Sharq al-Awsat*, highlighted the dangers of sectarian politics (see http://www.rasid.com/artc.php?id=45051); in *al-Watan*, Osama al-Qahtani praised Sunni-Shi'a coexistence (see http://www.rasid.com/artc.php?id=44883).

30. See Matthiesen, *The Other Saudis*.

31. As Jeff Colgan observes: "The sectarian nature of today's rivalries in the Middle East contrasts sharply with the last time Egypt and Saudi Arabia intervened in a Yemeni civil war. In the 1960s, Egyptian President Gamal Abdel Nasser led a pan-Arab nationalist movement that threatened the legitimacy of monarchies like Saudi Arabia. Egypt, along with Iraq and other Arab republics, supported North Yemen. Saudi Arabia and other monarchies, including Iran (which was a monarchy at the time), helped the royalists in South Yemen. Just like today, Yemen's battle was part of the larger political contest in the Middle East—but now the central cleavage has switched from regime type to sectarian identity": Jeff Colgan, "How Sectarianism Shapes Yemen's War," *The Monkey Cage* (*Washington Post* blog), April 13, 2015, available at www.washingtonpost.com/blogs/monkey-cage/wp/2015/04/13/how-sectarianism-shapes-yemens-war/.

32. See the chapters on these countries in this volume by Bassel F. Salloukh, Paulo Gabriel Hilu Pinto, Fanar Haddad, and Toby Matthiesen, respectively.

33. Ernest Gellner, *Muslim Society* (Cambridge: Cambridge University Press, 1981).

9. STRATEGIC DEPTH, COUNTERINSURGENCY, AND THE LOGIC OF SECTARIANIZATION: THE ISLAMIC REPUBLIC OF IRAN'S SECURITY DOCTRINE AND ITS REGIONAL IMPLICATIONS

1. The author would like to thank Nader Hashemi, Danny Postel, Anoushiravan Ehteshami, Nasser Mohajer, Fanar Haddad, Marc Valeri, Abdel Razzaq Takriti, Kamran Matin, Homa Katouzian, and Siavush Randjbar-Daemi for comments on an earlier draft of this chapter.
2. "Bayanat dar didar ba a'za-ye majles khebregan-e rahbari," 13 Shahrivar 1393 [September 4, 2014], available at farsi.khamenei.ir.
3. "Farmandeh-ye sepah: helal-e Shi'a dar hal sheklgiri ast," *Jahan News*, 17 Ordibehesht 1394 [May 7, 2015].
4. "Akharin mosahebeh-ye sardar Hamedani dar mored-e Surieh va fitneh 88," *Otagh-e Khabar* 24, October 10, 2015, available at http://otaghkhabar24.ir.
5. "Hassan Rouhani: Helal-e Shi'a nadarim," Radio Farda, 24 Mordad 1394 [August 15, 2015].
6. Soner Cagaptay, James F. Jeffrey, and Mehdi Khalaji, "Iran Won't Give up on its Revolution," *New York Times*, April 26, 2015, available at http://www.nytimes.com/2015/04/27/opinion/iran-wont-give-up-on-its-revolution.html.
7. Anoushiravan Ehteshami and Raymond A. Hinnebusch, *Syria and Iran: Middle Powers in a Penetrated Regional System* (London and New York: Routledge, 1997), p. 9.
8. Ehteshami and Hinnebusch, *Syria and Iran*, p. 6.
9. Barry Buzan and Ole Waever, *Regions and Powers: The Structure of International Security* (Cambridge and New York: Cambridge University Press, 2003), p. 41/Loc 1266.
10. Buzan and Waever, *Regions and Powers*, p. 49/Loc 1173.
11. F. Gregory Gause, III, *The International Relations of the Persian Gulf* (Cambridge: Cambridge University Press, 2010), p. 5/Loc 127.
12. Ehteshami and Hinnebusch, *Syria and Iran*, p. 9.
13. Adam Hanieh, *Capitalism and Class in the Gulf Arab States* (New York: Palgrave Macmillan, 2011), Loc 953.
14. Ehteshami and Hinnebusch, *Syria and Iran*, p. 10.
15. Ehteshami and Hinnebusch, *Syria and Iran*, p. 8.
16. Pierre Bourdieu, "Forms of Capital," in J. Richardson (ed.), *Handbook of Theory and Research for the Sociology of Education* (London: Greenwood Press, 1986), pp. 241–258.
17. See, for example, Eskandar Sadeghi-Boroujerdi, "IRGC Publication: 'Is the Revolutionary Guard after War?'", *Al-Monitor*: October 12, 2012, available at http://iranpulse.al-monitor.com/index.php/2012/10/482/irgc-publication-is-the-revolutionary-guard-after-war/.

18. "Goftogu ba moshaver-e omur-e beynolmelal-e rahbar-e enqelab-e Islami: tahdid-e nezami 'asl-e mozakerat' ra khatar mindazad," *Khamenei.ir*, 27 Ordibehesht 1394 [May 17, 2015]; "Akharin mosahebeh-ye sardar Hamedani dar mored-e Surieh va fitneh 88."

19. As Perry Anderson argues, however, the United States' conventional and nuclear military edge continues to dwarf powers such as Russia and China by a huge margin: Perry Anderson, *American Foreign Policy and its Thinkers* (London and New York: Verso, 2015), Loc 3767.

20. "Rahbar-e enqelab ba eshareh beh puch budan-e e'telaf-e zed-e Da'esh: Amrika dar Surieh shekast khord dar 'araq ham hich ghalati nemi tavanad bokonad," *Kayhan*, 24 Shahrivar 1393 [September 15, 2014].

21. It was framed in just this way by Brigadier-General Hossein Hamedani, who was killed in Aleppo in October 2015: "Akharin mosahebeh-ye sardar Hamedani dar mored-e Surieh va fitneh 88."

22. John Mearsheimer, *The Tragedy of Great Power Politics* (New York and London: W.W. Norton & Company, 2001), Loc 749.

23. Mearsheimer, *The Tragedy of Great Power Politics*, Loc 555.

24. Nadia von Maltzahn addresses the issue of cultural diplomacy and soft power in the Syria–Iran alliance: Nadia von Maltzahn, *The Syria–Iran Axis: Cultural Diplomacy and International Relations in the Middle East* (London and New York: I.B. Tauris, 2013).

25. Stephen M. Walt, *Taming American Power: The Global Response to US Primacy* (New York and London: W.W. Norton, 2005), p. 133.

26. Walt, *Taming American Power*, pp. 132–160.

27. Anthony H. Cordesman, "The Conventional Military," in *The Iran Primer*, United States Institute of Peace, 2010 (updated August 2015), available at http://iranprimer.usip.org/resource/conventional-military; Anthony H. Cordesman and Martin Kleiber, *Iran's Military Forces and Warfighting Capabilities* (Westport, CT and London: Praeger, 2007), chapter 3. It must be acknowledged that the Revolutionary Guards' numerous conglomerates, the best known of which is Khatam al-Anbia', are a crucial source of revenue for the organization, but reliable evidence indicating the extent to which its military operations are actually funded by business initiatives such as these remains elusive. The International Institute for Strategic Studies' estimate of Iranian military expenditure for 2013 is slightly higher, standing at $17.7 billion: "Giri Rajendran: 2013's Top Defence-Spenders," February 5, 2014, available at https://www.iiss.org/en/militarybalanceblog/blogsections/2014-3bea/february-f007/defence-spending-a132.

28. Stockholm International Peace Research Institute Military Expenditure Database, available at http://www.sipri.org/research/armaments/milex/milex_database.

29. Claude von Clausewitz, *On War* (Princeton: Princeton University Press, 1976), p. 87/Loc 1815.

30. "Commander-in-Chief of the Revolutionary Guards: The Islamic Revolution is Not Reducible to the Islamic Republic," *Nameh News*, 15 Mehr 1394 [October 7, 2015].

31. For the importance of framing processes to social movements see Doug McAdam, John D. McCarthy, and Mayer N. Zald, "Introduction," in Doug McAdam, John D. McCarthy, and Mayer N. Zald (eds.), *Comparative Perspectives on Social Movements: Political Opportunities, Mobilizing Structures, and Cultural Framings* (Cambridge and New York: Cambridge University Press, 1996), Loc 339.

32. Samia Nakhoul, "Iran Expands Regional 'Empire' Ahead of Nuclear Deal," Reuters, March 23, 2015, available at http://www.reuters.com/article/us-mideast-iran-region-insight-idUSKBN0MJ1G520150323.

33. Mearsheimer, *The Tragedy of Great Power Politics*, Loc 819.

34. Harriet Sherwood, "Hamas and Iran Rebuild Ties Three Years after Falling Out over Syria," *The Guardian*, January 9, 2014, available at http://www.theguardian.com/world/2014/jan/09/hamas-iran-rebuild-ties-falling-out-syria.

35. For a detailed account of SCIRI's history and its relationship to the post-revolutionary Iranian state see Elvire Corboz, *Guardians of Shi'ism: Sacred Authority and Transnational Family Networks* (Edinburgh: Edinburgh University Press, 2015), chapter 5.

36. Melani Cammett, Ishac Diwan, Alan Richards, and John Waterbury, *A Political Economy of the Middle East* (Boulder: Westview Press, 2015), Loc 920.

37. Barry R. Posen, "The Security Dilemma and Ethnic Conflict," *Survival* 35:1 (Spring 1993), p. 27.

38. Melani Cammett's important study addresses how social welfare can become a lens through which to study sectarian politics: Melani Cammett, *Compassionate Communalism: Welfare and Sectarianism in Lebanon* (Ithaca and London: Cornell University Press, 2014), Loc 164.

39. Anne Alexander, "ISIS and Counter-Revolution: Towards a Marxist Analysis," *International Socialism* 145 (January 2015), available at http://isj.org.uk/isis-and-counter-revolution-towards-a-marxist-analysis/.

40. Fanar Haddad, for example, has examined how certain elements within Iraq's Sunni community are convinced that the central government has discriminated against them in the educational system. While querying the validity of such perceptions, he convincingly shows how they can reinforce discontent with the Iraqi state. See Fanar Haddad, "Sectarian Relations and Sunni Identity in Post-Civil War Iraq," in Lawrence G. Potter (ed.), *Sectarian Politics in the Persian Gulf* (Oxford and New York: Oxford University Press, 2014), p. 97.

41. Posen, "The Security Dilemma and Ethnic Conflict," p. 27.

42. Rogers Brubaker, "Ethnicity, Race, and Nationalism," *Annual Review of Sociology* 35 (2009), Loc 256.

43. Sinisa Malesevic, *Identity as Ideology: Understanding Ethnicity and Nationalism* (New York: Palgrave-Macmillan, 2006), p. 27; quoted in Rasmus Christian Elling, *Minorities in Iran: Nationalism and Ethnicity after Khomeini* (New York: Palgrave-Macmillan, 2013), p. 6.

44. Charles Tilly and Sidney Tarrow, *Contentious Politics*, 2nd ed. (New York: Oxford University Press, 2015), Loc 279.

45. Cammett, *Compassionate Communalism*, Loc 297.

46. "Cultural Deputy Presides over Graduation of Popular Mobilization Unit Trainees at the University of Babel," 'Asa'ib Ahl al-Haqq official website, September 7, 2015, available at http://ahlualhaq.com/ [Arabic]; "Mojtaba Institute Announces Opening of Admissions for Preachers and Prayer Leaders for New Academic Year," 'Asa'ib Ahl al-Haqq official website, May 16, 2015, available at http://ahlualhaq.com/ [Arabic].

47. Fanar Haddad has adeptly examined the intersection of sectarianism and nationalism in Fanar Haddad, *Sectarianism in Iraq: Antagonistic Visions of Unity* (London and Oxford: Hurst/Oxford University Press, 2011).

48. Mearsheimer, *The Tragedy of Great Power Politics*, Loc 547.

49. Mearsheimer, *The Tragedy of Great Power Politics*, Loc 523.

50. Mearsheimer, *The Tragedy of Great Power Politics*, Loc 555.

51. Buzan and Waever, *Regions and Powers*, p. 64/Loc 1450.

52. Gause, *The International Relations of the Persian Gulf*, pp. 6–7.

53. Buzan and Waever, *Regions and Powers*, p. 64/Loc 1344.

54. Jubin M. Goodarzi, *Syria and Iran: Diplomatic Alliance and Power Politics in the Middle East* (London and New York: I.B. Tauris, 2009), pp. 18, 28.

55. Ehteshami and Hinnebusch, *Syria and Iran*, p. 88/Loc 1972.

56. Gause, *The International Relations of the Persian Gulf*, pp. 8, 191.

57. Anoushiravan Ehteshami, Raymond Hinnebusch, Heidi Huuhtanen, Paola Raunio, Maaike Warnaar, and Tina Zintl, "Authoritarian Resilience and International Linkages in Iran and Syria," in Steven Heydemann and Reinoud Leenders (eds.), *Middle East Authoritarianisms: Governance, Contestation, and Regime Resilience in Syria and Iran* (Stanford: Stanford University Press, 2013), p. 224/Loc 298.

58. "Syrian Army and Rebels Agree to New Truce in Zabadani," Al Jazeera, August 27, 2015, available at http://www.aljazeera.com/news/2015/08/syrian-army-rebels-agree-truce-zabadani-ceasefire-150827070432906.html; Michael Birnbaum, "The Secret Pact between Russia and Syria that gives Moscow Carte Blanche," *Washington Post*, January 15, 2016, available at https://www.washingtonpost.com/news/worldviews/wp/2016/01/15/the-secret-pact-between-russia-and-syria-that-gives-moscow-carte-blanche/.

59. For a copy of Appendix A: Iran's May 2003 Negotiation Proposal to the United States see Trita Parsi, *Treacherous Alliance: The Secret Dealings of Israel, Iran, and the US* (New Haven and London: Yale University Press, 2007), Loc 4753.

60. Lister goes even further, alleging the Syrian intelligence services' direct complicity in cultivating Sunni jihadist elements: Charles R. Lister, *The Syrian Jihad: Al-Qaeda, the Islamic State and the Evolution of an Insurgency* (London and New York: Hurst/Oxford University Press, 2015), chapter 3.

61. Hassan Hassan and Michael Weiss, *ISIS: Inside the Army of Terror* (New York: Regan Arts, 2015), Loc 494.

62. Joel Rayburn, *Iraq after America: Strongmen, Sectarians, Resistance* (Stanford: Hoover Institution Press, 2014), p. 191/Loc 2577.

63. Nicholas Krohley, *The Death of the Mahdi Army: The Rise, Fall, and Revival of Iraq's Most Powerful Militia* (London: Hurst, 2015), pp. 1–5.

64. Phillip Symth's work on this topic is one such example. Based predominantly on one-dimensional discourse analysis and iconography, he assumes several armed Shi'a groups to be advocates of an abstract ideology named "Khomeinism," and thus essentially clients of the Islamic Republic and adherents of *velayat-e faqih*. Phillip Smyth, *The Shiite Jihad in Syria and its Regional Effects*, Policy Focus 138, Washington Institute for Near East Policy, 2015.

65. For an interesting approach to affective politics and digital media see Zizi Papacharissi, *Affective Publics: Sentiment, Technology, and Politics* (Oxford and New York: Oxford University Press, 2015).

66. Joel Beinin and Frédéric Vairel, "Introduction: The Middle East and North Africa beyond Classical Social Movement Theory," in Joel Beinin and Frédéric Vairel (eds.), *Social Movements, Mobilization, and Contestation in the Middle East and North Africa*, 2nd ed. (Stanford: Stanford University Press, 2013), p. 7/ Loc 286.

67. This hypothesis is partially influenced by the analytical framework provided by Justin J. Gengler in the context of the domestic politics of the Gulf Arab states: Justin J. Gengler, "Understanding Sectarianism in the Persian Gulf," in Potter (ed.), *Sectarian Politics in the Persian Gulf*, Loc 780–794.

68. Charles Tilly, "War Making and State Making as Organized Crime," in Theda Skocpol, Peter B. Evans, and Dietrich Rueschemeyer (eds.), *Bringing the State Back In* (Cambridge and New York: Cambridge University Press, 1985), Loc 4536.

69. Ariel I. Ahram, *Proxy Warriors: The Rise and Fall of State-Sponsored Militias* (Stanford: Stanford University Press, 2011), p. 3/Loc 133.

70. Kirk H. Sowell, "Badr at the Forefront of Iraq's Shia Militias," *Sada*, Carnegie Endowment for International Peace, August 13, 2015, available at http:// carnegieendowment.org/sada/?fa=61016.

71. Ahram, *Proxy Warriors*, p. 15/Loc 354.

72. Charles Tilly, *The Politics of Collective Violence* (Cambridge and New York: Cambridge University Press, 2003), p. 34.

73. Tilly, *The Politics of Collective Violence*, p. 34.

74. Eric Hobsbawm, *Bandits* (London: Weidenfeld & Nicolson, 2010).

75. Janice E. Thompson, *Mercenaries, Pirates, and Sovereigns: State-Building and Extraterritorial Violence in Early Modern Europe* (Princeton: Princeton University Press, 1994).

76. Human Rights Watch, "Iraq: Militia Abuses Mar Fight Against ISIS," September 20, 2015, available at https://www.hrw.org/news/2015/09/20/iraq-militia-abuses-mar-fight-against-isis.

77. Kirk H. Sowell, "The Rise of Iraq's Militia State," *Sada*, Carnegie Endowment for International Peace, April 23, 2015, available at http://carnegieendowment.org/sada/?fa=59888. The figures pertaining to the number of Sunni members of the Hashd varies widely. Some figures are as high as 20,000, but are not easy to verify: "Safir-e 'Araq dar Tehran dar goftogu ba 'Qods': 20 hezar Sunni dar 'Hashd al-Sha'bi' hozur darand," *Qods Online*, 7 Bahman, 1393 [January 27, 2015], available at http://qudsonline.ir/detail/News/343092.

78. Beinin and Vairel, "Introduction," p. 28/Loc 706.

79. *Takfiri* as a term has generally come to denote Salafi–jihadi forces, and brings to the fore their theological excommunication of Muslims who fail to conform to their particular vision of "orthodoxy." It has been used to ideologically delegitimize fellow Muslim politico-military opponents, casting them instead as apostates, which in turn transforms the laws regulating conflict between them. The animosity expressed toward "Shi'a Muslims" has been particularly venomous and toxic in its consequences for sectarian relations. However, the designation *takfiri* has been used by official Iranian state media and Hezbollah to label forces with which Iran and its allies have been in conflict, effectively tarring all sub-state adversaries in Syria and Iraq with the same brush. This process in turn strips politico-military rivals of anything by way of identifiable political demands and depicts as unqualified sectarian fanatics. Both discursive interpellations turn one's opponent into an inhuman abstraction, and beyond the pale of rectitude and dialogue. For the theology of *takfir* see Daniel Lav, *Radical Islam and the Revival of Medieval Theology* (Cambridge and New York: Cambridge University Press, 2012).

80. Haddad, *Sectarianism in Iraq*, p. 50/Loc 1008.

81. Norman Cigar, *Iraq's Shia Warlords and their Militias: Political and Security Challenges and Options* (Kindle: Didactic Press, 2015), Loc 143.

82. Rayburn, *Iraq after America*, p. 85/Loc 1130; Toby Harnden, Aqeel Hussein, and Colin Freeman, "Iran 'Sponsors Assassination' of Sunni Pilots who

Bombed Teheran," *The Telegraph*, October 29, 2005, available at http://www.telegraph.co.uk/news/worldnews/middleeast/iran/1501837/Iran-sponsors-assassination-of-Sunni-pilots-who-bombed-Teheran.html.

83. Quoted in Cigar, *Iraq's Shia Warlords and their Militias*, Loc 332.

84. Corboz, *Guardians of Shi'ism*, p. 157.

85. Twelver Shi'a Muslims are the largest branch of Shi'a Muslims, which include the Ismailis, Zaydis, and also, but not always, the 'Alawis. They are "Twelvers" by virtue of the designated and sacrosanct sequence of twelve infallible Imams through the matrilineal line of Fatima, the Prophet Muhammad's daughter, and his cousin and son-in-law, 'Ali b. Abi Talib. Twelvers believe that the Twelfth Imam went into hiding in the ninth-century and remains in occultation to this day. It should be added that while one can refer to such groups as "Islamists," insofar as they believe that "Islam" has a role to play in the political ordering and management of society, it is far from clear whether groups such as ISCI subscribe to the official Iranian state doctrine of *velayat-e faqih*. In fact, many instances can be adduced where at least ISCI has explicitly distanced itself from the latter doctrine. Its change of name from the Supreme Council for the Islamic Revolution in Iraq to the Islamic Supreme Council of Iraq is just one such example. Similarly, the Islamic Da'wa Party, while often described as Islamist, has never subscribed to the doctrine of *velayat-e faqih* since their formation in the late 1950s.

86. Faleh A. Jabar, *The Shi'ite Movement in Iraq* (London: Saqi, 2003), p. 253.

87. Ned Parker, Babak Dehghanpisheh and Isabel Coles, "Special Report: How Iran's military chiefs operate in Iraq," Reuters, February 24, 2015, available at http://www.reuters.com/article/us-mideast-crisis-committee-specialrepor-idUSKBN0LS0VD20150224.

88. Meir Litvak, *Shi'i Scholars of Nineteenth-Century Iraq: The 'Ulama' of Najaf and Karbala'* (Cambridge and New York: Cambridge University Press, 1998), p. 123. Also see Juan R.I. Cole and Moojan Momen, "Mafia, Mob and Shiism in Iraq: The Rebellion of Ottoman Karbala 1824–1846," *Past and Present* 112:1 (1986): 112–143.

89. "Insight: Syrian Government Guerrilla Fighters Being Sent to Iran for Training," Reuters, April 4, 2013, available at http://uk.reuters.com/article/us-syria-iran-training-insight-idUSBRE9330DW20130404.

90. Aron Lund, "Who Are the Pro-Assad Militias?" Carnegie Endowment for International Peace, March 2, 2015, available at http://carnegieendowment.org/syriaincrisis/?fa=59215

91. Leon T. Goldsmith, *Cycle of Fear: Syria's Alawites in War and Peace* (London: Hurst, 2015), p. 6.

92. Thomas Pierret, "The Reluctant Sectarianism of Foreign States in the Syrian Conflict," Peace Brief 162, United States Institute of Peace, November 18, 2013, available at https://www.usip.org/sites/default/files/PB162.pdf

93. Aron Lund, "Chasing Ghosts: The *Shabiha* Phenomenon," in Michael Kerr and Craig Larkin (eds.), *The Alawis of Syria: War, Faith and Politics in the Levant* (London: Hurst, 2015), p. 208.

94. "Janeshin-e farmandeh-ye qods dekhalat-e sepah dar havades-e surieh ra ta'id kard," Radio Farda, 7 Khordad 1391 [May 27, 2012].

95. Lund, "Chasing Ghosts," p. 212.

96. Nicolas Blanford, "Leaked Video: Iran Guiding Thousands of Shiite Fighters to Syria," *Christian Science Monitor*, September 23, 2013, available at http://www.csmonitor.com/World/Security-Watch/2013/0923/Leaked-video-Iran-guiding-thousands-of-Shiite-fighters-to-Syria.

97. "Farmandeh-ye arshad-e Sepah: Iran Hezbollah-ye dovvom ra dar Surich tashkil dad," BBC Persian, May 5, 2014.

98. Hossein Bastani, "Iran Quietly Deepens Involvement in Syria's War," BBC News, October 20, 2015, available at http://www.bbc.co.uk/news/world-middle-east-34572756.

99. For the importance of framing processes to social movements see McAdam, McCarthy, and Zald, "Introduction," Loc 340.

100. I am adapting the dichotomy elaborated upon by Alexander Wendt. See Alexander Wendt, *Social Theory of International Politics* (Cambridge and New York: Cambridge University Press, 1999), p. 298/Loc 6754.

10. SECTARIANIZATION, ISLAMIST REPUBLICANISM, AND INTERNATIONAL MISRECOGNITION IN YEMEN

1. Pierre Bourdieu, "On Symbolic Power," in *Language and Symbolic Power*, edited by John P. Thompson and translated by Gino Raymon and Matthew Adamson (Cambridge, MA: Harvard University Press, 1991), p. 169.

2. Bourdieu, "On Symbolic Power," p. 169.

3. A term used to describe a transnational capitalist class spanning the member states of the GCC that has been central to the construction of the Gulf states and the formation and continuation of existing political regimes. See Adam Hanieh, *Capitalism and Class in the Gulf Arab States* (London: Routledge, 2009).

4. Zaydi Muslims have historically comprised roughly 30 per cent of the Yemeni population, predominantly concentrated in provinces located in the Northern highlands. Sunni Yemenis have largely followed the Shafi'i legal school, though the rise of a non-denominational Salafi trend has affected the identities and practices of both Zaydi and Shafi'i Muslims in notable ways, especially since the 1980s: Paul Dresch, *A History of Modern Yemen* (Cambridge: Cambridge University Press, 2000).

5. Lisa Wedeen, *Peripheral Visions: Publics, Power, and Performance in Yemen* (Chicago: University of Chicago Press, 2008), pp. 152–162; Barak A. Salmoni, Bryce Loidolt, and Madeleine Wells, *Regime and Periphery in Northern Yemen: The Huthi*

Phenomenon (Santa Monica, CA: RAND Corporation, 2010); Christopher Boucek, "War in Saada: From Local Insurrection to National Challenge," in Christopher Boucek and Marina Ottoway (eds.), *Yemen on the Brink* (Washington, DC: Carnegie Endowment for International Peace, 2010), pp. 45–59.

6. Jillian Schwedler, *Faith in Moderation: Islamist Parties in Jordan and Yemen* (Cambridge: Cambridge University Press, 2006).
7. Salmoni et al., *Regime and Periphery in Northern Yemen*; Boucek, "War in Saada."
8. Salmoni et al., *Regime and Periphery in Northern Yemen*, pp. 89–94.
9. Shelagh Weir, *A Tribal Order: Politics and Law in the Mountains of Yemen* (Austin: University of Texas Press, 2007), pp. 296–303.
10. Weir, *A Tribal Order*, p. 297.
11. Salmoni et al. *Regime and Periphery in Northern Yemen*, p. 100.
12. Wedeen, *Peripheral Visions*, p. 153.
13. Wedeen, *Peripheral Visions*, p. 161.
14. Stacey Philbrick Yadav, *Islamists and the State: Legitimacy and Institutions in Yemen and Lebanon* (London: I.B. Tauris, 2013), pp. 52–55.
15. Muhammed Qahtan, interview with author, Sana'a, August 24, 2005. It is no small irony that Muhammed Qahtan was himself abducted by Houthi gunmen in April 2015; his whereabouts remain unknown at time of publication.
16. Field notes, March 10, 2005.
17. Gabrielle vom Bruck, *Islam, Memory, and Morality in Yemen: Ruling Families in Transition* (London: Palgrave, 2005), p. 61.
18. Dresch, *A History of Modern Yemen*, pp. 186–198.
19. It is important to note that Yemen's Salafi movement is diverse, both in the extent of its political mobilization and in its relationship to the regime. By no means are all Salafis aligned with the Islah party. Some (very religiously influential) Salafis have withdrawn from politics; some aligned with the General People's Congress (GPC, Salih's party); and some with Islah. A small number of southern Salafis eventually aligned with the Southern Movement, following its emergence in 2007. The Salafi faction within Islah, however, grew out of the organized Islamist faction under the GPC umbrella in the 1980s, and was solidified by an intra-Salafi debate at the time of unification about the nature of *hizbiyya*, or partisanship, and the permissibility of participation in multi-party competition. Those Salafis in Islah sided "with" partisan competition, but even still left the imprint of their reservations on the party's name: The Yemeni Congregation for Reform. While colloquially referred to by those outside the party (and some within the Brotherhood faction, as well) as the Islah party, senior party leaders insist that the party is a "congregation," where the term connotes a coming together, as opposed to a partisan fracturing (Yadav, *Islamists and the State*, pp. 23–35).

20. Stephen Day, *Regionalism and Rebellion in Yemen: A Troubled National Union* (Cambridge: Cambridge University Press, 2012); Sarah Phillips, *Yemen and the Politics of Permanent Crisis* (London: Routledge/International Institute for Strategic Studies, 2011).

21. W. Flagg Miller, "Invention (Ibtidaa') or Convention (Itibaa')? Islamist Cassettes and Tradition in Yemen," paper delivered at the annual meeting of the American Anthropological Association, November 2000, available at http://www.mafhoum.com/press3/103C31.htm.

22. Stacey Philbrick Yadav, "Antecedents of the Revolution: Intersectoral Networks and Post-Partisanship in Yemen," *Studies in Ethnicity and Nationalism* 11:3 (2011): 550–563.

23. Yadav, *Islamists and the State*.

24. Stacey Philbrick Yadav, "Segmented Publics and Islamist Women in Yemen: Rethinking Space and Activism," *Journal of Middle East Women's Studies* 6:2 (2010): 1–30.

25. Laurent Bonnefoy, *Salafism in Yemen: Transnationalism and Religious Identity* (New York: Columbia University Press, 2011).

26. Michaelle Browers, *Political Ideology in the Arab World: Accommodation and Transformation* (Cambridge: Cambridge University Press, 2009), pp. 154–155. For more on the doctrine itself see Bernard Haykel, *Revival and Reform in Islam: The Legacy of Muhammad al-Shawkani* (Cambridge: Cambridge University Press, 2003), p. 6.

27. Yadav, *Islamists and the State*, pp. 208–210.

28. Wedeen, *Peripheral Visions*, pp. 152–162.

29. Salmoni et al., *Regime and Periphery in Northern Yemen*, p. 122.

30. Vom Bruck, *Islam, Memory, and Morality in Yemen*, pp. 243–246.

31. These workshops were held under Chatham House rules, according to which statements and practices, but not individual participants, may be characterized. Workshops in question were sponsored by Chatham House, the Project on Middle East Democracy, the Atlantic Council, and the American Institute of Yemeni Studies, and interviews were held in Washington DC, London, Amman, and Istanbul between June 2011 and March 2013. The impressions characterized here were also reflected in personal correspondence and social media involving participants in the same workshops and their colleagues.

32. All three terms are negative descriptions of undue preference for one's own, variously described. *Ta'ifiyya* is usually translated as sectarianism or communalism, whereas *madhabiyya* refers to loyalty to doctrinal schools of law, such as the descriptor "Shafi'i" would indicate. *'Unsuriyya* is the most multivalent—it might literally be understood as simply "factionalism" but is more frequently used to describe racism.

33. Atiaf Z. Alwazir, "Yemen's Enduring Resistance: Youth between Politics and Informal Mobilization," *Mediterranean Politics*, October 13, 2015, p. 17.

34. Alwazir, "Yemen's Enduring Resistance," p. 17.
35. Consider, for example, the genuinely momentous protest march from Taiz to Sana'a at the very end of 2011, in which a group of several hundred protesters grew to tens of thousands as they marched over hundreds of kilometers to the capital to signal their rejection of the transitional framework's immunity provision, in particular. See *Global Voices*, "Yemen: The Amazing Life March Arrives in Sanaa," December 24, 2011, available at https://globalvoices.org/2011/12/24/yemen-the-amazing-march-of-life-arrives-in-sanaa/.
36. Erica Gaston, "Process Lessons Learned in Yemen's National Dialogue," United States Institute of Peace, Special Report 342, February 2014, pp. 3–8, available at https://www.usip.org/sites/default/files/SR342_Process-Lessons-Learned-in-Yemens-National-Dialogue.pdf.
37. Lest there be any doubt about this, a member of the US National Security Council contacted American participants in one of the aforementioned workshops sponsored by Chatham House in order to alert participants to President Obama's executive order issuing sanctions against transitional spoilers. In response to the question of whether spoiling extended to peaceful nonviolent opposition to the terms of the transitional agreement, the NSC representative responded inconclusively that "The [President's executive order] provides us with a tool to help ensure the Yemenis meet the transition benchmarks they agreed to in their political agreement: convening an inclusive National Dialogue, reforming their constitution and electoral laws, reorganizing their military, and holding truly democratic elections." The issue for many critics of the framework, of course, was that they did not feel themselves to be a part of the "they" that concluded the agreement. See Steph Speirs, "RE: President's Executive Order on Yemen," electronic correspondence with author, May 22, 2012.
38. Wedeen, *Peripheral Visions*, p. 151.
39. Marc Lynch, "Why Saudi Arabia Escalated the Middle East's Sectarian Conflict," *The Monkey Cage* (*Washington Post* blog), January 4, 2016, available at https://www.washingtonpost.com/news/monkey-cage/wp/2016/01/04/why-saudi-arabia-escalated-the-middle-easts-sectarian-conflict/.
40. Boucek, "War in Saada."
41. Boucek, "War in Saada," p. 56.
42. Ala Qasem, "Five Barriers to Youth Engagement, Decision-Making, and Leadership in Yemen's Political Parties," Saferworld, 2013, available at http://www.saferworld.org.uk/resources/view-resource/785-five-barriers-to-youth-engagement-decision-making-and-leadership-in-yemens-political-parties.
43. Ishaan Tharoor, "Top Yemen Scholars in the West Condemn Saudi Arabia's

War," *Washington Post*, April 18, 2015, available at https://www.washington-post.com/news/worldviews/wp/2015/04/18/top-yemen-scholars-in-the-west-condemn-saudi-arabias-war/.

44. It is no small irony that over the course of the war, units of the Yemeni armed forces and tribes with loyalties to former President Salih aligned themselves with the Houthis, against whom they previously fought for the better part of a decade. This is undoubtedly a pragmatic alliance, driven by shared opposition to the transitional government now operating largely in exile in Riyadh.

45. See Human Rights Watch, "Targeting Saada: Unlawful Coalition Airstrikes on Saada City in Yemen," June 30, 2015, available at https://www.hrw.org/report/2015/06/30/targeting-saada/unlawful-coalition-airstrikes-saada-city-yemen. For the siege of Taiz see Ghaith Abdul-Ahad, "Life under Siege: Inside Taiz, the Yemeni City Being Slowly Strangled," *The Guardian*, December 28, 2015, available at http://www.theguardian.com/world/2015/dec/28/life-under-siege-inside-taiz-yemen-houthi.

46. Kareem Fahim, "Bitterness Abounds in Yemen's North, a Houthi Stronghold," *New York Times*, October 13, 2015, available at http://www.nytimes.com/2015/10/14/world/middleeast/bitterness-abounds-in-yemens-north-a-houthi-stronghold.html.

47. Lynch, "Why Saudi Arabia Escalated the Middle East's Sectarian Conflict." For an elaboration see Toby Matthiesen, *Sectarian Gulf: Bahrain, Saudi Arabia, and the Arab Spring That Wasn't* (Stanford: Stanford University Press, 2013).

11. SECTARIANIZATION AS SECURITIZATION: IDENTITY POLITICS AND COUNTER-REVOLUTION IN BAHRAIN

1. The demographics of Bahrain are disputed. Estimates of sectarian affiliation put the percentage of Shi'a Muslims somewhere between 55 and 70 per cent, with the Sunnis being the respective other part. What is clear is that the percentage of Shi'a Muslims is declining as a result of social engineering and naturalization of Sunnis.

2. For an early account see Barry Buzan, Ole Wæver, and Jaap de Wilde, *Security: A New Framework for Analysis* (Boulder, CO: Lynne Rienner, 1998).

3. To cite a few examples: German-speaking communities outside Germany before World War II; the Danish-speaking communities in Germany; the cultural ties between different linguistic groups in Switzerland and Belgium with neighboring countries; and the Russian-speaking communities in the Baltic states and Eastern Europe.

4. Raymond Hinnebusch, "Sectarianization and the Syrian Case," paper delivered at a workshop on Sectarianism in the Wake of the Arab Revolts, Aarhus University, November 11, 2015.

5. The notion of Gulf cosmopolitanism was highlighted by the Kuwaiti author and scholar Mai al-Nakib in her book of short stories *The Hidden Light of Objects* and her talk "Hidden Light: A View from Cosmopolitan Kuwait," LMEI (London Middle East Institute) Lecture Programme on the Contemporary Middle East, October 6, 2015, SOAS, London.

6. See, for example, Nelida Fuccaro, *Histories of City and State in the Persian Gulf: Manama since 1800* (Cambridge: Cambridge University Press, 2009).

7. For one such case see James Onley, "Transnational Merchants in the Nineteenth Century Gulf: The Case of the Safar Family," in Madawi Al-Rasheed (ed.), *Transnational Connections and the Arab Gulf* (London: Routledge, 2004), pp. 59–89.

8. See, for example, Muhammad Alhabib, "The Formation of the Shi'a Community in Kuwait: Migration, Settlement and Contribution between 1880 and 1938," Ph.D. thesis, Royal Holloway.

9. For more on this period see, for example, 'Abd al-Hadi Khalaf, "Labor Movements in Bahrain", *Middle East Report* (Middle East Research and Information Project) 132 (1985): 24–29; Toby Matthiesen, "Migration, Minorities and Radical Networks: Labour Movements and Opposition Groups in Saudi Arabia, 1950–1975," *International Review of Social History* 59:3 (Autumn 2014): 473–504; Omar Hesham Alshehabi, "Divide and Rule in Bahrain and the Elusive Pursuit for a United Front: The Experience of the Constitutive Committee and the 1972 Uprising," *Historical Materialism* 21:1 (2013): 94–127; Abdel Razzaq Takriti, *Monsoon Revolution: Republicans, Sultans, and Empires in Oman 1965–1976* (Oxford: Oxford University Press, 2013), available at http://www.merip.org/mer/mer132/labor-movements-bahrain.

10. For more see Toby Matthiesen, *The Other Saudis: Shiism, Dissent and Sectarianism* (Cambridge: Cambridge University Press, 2015), chapter 1.

11. The authoritative account of this aspect of Bahraini history is Fuad I. Khuri, *Tribe and State in Bahrain: The Transformation of Social and Political Authority in an Arab State* (Chicago: University of Chicago Press, 1980).

12. Fuccaro, *Histories of City and State*.

13. Fuccaro, *Histories of City and State*, p. 172.

14. See the remarkable biography of one of the leaders of the HEC: 'Abd al-Rahman al-Bakir, *Min al-Bahrayn ila al-manfa "Sant Hilana"* (Beirut: Dar Maktabat al-Haya, 1965).

15. See editorial of *al-Jamahir* (December 1, 1962). This issue also contained the first general program of the BNLF.

16. See, amongst others, Basil Raouf al-Kubaisi, "The Arab Nationalist Movement 1951–1971: from Pressure Group to Socialist Party," Ph.D. thesis, The American University, Washington DC, 1971; Falah al-Mdairis, "The Arab Nationalist Movement in Kuwait from its Origins to 1970," D.Phil. thesis, University of Oxford, 1987.

17. Ian Henderson remained in charge of Bahrain's internal security services until 1998, long after formal independence in 1971, and became infamous amongst the opposition for the brutal interrogation techniques he was said to have authorized: Kristian Coates Ulrichsen, "The Hollow Shell of Security Reform in Bahrain," *Foreign Policy*, April 12, 2012, available at http://mideast.foreignpolicy.com/posts/2012/04/12/the_hollow_shell_of_security_reform_in_bahrain.

18. Interview with Abdulhadi Khalaf, MP in the 1973 parliament and BNLF cadre, London, 2015. There was, however, also cooperation between the communists and the Shi'a religious bloc in parliament, in particular in 1975 over the issue of the new state security law. Both blocs opposed it, and this issue ultimately led to the dissolution of the parliament later that year. See R.M. Tesh, Bahrain, to I.T.M. Lucas, MED, FCO, 16 June, 1975, FCO 8/2415/8, The National Archives, Kew.

19. See Staci Strobl, "From Colonial Policing to Community Policing in Bahrain: The Historical Persistence of Sectarianism," *International Journal of Comparative and Applied Criminal Justice* 35:1 (February 2011): 19–37.

20. Munira Fakhro, "The Uprising in Bahrain: An Assessment," in Gary Sick and Lawrence Potter (eds.), *The Persian Gulf at the Millennium: Essays in Politics, Economy, Security, and Religion* (Basingstoke: Macmillan, 1997), pp. 167–188; Ute Meinel, *Die Intifada im Ölscheichtum Bahrain: Hintergründe des Aufbegehrens von 1994–98* (Münster: LIT-Verlag, 2003).

21. Justin Gengler, *Group Conflict and Political Mobilization in Bahrain and the Arab Gulf: Rethinking the Rentier State* (Bloomington: Indiana University Press 2015), p. 32.

22. Physicians for Human Rights, *Weaponizing Tear Gas: Bahrain's Unprecedented Use of Toxic Chemical Agents Against Civilians*, August 2012, available at https://s3.amazonaws.com/PHR_Reports/Bahrain-TearGas-Aug2012-small.pdf.

23. See Omar Hesham Alshehabi, "Radical Transformations and Radical Contestations: Bahrain's Spatial–Demographic Revolution," *Middle East Critique* 23:1 (2014): 29–51.

24. While still heavily disputed in Bahrain and the wider Gulf region, the broad trajectories of the events in 2011 have now been established in the academic literature as well as in reports by international NGOs and the Bassiouni Commission appointed by King Hamad. Therefore, I will not recount events in this chapter. For authoritative accounts of events since 2011 see Bahrain Independent Commission of Inquiry, *Report of the Bahrain Independent Commission of Inquiry*, November 23, 2011, available at www.bici.org.bh; International Crisis Group, *Popular Protests in North Africa and the Middle East (III): The Bahrain Revolt*, Middle East/North Africa Report no. 105, April 6, 2011, available at http://goo.gl/GbX5f3; International Crisis Group, *Popular Protest in North*

Africa and the Middle East (VIII): Bahrain's Rocky Road to Reform, Middle East/ North Africa Report no. 111, July 28, 2011, available at https://www.crisis- group.org/middle-east-north-africa/gulf-and-arabian-peninsula/bahrain/ popular-protest-north-africa-and-middle-east-viii-bahrain-s-rocky-road- reform; Ala'a Shehabi and Marc Owen Jones (eds.), *Bahrain's Uprising: Resistance and Repression in the Gulf* (London: Zed Books, 2015); Kristian Coates Ulrichsen, "Bahrain," in Larbi Sadiki (ed.), *Routledge Handbook of the Arab Spring: Rethinking Democratization* (New York: Routledge, 2014), pp. 133–144.

25. For the symbolism of the Pearl Monument and its many afterlives see Amal Khalaf, "Squaring the Circle: Bahrain's Pearl Roundabout," *Middle East Critique* 22:3 (2013): 265–280.

26. Toby Matthiesen, "(No) Dialogue in Bahrain," *Middle East Report Online*, February 13, 2014, available at http://www.merip.org/mero/mero021314.

27. Toby Matthiesen, "Wanted: An inclusive Bahraini social contract", *Middle East Eye*, November 21, 2014, available at http://www.middleeasteye.net/ columns/wanted-inclusive-bahraini-social-contract-856097571.

28. For a good account of how media was used in counter-revolution see Elham Fakhro, "Revolution and Counter-Revolution in Bahrain," in Adam Roberts, Michael J. Willis, Rory McCarthy, and Timothy Garton Ash (eds.), *Civil Resistance in the Arab Spring: Triumphs and Disasters* (Oxford: Oxford University Press, 2016), pp. 88–115.

29. Marc Owen Jones, "Social Media, Surveillance, and Cyberpolitics in the Bahrain Uprising," in Shehabi and Owen Jones (eds.), *Bahrain's Uprising*, pp. 239–262.

30. See, for example, Justin Gengler, "Bahrain's Sunni Awakening," *Middle East Report* (Middle East Research and Information Project), January 17, 2012, available at http://www.merip.org/mero/mero011712; Justin Gengler, "Electoral Rules (and Threats) Cure Bahrain's Sectarian Parliament," *The Monkey Cage* (*Washington Post* blog), December 1, 2014, available at https:// www.washingtonpost.com/blogs/monkey-cage/wp/2014/12/01/electoral- rules-and-threats-cure-bahrains-sectarian-parliament/.

31. Justin J. Gengler, "Royal Factionalism, the Khawalid, and the Securitization of 'the Shī'a Problem' in Bahrain," *Journal of Arabian Studies: Arabia, the Gulf and the Red Sea* 3:1 (2013): 53–79.

32. One should not forget, however, that King Hamad had his power base in the BDF. The BDF were founded in 1968 in anticipation of British with- drawal and his personal rise in prominence was closely associated with the expansion of the BDF. The king is thus also a military man, while his son, the crown prince, is not. For an excellent account of the recent history of Bahrain, intra-elite power struggles, and the use of sectarianism in the polit- ical economy of Bahrain see Kristin Smith Diwan, "Royal Factions, Ruling

Strategies, and Sectarianism in Bahrain," in Lawrence G. Potter (ed.), *Sectarian Politics in the Persian Gulf* (London: Hurst, 2013), pp. 143–177.

33. See, amongst others, Toby Matthiesen, "EU Foreign Policy towards Bahrain in the Aftermath of the Uprising," in Ana Echagüe (ed.), *The Gulf States and the Arab Uprisings* (Madrid: FRIDE, 2013), pp. 77–85; Zoe Holman, "On the Side of Decency and Democracy: The History of British–Bahraini Relations and Transnational Contestation," in Shehabi and Owen Jones (eds.), *Bahrain's Uprising*, pp. 175–206.

34. See Hillary Rodham Clinton, *Hard Choices* (New York: Simon & Schuster, 2014), pp. 355–359, 373.

35. "Bahrain Hardliners to Put Shi'a MPs on Trial," *The Telegraph*, March 30, 2011, available at http://www.telegraph.co.uk/news/worldnews/middlee-ast/bahrain/8416953/Bahrain-hardliners-to-put-Shia-MPs-on-trial.html.

36. For more on sectarianism as a political strategy see Justin J. Gengler, "Understanding Sectarianism in the Persian Gulf," in Potter (ed.), *Sectarian Politics in the Persian Gulf*, pp. 31–66; Toby Matthiesen, *Sectarian Gulf: Bahrain, Saudi Arabia and the Arab Spring That Wasn't* (Stanford: Stanford University Press, 2013).

37. Claire Beaugrand, "Deconstructing Minorities/Majorities in Parliamentary Gulf States (Kuwait and Bahrain)", *British Journal of Middle Eastern Studies* 43:2 (2016): 232–249.

38. Fakhro, "Revolution and Counter-Revolution in Bahrain."

39. Amy Austin Holmes, "Working on the Revolution in Bahrain: From the Mass Strike to Everyday Forms of Medical Provision," *Social Movement Studies* 15: 1 (2016): 105–114.

40. Michael Weiss and Hassan Hassan, *ISIS: Inside the Army of Terror* (New York: Regan Arts, 2015), pp. ix–xii.

41. Cole Bunzel, "The Caliphate's Scholar-in-Arms," Jihadica, July 23, 2014, http://www.jihadica.com/the-caliphate%E2%80%99s-scholar-in-arms/

42. "Bomb Kills Two Policemen in Worst Bahrain Bombing in Months," Reuters, July 28, 2015, available at http://www.reuters.com/article/us-bahrain-security-blast-idUSKCN0Q20HJ20150728.

43. For the best discussion of Bahrain's political economy and its policies of inclusion and exclusion see Gengler, *Group Conflict and Political Mobilization*.

12. THE ARCHITECTURE OF SECTARIANIZATION IN LEBANON

1. See Bassel F. Salloukh, "The Sectarianization of Geopolitics in the Middle East," chapter 2 in this volume; Toby Matthiesen, *Sectarian Gulf: Bahrain, Saudi Arabia, and the Arab Spring That Wasn't* (California: Stanford University Press, 2013); and Raymond Hinnebusch, "Syria's Alawis and the Ba'ath Party," in

Michael Kerr and Craig Larkin (eds.), *The Alawis of Syria: War, Faith and Politics in the Levant* (London: Hurst, 2015), pp. 107–124.

2. See Bassel F. Salloukh, Rabie Barakat, Jinan S. al-Habbal, Lara W. Khattab, and Shoghig Mikaelian, *The Politics of Sectarianism in Postwar Lebanon* (London: Pluto Press, 2015).

3. See Ussama Makdisi, *The Culture of Sectarianism: Community, History, and Violence in Nineteenth-Century Ottoman Lebanon* (Berkeley: University of California Press, 2000).

4. See Makdisi, *The Culture of Sectarianism*; Caesar E. Farah, *The Politics of Interventionism in Ottoman Lebanon: 1830–1861* (London: I.B. Tauris, 2000); and Leila Tarazi Fawaz, *An Occasion for War: Civil Conflict in Lebanon and Damascus in 1860* (Berkeley: University of California Press, 1995).

5. Makdisi, *The Culture of Sectarianism*, p. 161.

6. Makdisi, *The Culture of Sectarianism*, p. 162.

7. For 1913 figures see Ghassan Salamé, *al-Mujtama' wal-dawla fil-Mashriq al-'Arabi* (Beirut: Markaz Dirasat al-Wihda al-'Arabiya, 1987), p. 103. For 1932 and 1975 see Helena Cobban, *The Making of Modern Lebanon* (London: Hutchinson, 1985), p. 16. For 2011 see "Min ayna yabda' ilgha' al-nizam al-Ta'ifi fi Lubnan," *al-Safir*, June 2, 2011.

8. For a discussion of how ethnic entrepreneurs deploy identity for instrumental material and political ends see Ashutosh Varshney, "Ethnicity and Ethnic Conflict," in Carles Boix and Susan C. Stokes (eds.), *The Oxford Handbook of Comparative Politics* (Oxford: Oxford University Press, 2007), pp. 274–294; and Matthiesen, *Sectarian Gulf*.

9. See Meir Zamir, *The Formation of Modern Lebanon* (Ithaca: Cornell University Press, 1985).

10. See Kanchan Chandra, "Introduction," in Kanchan Chandra (ed.), *Constructivist Theories of Ethnic Politics* (Oxford: Oxford University Press, 2012), pp. 1–50; and John McGarry and Brendan O'Leary, "Iraq's Constitution of 2005: Liberal Consociation as Political Prescription," *International Journal of Constitutional Law* 5:4 (2007): 670–698.

11. See John Nagle, "Between Entrenchment, Reform and Transformation: Ethnicity and Lebanon's Consociational Democracy," *Democratization* 22 (2015): 1–21.

12. For a comprehensive discussion see Salloukh et al., *The Politics of Sectarianism in Postwar Lebanon*.

13. See Basem al-Jisr, *Mithaq 1943: Limaza kan? Wa hal saqata?* 2nd ed. (Beirut: Dar al-Nahar lil-Nashr, 1997), pp. 485–495.

14. See Fawwaz Traboulsi, *A History of Modern Lebanon* (London: Pluto Press, 2007), pp. 110 and 244.

15. See Bassel F. Salloukh, "The Limits of Electoral Engineering in Divided

Societies: Elections in Postwar Lebanon," *Canadian Journal of Political Science* 39:3 (September 2006): 635–655.

16. See Shafiq Jiha (ed.), *al-Dustur al-Lubnani: tarikhuhu, ta'dilatuhu, nasuhu al-hali, 1926–1991* (Beirut: Dar al-'Elm lil-Malayin, 1991), p. 66.

17. See Article 55 of the constitution as amended in 1929 in Jiha (ed.), *al-Dustur al-Lubnani*, p. 68.

18. Jiha (ed.), *al-Dustur al-Lubnani*, p. 39.

19. For an explanation see Salloukh et al., *The Politics of Sectarianism in Postwar Lebanon*, chapter 3 ("Institutions, Sectarian Populism, and the Production of Docile Subjects").

20. See Jiha (ed.), *al-Dustur al-Lubnani*, p. 39.

21. See Albert Hourani, "Visions of Lebanon," in Halim Barakat (ed.), *Toward a Viable Lebanon* (Washington, DC: Georgetown University Press, 1988), pp. 3–11.

22. For an elaboration see Salloukh et al., *The Politics of Sectarianism in Postwar Lebanon*.

23. See 'Isma Sulayman, *al-Jumhuriya al-thaniya bayn al-nusus wa-l-mumarasa* (Beirut: n.p., 1998); Michael C. Hudson, "Trying Again: Power-Sharing in Post-Civil War Lebanon," *International Negotiation* 2:1 (1997): 103–122; and Joseph Maïla, "Le 'Document d'Entente Nationale:' un commentaire," *Les Cahiers de l'Orient* 16–17 (1989–1990): 135–217.

24. The preamble of the constitution reads: "Illegitimate is the authority that negates the covenant of mutual coexistence." See Jiha (ed.), *al-Dustur al-Lubnani*, p. 34.

25. See the preamble of the constitution, in Jiha (ed.), *al-Dustur al-Lubnani*, p. 33.

26. See articles 55, 56, and 65 of the 1990 Constitution in Jiha (ed.), *al-Dustur al-Lubnani*, pp. 67–69 and 75–76.

27. See Jiha (ed.), *al-Dustur al-Lubnani*, p. 76.

28. See Article 56 in Jiha (ed.), *al-Dustur al-Lubnani*, p. 69.

29. As stipulated in Article 53 of the Constitution in Jiha (ed.), *al-Dustur al-Lubnani*, p. 65.

30. See Article 44 of the constitution in Jiha (ed.), *al-Dustur al-Lubnani*, p. 58.

31. See Salloukh et al., *The Politics of Sectarianism in Postwar Lebanon*, p. 99.

32. See, respectively, Michael Johnson, *All Honourable Men: The Social Origins of War in Lebanon* (London: I.B. Tauris, 2001); Traboulsi, *A History of Modern Lebanon*; and Roschanack Shaery-Eisenlohr, *Shi'ite Lebanon: Transnational Religion and the Making of National Identities* (New York: Columbia University Press, 2008).

33. See Melani Cammett and Sukriti Issar, "Bricks and Mortar Clientelism: Sectarianism and the Logics of Welfare Allocation in Lebanon," *World Politics* 62:3 (June 2010): 381–421; Nisreen Salti and Jad Chaaban, "The Role of

Sectarianism in the Allocation of Public Expenditures in Postwar Lebanon," *International Journal of Middle East Studies* 42:4 (October 2010): 637–655; and Melani Cammett, *Compassionate Communalism: Welfare and Sectarianism in Lebanon* (Ithaca: Cornell University Press, 2014).

34. See Paul W.T. Kingston, *Reproducing Sectarianism: Advocacy Networks and the Politics of Civil Society in Post-Civil War Lebanon* (New York: State University of New York Press, 2014); and Janine Clark and Bassel F. Salloukh, "Elite Strategies, Civil Society, and Sectarian Identities in Postwar Lebanon," *International Journal of Middle East Studies* 45:4 (November 2013): 731–749.

35. Suad Joseph, "Working-Class Women's Networks in a Sectarian State: A Political Paradox," *American Ethnologist* 10:1 (February 1983), p. 11.

36. See Fawwaz Traboulsi, *al-Tabaqat al-ijtimaʻiya fi Lubnan: ithbat wujood* (Beirut: Heinrich Böll Stftung, 2014).

37. For comparative perspectives see Lisa Anderson, "Prospects for Liberalism in North Africa: Identities and Interests in Preindustrial Welfare States," in John P. Entelis (ed.), *Islam, Democracy, and the State in North Africa* (Bloomington: Indiana University Press, 1997), pp. 127–140; and Dietrich Rueschemeyer, Evelyne Huber Stephens, and John D. Stephens, *Capitalist Development and Democracy* (Chicago: University of Chicago Press, 1992).

38. See Danyel Reiche, "War Minus the Shooting? The Politics of Sport in Lebanon as a Unique Case in Comparative Politics," *Third World Quarterly* 32:2 (2011): 261–277.

39. For a comprehensive discussion see Salloukh et al., *The Politics of Sectarianism in Postwar Lebanon*; and Bassel F. Salloukh, "The Disciplinary Violence of Sectarianism in Lebanon," Pluto Press Blog, July 14, 2015, available at https://plutopress.wordpress.com/2015/07/14/the-disciplinary-violence-of-sectarianism-in-lebanon/, on which this section is based.

40. See Salloukh et al., *The Politics of Sectarianism in Postwar Lebanon*, chapter 4 ("Neoliberal Sectarianism and Associational Life").

41. See Salloukh et al., *The Politics of Sectarianism in Postwar Lebanon*, chapter 8 ("The Postwar Mediascape and Sectarian Demonizing").

42. See Aram Nerguizian, "Between Sectarianism and Military Development: The Paradox of the Lebanese Armed Forces," in Salloukh et al., *The Politics of Sectarianism in Postwar Lebanon*, pp. 108–135.

43. See Michel Foucault, "The Subject and Power," in Hubert L. Dreyfus and Paul Rabinow (eds.), *Michel Foucault: Beyond Structuralism and Hermeneutics* (Chicago: University of Chicago Press, 1983), pp. 208–226; James Tully, "Political Philosophy as a Critical Activity," *Political Theory* 30:4 (August 2002): 533–555; Antonio Gramsci, *Selections from the Prison Notebooks*, translated and edited by Q. Hoare and G.N. Smith (New York: International Publishers, 1971); and Gauri Viswanathan (ed.), *Power, Politics, and Culture: Interviews with Edward W. Said* (New York: Vintage, 2001).

44. See Salloukh et al., *The Politics of Sectarianism in Postwar Lebanon.*

45. See Bassel F. Salloukh, "Lebanese Protesters United against Garbage … and Sectarianism," *The Monkey Cage* (*Washington Post* blog), September 14, 2015, available at http://www.washingtonpost.com/blogs/monkey-cage/wp/2015/09/14/lebanese-protesters-united-against-garbage-and-sectarianism/.

46. See Hugh Naylor and Suzan Haidamous, "Trash Crisis Sparks Clashes over Corruption, Dysfunction in Lebanon," *Washington Post*, August 23, 2015, available at https://www.washingtonpost.com/world/middle_east/lebanon-rattled-by-protests-over-trash-crisis-corruption/2015/08/23/9d309ef8–2c2f-447b-9fff-3c5c62543da9_story.html.

47. See Hugh Naylor, "Thousands of Demonstrators Continue Protests in Lebanese Capital," *Washington Post*, August 29, 2015, available at https://www.washingtonpost.com/world/middle_east/thousands-of-demonstrators-gather-in-lebanese-capital/2015/08/29/b82b92b0–4cf0–11e5–80c2–106ea7fb80d4_story.html.

48. See Rima S. Aboulmona and Nizar Hassan, "Protest Ongoing as Police Clear Ministry of Environment," *Daily Star*, September 1, 2015, available at http://www.dailystar.com.lb/News/Lebanon-News/2015/Sep-01/313556-you-stink-campaign-protesters-storm-into-ministry-of-environment-building-in-downtown-beirut.ashx.

49. See Bassel F. Salloukh, "Democracy in Lebanon: The Primacy of the Sectarian System," in Nathan Brown and Emad El-Din Shahin (eds.), *The Struggle over Democracy in the Middle East* (London: Routledge, 2009), pp. 134–150.

50. The name is in reference to the popular demonstration in downtown Beirut commemorating the one-month anniversary of Hariri's assassination. It later gathered Sa'd al-Hariri's and Walid Jumblatt's parliamentary blocs, the Lebanese Forces, the reunited Kata'eb, most of the members of Liqa' Qornat Shihwan, Haraket al-Yasar al-Dimuqrati, Harkat al-Tajadud al-Dimuqrati, and a number of independent MPs.

51. Then gathering mainly Hezbollah, Amal, 'Awn's Free Patriotic Movement, Slayman Franjieh, Talal Arslan, Omar Karamé, Nazih al-Bizri, Usama al-Sa'd, and a number of other political groups.

52. See, for example, Jean 'Aziz, "Sarkozy karara risalat al-malek Louis wa Sfeir aqsama 'ala salibih," *al-Akhbar*, November 10, 2007.

53. For details see Salloukh, "Democracy in Lebanon."

54. See Joseph Smaha, "al-Ihtiqan al-mazhabi bayna al-hizb wa-l-tayyar," *al-Akhbar*, December 12, 2006.

55. See Bassel F. Salloukh, "The Arab Uprisings and the Geopolitics of the Middle East," *The International Spectator* 48:2 (June 2013): 32–46; and F. Gregory Gause III, *Beyond Sectarianism: The New Middle East Cold War*, Brookings Doha

Center Analysis Paper, July 11, 2014, available at https://www.brookings.edu/wp-content/uploads/2016/06/English-PDF-1.pdf.

56. See Bassel F. Salloukh, "The Sectarianization of Geopolitics in the Middle East," chapter 2 in this volume.

57. See Steven Heydemann, *Syria's Uprising: Sectarianism, Regionalisation, and State Order in the Levant*, Fride and Hivos Working Paper no. 119 (May 2013), available at http://fride.org/descarga/WP_119_Syria_Uprising.pdf; and Bassel F. Salloukh, "The Geopolitics of the Struggle for Syria," *E-International Relations*, September 23, 2013, available at http://www.e-ir.info/2013/09/23/the-geopolitics-of-the-struggle-for-syria/.

58. See Aram Nerguizian, "Assessing the Consequences of Hezbollah's Necessary War of Choice in Syria," Center for Strategic and International Studies, June 17, 2013, available at http://csis.org/publication/assessing-consequences-hezbollahs-necessary-war-choice-syria; and Shoghig Mikaelian and Bassel F. Salloukh, "Strong Actor in a Weak State: The Geopolitics of Hezbollah," in Mehran Kamrava (ed.), *Fragile Politics: Weak States in the Greater Middle East* (New York: Oxford University Press, 2016), pp. 119–143.

59. See Ibrahim al-Amin, "Hezbollah fi Suriya," *al-Akhbar*, March 22, 2013.

60. See Ali Shehab, "al-Qusayr Isra'eliyan: Hezbollah min al-difaʻ ila al-hujoom," *al-Safir*, June 6, 2013.

61. See International Crisis Group, *Lebanon's Hizbollah Turns Eastward to Syria*, Report No. 153, Middle East & North Africa, 27 May 2014, available at https://www.crisisgroup.org/middle-east-north-africa/eastern-mediterranean/lebanon/lebanon-s-hizbollah-turns-eastward-syria; and Sahar Atrache, "How Hezbollah is Changing the War in Syria—and Vice Versa," Huffington Post, June 6, 2014, available at http://www.huffingtonpost.com/sahar-atrache/hezbollah-war-syria_b_5455850.html.

62. See Bassel F. Salloukh, "Lebanon—Where Next for Hezbollah: Resistance or Reform?" in Alexander Ramsbotham and Achim Wennmann (eds.), *Legitimacy and Peace Processes: From Coercion to Consent*, Accord Issue 25 (London: Conciliation Resources, April 2014), pp. 100–104.

63. International Crisis Group, *Tentative Jihad: Syria's Fundamentalist Opposition*, Report No. 131, Middle East & North Africa, 12 October 2012, available at https://www.crisisgroup.org/middle-east-north-africa/eastern-mediterranean/syria/tentative-jihad-syria-s-fundamentalist-opposition.

64. See Alexander Corbeil and Amarnath Amarasingam, "The Houthi Hezbollah: Iran's Train-and-Equip Program in Sanaa," *Foreign Affairs*, March 31, 2016, available at https://www.foreignaffairs.com/articles/2016–03–31/houthi-hezbollah?cid=soc-tw-rdr.

65. See Salloukh et al., *The Politics of Sectarianism in Postwar Lebanon*, pp. 178–179.

66. Nagle, "Between Entrenchment, Reform and Transformation," p. 9.
67. Nagle, "Between Entrenchment, Reform and Transformation," p. 9.
68. Nagle, "Between Entrenchment, Reform and Transformation," p. 9.
69. See his comments quoted in *al-Safir*, April 6, 2016.
70. For a discussion see Salloukh et al., *The Politics of Sectarianism in Postwar Lebanon*, chapter 10 ("Conclusion").
71. See their website at: http://beirutmadinati.com/about-beirut-madinati/.

13. SECTARIANISM, AUTHORITARIANISM, AND OPPOSITION IN KUWAIT

1. Disclaimer: The views expressed in this chapter are those of the author and not necessarily those of the US government.
2. For examples of theoretical literature on the treatment of ethnic minorities or non-core groups with perceived links to "lobby powers" or "external powers" see Harris Mylonas, *The Politics of Nation-Building: Making Co-Nationals, Refugees, and Minorities* (New York: Cambridge University Press, 2013); Erin K. Jenne, *Ethnic Bargaining: The Paradox of Minority Empowerment* (Ithaca: Cornell University Press, 2006); Rogers Brubaker, *Nationalism Reframed: Nationhood and the National Question in the New Europe* (New York: Cambridge University Press, 1996).
3. Interviews with ten Kuwaiti liberals at a *diwaniyya*, Kuwait City, Kuwait, February 2013.
4. Mylonas, *The Politics of Nation-Building*. Mylonas defines a non-core group as "any aggregation of individuals that is perceived as an unassimilated ethnic group (on a linguistic, religious, physical, or ideological basis) by the ruling political elite of a country."
5. Mylonas, *The Politics of Nation-Building*. Accommodation refers to granting non-core groups official minority status or quotas and/or giving access to separate institutions in education or in religious, cultural, or legal realms.
6. If we consider a regime's treatment of a sectarian minority or non-core group on a scale from exclusionary to inclusionary, full exclusion is on one end of the spectrum, followed by accommodation, then co-optation, then full inclusion.
7. This is Azoulay's argument: Rivka Azoulay, "The Politics of Shi'i Merchants in Kuwait," in Steffen Hertog, Giacomo Luciani, and Marc Valeri (eds.), *Business Politics in the Middle East* (London: Hurst, 2015).
8. Nathan Brown defines semi-authoritarianism as a "category of regimes whose defining characteristic is that opposition parties can organize, propagandize, canvass, convene, publish, and complain—but never win": Nathan J. Brown, "Dictatorship and Democracy," in Nathan J. Brown (ed.), *The Dynamics of Democratization: Dictatorship, Development, and Diffusion* (Baltimore: Johns Hopkins University Press, 2011), p. 57.

9. Michael Herb, *The Wages of Oil: Parliaments and Economic Development in Kuwait and the UAE* (Ithaca: Cornell University Press, 2014), p. 50.

10. In December 2009 Shaykh Nasser al-Mohammed al-Sabah was the first prime minister to actually undergo a vote of confidence, which he won easily.

11. Mary Ann Tetreault, *Stories of Democracy: Politics and Society in Contemporary Kuwait* (New York: Columbia University Press, 2000), p. 146.

12. Shi'a in Kuwait cannot obtain high-ranking positions in what are known as "sovereign" ministries such as Defense, Interior, or Foreign Affairs, and have less access to permits for mosque building and little hope of changing the dominant Sunni educational curriculum. Barring these things, they have access to all of the other spoils of the welfare state in equal measure to Sunnis. Interviews with multiple Shi'a respondents, Kuwait City, Kuwait, spring 2013.

13. For example, in the late 1960s through 1970s the Kuwaiti government engineered the mass naturalization (*al-tajnis*) of Saudi tribes, giving them full voting rights to offset Arab nationalist opposition. For an excellent source on this see Farah al-Nakib, "Revisiting Hadar and Badu in Kuwait: Citizenship, Housing, and the Construction of a Dichotomy," *International Journal of Middle East Studies* 46:1 (2014): 5–30.

14. Two Shi'a Islamist trends, the Shiraziyyin and Da'wa branches, originated in Iraq but spread to the rest of the Gulf in the 1960s and 1970s. Both trends were initially apolitical and focused solely on benefits for Shi'a in Kuwait. The Da'wa trend, however, had a number of young followers who were interested in increasing their representation in Kuwaiti political life as well. These activist youth effectively took control over the important Social and Cultural Society of Shi'a and then further politicized the movement. Both movements were affected by the Iranian Islamic revolution in that they had to decide how deeply they identified with the political values of Khomeini's Islamic revolutionary ideology. The Shirazi followers in Kuwait initially followed Khomeini while Da'wa was much more independent of Iran. In the late 1990s, however, Iran ended up supporting the Da'wa trend in Kuwait, which was seen as much more autonomous. As such, the Kuwaiti Shiraziyyin ended up becoming politically quietist in their interactions with the government. For an in-depth explanation see Laurence Louër, *Transnational Shia Politics: Religious and Political Networks in the Gulf* (New York: Columbia University Press, 2008).

15. See September 12, 1976, Kuwait Tel 316 and 317: Constitutional Crisis, Milton, in FCO 8/2674, Kuwait: Internal Political Situation, Political Internal Memo from Kuwaiti Ambassador AT Lamb, 12 September 1976, TNA: PRO, Richmond, UK.

16. Ahmed al-Sadoun held the position of speaker of the house from 1982 through 1999. MP Musallam al-Barak announced the group's formation on March 16, 1999.

17. Laurence Louër, "Activism in Bahrain: Between Sectarian and Issue Politics," in Lina Khatib and Ellen Lust (eds.), *Taking to the Streets: The Transformation of Arab Activism* (Baltimore: Johns Hopkins University Press, 2014), p. 176.

18. Major Sunni personalities in the bloc included Musallam al-Barak and Ahmed al-Sadoun; Shi'a figures included members of al-Tahaluf al-Islami al-Watani such as Adnan 'Abd al-Samad. Musallam al-Barak is well known today both for his outspoken opposition to the Kuwaiti regime and for his public role in the 2011 and 2012 protests. Al-Sadoun is currently the speaker of the Kuwaiti National Assembly (as of 2012), and was previously speaker from 1985 to 1999. Adnan 'Abd al-Samad was a leader of the 2007 commemoration of 'Imad Mughniyah, to be discussed below.

19. Louër, *Transnational Shia Politics*, p. 208.

20. Louër, *Transnational Shia Politics*, p. 204. In the 1980s these activists had each gone on to successful political careers despite the political climate, and remained committed to participatory politics even though their civil society base in the Shi'a Cultural and Social Society had been forcibly shut down in 1989.

21. The Da'wa line and its modern incarnation in al-Tahaluf is sometimes called the "Hezbollah trend" by Sunnis in reference to Shi'a with whom they disagree. This does not mean they were all members or believers, but rather refers to their alleged ideological and political affinity toward the Hezbollah-aligned Shi'a in the 1980s who carried out several acts of terrorism in Kuwait, in hopes of forcing the government to free Da'wa prisoners.

22. Louër, *Transnational Shia Politics*, p. 208.

23. Azoulay, "The Politics of Shi'i Merchants." For more on the historical identity split between *hadhar* (urbanites) and *badu* (tribes), see al-Nakib, "Revisiting Hadar and Badu in Kuwait."

24. Interviews at a liberal *diwaniyya*, Kuwait City, Kuwait, February 2013.

25. My Shi'a respondents uniformly referred to the 2003 invasion as "*tahrir 'Iraq*," the liberation of Iraq, and particularly its Shi'a, whereas Sunni respondents were comfortable using *tahrir* to describe the initial event in 2003, but referring to events afterward using multiple terms, including *ihtilal* (occupation).

26. Interview with member of the Islamic Constitutional Movement, Kuwait City, Kuwait, April 24, 2013.

27. Frederic Wehrey, *Sectarian Politics in the Gulf: From the Iraq War to the Arab Uprisings* (New York: Columbia University Press, 2014), p. 163.

28. Sovereign ministries refer to those reserved for members of the Al Sabah regime, including Interior, Defense, and Foreign Affairs.

29. Shi'a have most often served as the ministers of relatively uncontroversial ministries (i.e. ones that do not have to do with security and are not linked to foreign affairs), such as Commerce and Industry, Finance, Oil, Health, Information, Housing Affairs, Planning, Public Works, and Municipal Affairs.

30. The second ever female Shi'a Kuwaiti minister, Rola Dashti, was appointed in 2012.

31. Information for the table came from Michael Herb, Kuwait Politics Database, available at http://www2.gsu.edu/~polmfh/database/shiiministers.htm. Calculations and counts are mine. I have not included 2012 through 2014 in the data due to the complicated nature of post-Arab Spring politics in Kuwait, particularly the boycott of the December 2012 elections.

32. For example, Article 29 of the constitution says that there shall be "no discrimination on the basis of sex or origin or language or religion," and Article 35 guarantees freedom of religious belief.

33. No official number was available during fieldwork. Estimates are based on speaking with Sunni and Shi'a officials in the *awqaf* as well as assessments from religious leaders. People usually thought that there were at least 1,000–1,600 Sunni mosques and 36–42 Shi'a mosques. The Kuwaiti state permitted a remarkable number of Shi'a mosques to be built. By the 1970s around thirty-five out of the eighty-five mosques in the country were Shi'a mosques—which meant that around 41 per cent of the mosques in Kuwait were designated for a religious minority that supposedly made up only 30 per cent of the population.

34. The processions were banned again by 2010 as part of a general ban on public gatherings, partially as a result of sectarian tension. For example, reports suggest the Kuwaiti police took significant efforts to protect Shi'a religious affairs from sectarian violence.

35. Interview with former editor of a Shi'a newspaper, Kuwait City, Kuwait, January 29, 2013.

36. Kuwaiti religious courts handle family law issues. The current Ja'fari Court (established in the 1970s) is a primary court with no appeal system. The Muhakema al-Tamayyaz (Court of Cassation) and Muhakema al-Isti'anaf (Court of Appeal) have no separate Ja'fari authority, so if Shi'a want to appeal a decision, they are dealing with jurists unfamiliar with Ja'fari jurisprudence. People have been pressing for a law in the parliament to give the Ja'fari Court more power as the Shi'a feel discriminated against in this respect. Interview with member of traditional notable Shi'a merchant family, Kuwait City, Kuwait, April 15, 2013.

37. "Q&A: Kuwait Parliamentary Election," BBC News, July 26, 2013, available at http://www.bbc.co.uk/news/world-middle-east-23449066.

38. The Behbehani family is an important Shi'a merchant family who, like the

majority of Kuwaiti Shiʻa, came from western Iran between the eighteenth and twentieth centuries. They applied for a mosque in 1987 to honor an elder family member, Sayyid Hashim Behbehani. They submitted their application near the end of the Iran-Iraq war—during the period of the highest political exclusion in Kuwait. At that time, when there was only one Awqaf (state institution for handling religious affairs) for all Kuwaitis (Sunni and Shiʻa), it took over seven years to approve the application. During those seven years the Behbehanis received various "verbal" responses from the ministry that a mosque was "unnecessary," but they never received official written responses. The next step was for the local municipal council to approve the building, and this is where my respondents argued that sectarianism permeated the process. The neighborhood of al-Qurain is mostly Sunni, and there were already forty-five Sunni mosques (and five "semi-permanent mosque structures" as of 1997, when the Behbehani family applied for their first one). When the municipal council took the issue up in 1994, its members immediately began fighting over the location of the mosque and formed a special committee to deal with the issue. The mosque was finally approved with the personal help of Sabah al-Ahmed.

39. Interview with member of the Behbehani-Maarafi family, Kuwait City, Kuwait, spring 2013.

40. Wehrey, *Sectarian Politics in the Gulf*, p. 174.

41. Leadership has generally alternated between two main branches of the Al Sabah family, the Al Salim branch and the Al Jaber branch. Saʻad al-Salem, the crown prince and technically successor to the emir who passed away in 2006, abdicated and was voted out as emir after only nine days, leading to a skipping of the Al Salim branch and the succession of the current emir, Sabah al-Ahmed al-Jaber. One branch, embodied by Shaykh Ahmed al-Fahd, a rival of prime minister Nasser al-Mohammed, allegedly responded to the Al Jaber branch's courting of the Shiʻa by forming alliances with sectarian Salafis in parliament, especially after 2008. For an excellent explanation of this dynamic see Rivka Azoulay and Claire Beaugrand, "Limits of Political Clientelism: Elites' Struggles in Kuwait Fragmenting Politics," *Arabian Humanities* 4 (Spring 2015).

42. Azoulay, "The Politics of Shiʻi Merchants," p. 87.

43. For the most recent information on this killing, see Alan Goldman and Ellen Nakashima, "CIA and Mossad Killed Senior Hezbollah Figure in Car Bombing," *Washington Post*, January 30, 2015, available at https://www.washingtonpost.com/world/national-security/cia-and-mossad-killed-senior-hezbollah-figure-in-car-bombing/2015/01/30/ebb88682-968a-11e4-8005-1924ede3e54a_story.html

44. This hijacking resulted in the death of two Kuwaiti passengers. For more

information see Lori Plotkin Boghardt, *Kuwait amid War, Peace and Revolution: 1979–1991* (New York: Palgrave, 2006).

45. Interviews with respondents from Kuwait's Islamic Constitutional Movement, National Security Bureau, and members of al-Tahaluf, Kuwait City, Kuwait, February–March, 2013; telephone interview with historian at the Kuwaiti National Security Bureau, February 6, 2014.

46. On February 18, 2008 the bloc published a statement that it was expelling Lari and Adnan 'Abd al-Samad because they would not apologize.

47. Wehrey, *Sectarian Politics in the Gulf*, p. 18.

48. Telephone interview with historian at the Kuwaiti National Security Bureau, February 6, 2014.

49. Additionally, several political activists were imprisoned, including high-ranking members of al-Tahaluf: Shaykh Husayn Ma'touk, Saleh Musi, Fadhal Safar Ali Safar, Hassan Salman, and 'Abdalmuhsin Jamal. Many Shi'a demonstrated in front of the state's Security Services building demanding their release.

50. So was the secretary general of al-Tahaluf, Nasr Sarkhwa, who had served previously as an MP in 1981, 1985, and 1992.

51. He remained in this position until December 2012, despite a high level of political upheaval.

52. Azoulay, "The Politics of Shi'a Merchants in Kuwait," p. 96.

53. Interviews at liberal *diwaniyya*, Kuwait City, Kuwait, February 2013; interviews with members of the Islamic Constitutional Movement, Kuwait City, Kuwait, April 2013.

54. Bandar Report; obviously, the demographic balance in Bahrain influenced this decision, too.

55. Azoulay, "The Politics of Shi'i Merchants in Kuwait," p. 88.

56. Azoulay and Beaugrandt, "Limits of Political Clientelism."

57. Interviews with two participants in the Mughniyah commemoration, Kuwait City, Kuwait, March 11 and 12, 2013.

58. Wehrey, *Sectarian Politics in the Gulf*, p. 172.

59. Wehrey, *Sectarian Politics in the Gulf*, p. 185.

60. Wehrey, *Sectarian Politics in the Gulf*, p. 185. Eight seats also went to "independent Sunnis" who were basically tribal Salafis.

61. Wehrey, *Sectarian Politics in the Gulf*, p. 185.

62. The majority of this section was adapted from Madeleine Wells, "Sectarianism and Authoritarianism in Kuwait," *The Monkey Cage* (*Washington Post* blog), April 13, 2015, available at https://www.washingtonpost.com/news/monkey-cage/wp/2015/04/13/sectarianism-and-authoritarianism-in-kuwait/.

63. Interview with former Sunni tribal MP, Kuwait City, April 2015.

64. Although beyond the scope of inquiry in this chapter, another important ele-

ment of Kuwait's protest movement that significantly pre-dated the Arab Spring was the rising up of stateless Kuwaitis to form a reform and rights movement in 2008 that also peaked around 2011 and 2012, sometimes aligning with tribal oppositionists.

65. For more on tribal primaries see Tetreault, *Stories of Democracy*, especially chapter 6 on the election of 1992.

66. "Kuwait's Shia MPs Boycott Parliament Session," *Middle East Eye*, January 13, 2016, available at http://www.middleeasteye.net/news/kuwaits-shia-mps-boycott-parliament-session-1636491037.

67. Amnesty International, "Kuwait at Risk of Sliding into Deeper Repression Amid Growing Clampdown on Critics," December 14, 2015, available at https://www.amnesty.org/en/latest/news/2015/12/kuwait-at-risk-of-sliding-into-deeper-repression-amid-growing-clampdown-on-critics/.

68. See "Kuwait Activist Sentenced for Insulting Emir," Al Jazeera English, June 22, 2015, available at http://www.aljazeera.com/news/2015/06/kuwait-activist-sentenced-insulting-emir-150622074745029.html.

69. Of the twenty-nine conspirators arrested in the ISIS-claimed bombings, thirteen were stateless and seven were citizens.

70. *Bidun* used to get regular Kuwaiti passports with a special designation that they were stateless. Most had the same benefits as other GCC travelers. Later, the system became more restrictive and *bidun* were issued "Article 17" gray passports which were only obtainable under specific conditions (such as grave health problems or the need to travel for higher education), and were valid for only one destination at a time. See, for example, Research Directorate, Immigration and Refugee Board, Canada, "Kuwait: Information on Article 17 passports," June 11, 2001, available at http://www.refworld.org/docid/3df4be5914.html; Sebastian Kohn, "Stateless in Kuwait: Who Are the Bidoon?" Open Society Foundations, March 24, 2011, available at https://www.opensocietyfoundations.org/voices/stateless-kuwait-who-are-bidoon.

71. Madeleine Wells, "The Danger to Kuwait is Authoritarianism," *Sada*, Carnegie Endowment for International Peace, July 21, 2015, available at http://carnegieendowment.org/sada/?fa=60802.

72. "Former Kuwaiti MP sentenced in absentia for insulting Saudi Arabia and Bahrain," *Middle East Monitor*, October 11, 2016, available at https://www.middleeastmonitor.com/20161011-former-kuwaiti-mp-sentenced-in-absentia-for-insulting-saudi-arabia-and-bahrain/.

73. See Habib Toumi, "Kuwait former MP sentenced for insulting UAE," Gulf News, April 13, 2016, http://gulfnews.com/news/gulf/kuwait/kuwait-former-mp-sentenced-for-insulting-uae-1.1710578.

74. Madawi Al-Rasheed, "Kuwaiti Activists Targeted under GCC Security Pact," *Al-Monitor*, March 20, 2015, available at http://www.al-monitor.com/pulse/

originals/2015/03/saudi-gcc-security-dissident-activism-detention-opposition.html.

14. CONCLUSION: PEACEBUILDING IN SECTARIANIZED CONFLICTS: FINDINGS AND IMPLICATIONS FOR THEORY AND PRACTICE

1. Benedict Anderson, *Imagined Communities: Reflections on the Origin and Spread of Nationalism* (London: Verso, 1983).

2. See, for example, David Little, *Sri Lanka: The Invention of Enmity* (Washington, DC: United States Institute of Peace Press, 1993).

3. Donald Rothchild, *Managing Ethnic Conflict in Africa: Pressures and Incentives for Cooperation* (Washington, DC: Brookings Institution Press, 1997), pp. 36–37.

4. By way of definition, peacebuilding refers to preventing the recurrence of conflict through implementation of peace agreements and efforts to build the basis for peace by addressing the multi-dimensional or complex root causes of conflict that may arise from underlying drivers, such as pervasive social discrimination and fear, economic inequalities and perceptions of economic injustice perpetrated by greedy and manipulative elites. For more on the concept see Vincent Chetail (ed.), *Post-Conflict Peacebuilding: A Lexicon* (Oxford: Oxford University Press, 2009).

5. Timothy D. Sisk (ed.), *Between Terror and Tolerance: Religious Leaders, Conflict, and Peacemaking* (Washington, DC: Georgetown University Press, 2011).

6. Scott Gates, Håvard Mokleiv Nygård, Håvard Strand, and Henrik Urdal, "Trends in Armed Conflict, 1946–2014," *Conflict Trends* 1, Peace Research Institute Oslo, PRIO Policy Brief, 2016, available at http://file.prio.no/publication_files/prio/Gates,%20Nyg%C3%A5rd,%20Strand,%20Urdal%20-%20Trends%20in%20Armed%20Conflict,%20Conflict%20Trends%201-2016.pdf. The authors note that in conflicts in 2014, "90% of all casualties occurred in countries where [political Islam] was present" (p. 3).

7. Pew Research Center, *Religious Hostilities Reach Six-Year High*, January 14, 2014, available at http://www.pewforum.org/2014/01/14/religious-hostilities-reach-six-year-high.

8. This paradox has been identified in other contexts: see Jack Snyder, *From Voting to Violence: Democratization and Nationalist Conflict* (New York: W.W. Norton, 2000); and Michael Mann, *The Dark Side of Democracy: Explaining Ethnic Cleansing* (Cambridge: Cambridge University Press, 2005).

9. See, for example, Iftikhar H. Malik, "Religious Minorities in Pakistan," Minority Rights Group International, 2002, available at http://minority-rights.org/wp-content/uploads/old-site-downloads/download-139-Religious-Minorities-in-Pakistan.pdf; and Human Rights Watch, "Iraq: Forced Marriage, Conversion for Yezidis," October 11, 2014, available at https://www.hrw.org/news/2014/10/11/iraq-forced-marriage-conversion-yezidis.

10. Anna Jarstad and Timothy D. Sisk (eds.), *From War to Democracy: Dilemmas of Peacebuilding* (Cambridge: Cambridge University Press, 2008).

11. On the case for partitioning Iraq see Peter W. Galbraith, *The End of Iraq* (New York: Simon & Schuster, 2006); and Adam Taylor, "People Have Talked about Iraq Breaking Up for Years. Now it May Actually Happen," *Washington Post*, June 13, 2014, available at https://www.washingtonpost.com/news/worldviews/wp/2014/06/13/people-have-talked-about-iraq-breaking-up-for-years-now-it-may-actually-happen/. On the case for partitioning Syria see "On GPS: Landis on a Syria Solution—Fareed Goes 1-on-1 with Syria Expert Joshua Landis to Discuss an Innovative Solution to the Ongoing Syrian Crisis," *Fareed Zakaria GPS* (CNN), November 8, 2014, available at http://www.cnn.com/videos/bestoftv/2014/11/08/exp-gps-landis-sot-syria.cnn.

12. Dean Pruitt and Jeffrey Z. Rubin, *Social Conflict: Escalation, Stalemate, Settlement* (New York: Random House, 1986).

13. For a succinct overview see Andreas Wimmer, Richard Goldstone, Donald Horowitz, Ulrike Joras, and Conrad Schetter (eds.), *Facing Ethnic Conflict: Toward a New Realism* (Lanham, MD: Rowman & Littlefield, 2004).

14. United Nations Development Programme (UNDP), *Toward a Citizen's State: Lebanon National Human Development Report, 2008–2009* (New York: United Nations, 2009), available at http://www.lb.undp.org/content/lebanon/en/home/library/democratic_governance/the-national-human-development-report-2008-2009—toward-a-citize0.html; see also Bassel F. Salloukh's two chapters in this volume: "The Sectarianization of Geopolitics in the Middle East" and "The Architecture of Sectarianization in Lebanon."

15. Such is the conclusion of the authors in Bassel F. Salloukh et al., *The Politics of Sectarianism in Postwar Lebanon* (London: Pluto Press, 2015).

16. See David Smock (ed.), *Religious Contributions to Peacemaking: When Religion Brings Peace, Not War* (Washington, DC: United States Institute of Peace, 2006), which includes case studies of Kashmir, Nigeria, Macedonia, Sudan, Iraq and Israel/Palestine, available at http://www.usip.org/sites/default/files/PWJan2006.pdf.

17. "Sheikh Nimr al-Nimr: Saudi Arabia Executes Top Shi'a Cleric," BBC World News, January 2, 2016, available at http://www.bbc.com/news/world-middle-east-35213244.

18. Marc Lynch, "Why Saudi Arabia Escalated the Middle East's Sectarian Conflict," *The Monkey Cage* (*Washington Post* blog), January 3, 2016, available at https://www.washingtonpost.com/news/monkey-cage/wp/2016/01/04/why-saudi-arabia-escalated-the-middle-easts-sectarian-conflict/.

19. A similar debate between primordialists and essentialists occurred in the Balkans in the 1990s. A champion of the primordialist perspective was Robert

Kaplan, whose widely read book *Balkan Ghosts* presented the "ancient hatreds" perspective—and was the subject of much debate. See Robert D. Kaplan, *Balkan Ghosts: A Journey through History* (New York: Picador, 2005).

20. See Karen Barkey, *Empire of Difference: The Ottomans in Comparative Perspective* (Cambridge: Cambridge University Press, 2008).
21. See Jörg Neuheiser and Stefan Wolff (eds.), *Peace at Last? The Impact of the Good Friday Agreement on Northern Ireland* (New York: Berghahn Books, 2002).
22. Marie Fitzduff, "Just Enough to Hate—Not Enough to Love: Religious Leaders in Northern Ireland," in Sisk (ed.), *Between Terror and Tolerance*.
23. See Bogdan Denitch, *Ethnic Nationalism: The Tragic Death of Yugoslavia* (Minneapolis: University of Minnesota Press, 1996).
24. Martina Fischer (ed.), *Peacebuilding and Civil Society in Bosnia-Herzegovina* (Berlin: Berghof Center for Conflict Transformation, 2006).
25. See, for example, International Dialogue on Peacebuilding and Statebuilding, *A New Deal for Engagement in Fragile States* (Paris: OECD Publishing, 2011), available at https://www.pbsbdialogue.org/media/filer_public/07/69/07692de0-3557-494e-918e-18df00e9ef73/the_new_deal.pdf.
26. The RBAS serves as the headquarters for the UNDP's regional programs and country offices in seventeen Arab countries (plus the Occupied Palestinian Territories). On the work of its important Promoting Social Cohesion Project see http://www.arabstates.undp.org/content/rbas/en/home/operations/regional-hub-in-amman/our-regional-programme/.
27. Sue Ingram, "Political Settlements: The History of an Idea in Policy and Theory," SSGM (State, Society and Governance in Melanasia) Discussion Paper, Australian National University, 2014/2015, available at http://ips.cap.anu.edu.au/sites/default/files/DP-2014-5-Ingram-ONLINE.pdf.
28. Security Council briefing on the situation in Syria, Special Envoy for Syria Staffan de Mistura, July 29, 2015, available at http://www.un.org/undpa/speeches-statements/29072015/syria.
29. Robert Muggah, Timothy D. Sisk, Eugenia Piza-Lopez, Jago Salmon, and Patrick Keuleers, *Governance for Peace: Securing the Social Contract* (New York: UNDP, 2012), available at http://www.undp.org/content/dam/undp/library/crisis%20prevention/governance-for-peace_2011-12-15_web.pdf
30. Fletcher Cox, Catherine Orsborn, and Timothy D. Sisk, "Religion, Peacebuilding, and Social Cohesion in Conflict-Affected Countries," Sié Chéou Kang Center for International Security and Diplomacy, Josef Korbel School of International Studies, University of Denver, 2015, available at http://www.du.edu/korbel/sie/media/documents/faculty_pubs/sisk/religion-and-social-cohesion-reports/rsc-researchreport.pdf.
31. For a finding from India that supports this hypothesis see Ashutosh Varshney, "Ethnic Conflict and Civil Society: India and Beyond," *World Politics* 53:3 (April 2001): 362–398.

32. See Hassan Hassan, "The Sectarianism of the Islamic State: Ideological Roots and Political Context," Carnegie Endowment for International Peace, June 13, 2016, available at http://carnegieendowment.org/2016/06/13/sectarianism-of-islamic-state-ideological-roots-and-political-context-pub-63746.

33. Jean-Marie Guéhenno, "Tackle Early the Conditions that Breed Extremism," *Nikkei Asian Review*, February 4, 2015, available at http://www.crisisgroup.org/en/regions/op-eds/2015/guehenno-tackle-early-the-conditions-that-breed-extremism.aspx.

34. "Syria in Flames: Leila Al-Shami and Robin Yassin-Kassab with Ella Wind," *The Brooklyn Rail*, May 3, 2016, available at http://www.brooklynrail.org/2016/05/field-notes/syria-in-flames.

35. Bassel F. Salloukh, "Lebanese Protestors United against Garbage … and Sectarianism," *The Monkey Cage* (*Washington Post* blog), September 14, 2015, available at https://www.washingtonpost.com/blogs/monkey-cage/wp/2015/09/14/lebanese-protesters-united-against-garbage-and-sectarianism/.

36. See Bassel F. Salloukh, "The End of the Arab Affair," *The New Arab*, March 28, 2016, available at https://www.alaraby.co.uk/english/comment/2016/3/28/the-end-of-the-arab-affair.

SELECT BIBLIOGRAPHY

Abou El Fadl, Khaled. *Reasoning with God: Reclaiming Shari'ah in the Modern Age.* Lanham, MD: Rowman & Littlefield, 2014.

Adam, Karla. "Obama ridiculed for saying conflicts in the Middle East 'date back millennia.' (Some don't date back a decade.)" *Washington Post,* January 13, 2016, https://www.washingtonpost.com/news/worldviews/wp/2016/01/13/obama-ridiculed-for-saying-conflicts-in-the-middle-east-date-back-millennia-some-dont-date-back-a-decade/.

al-Ali, Zaid. "The Only Way to Solve Iraq's Political Crisis." *New York Times,* May 5, 2016, http://www.nytimes.com/2016/05/06/opinion/the-only-way-to-solve-iraqs-political-crisis.html.

Al Jazeera, *Bahrain: Shouting in the Dark.* Al Jazeera documentary, http://www.aljazeera.com/programmes/2011/08/201184144547798162.html.

Allawi, Ali A. *The Occupation of Iraq: Winning the War, Losing the Peace.* New Haven, CT: Yale University Press, 2007.

Alshehabi, Omar Hesham. "Radical Transformations and Radical Contestations: Bahrain's Spatial–Demographic Revolution." *Middle East Critique* 23:1 (2014): 29–51.

Ayoub, Mahmoud. *The Crisis of Muslim History: Religion and Politics in Early Islam.* Oxford: Oneworld, 2003.

Azoulay, Rivka. "The Politics of Shi'i Merchants in Kuwait." In Steffen Hertog, Giacomo Luciani, and Marc Valeri (eds.), *Business Politics in the Middle East.* London: Hurst, 2015, pp. 67–100.

Bahrain Independent Commission of Inquiry. *Report of the Bahrain Independent Commission of Inquiry,* November 23, 2011, http://www.bici.org.bh/BICIreportEN.pdf.

Barkey, Karen. *Empire of Difference: The Ottomans in Comparative Perspective.* Cambridge: Cambridge University Press, 2008.

Batatu, Hanna. *The Old Social Classes and the Revolutionary Movements of Iraq: A Study of Iraq's Old Landed and Commercial Classes and of its Communists, Ba'thists, and Free Officers*. Princeton: Princeton University Press, 1979.

Bazzi, Mohamad. "Lebanon and the Start of Iran and Saudi Arabia's Proxy War." *The New Yorker*, May 20, 2015, http://www.newyorker.com/news/news-desk/labanon-and-the-start-of-iran-and-saudi-arabias-proxy-war.

Beaugrand, Claire. "Deconstructing Minorities/Majorities in Parliamentary Gulf States (Kuwait and Bahrain)." *British Journal of Middle Eastern Studies* 43:2 (2016): 234–249.

Beinin, Joel and Frédéric Vairel (eds.). *Social Movements, Mobilization, and Contestation in the Middle East and North Africa*, 2nd ed. Stanford: Stanford University Press, 2013.

Black, Ian. "Fear of a Shia Full Moon." *The Guardian*, January 27, 2007, http://theguardian.com/world/2007/jan/26/worlddispatch.ian.black.

Bonnefoy, Laurent. *Salafism in Yemen: Transnationalism and Religious Identity*. New York: Columbia University Press, 2011.

Borowitz, Andy. "Pressure on Obama to Quickly Resolve Centuries-old Sunni–Shiite Conflict." *The New Yorker*, June 18, 2014, http://www.newyorker.com/humor/borowitz-report/pressure-on-obama-to-quickly-resolve-centuries-old-sunni-shiite-conflict.

Boucek, Christopher. "War in Saada: From Local Insurrection to National Challenge." In Christopher Boucek and Marina Ottoway (eds.), *Yemen on the Brink*. Washington, DC: Carnegie Endowment for International Peace, 2010, pp. 45–59. http://carnegieendowment.org/2010/05/05/war-in-saada-from-local-insurrection-to-national-challenge.

Bowen, Jeremy. "Sharpening Sunni–Shia Schism Bodes Ill for the Middle East." BBC News, December 20, 2013, http://www.bbc.com/news/world-middle-east-25458755.

Bozarslan, Hamit. "Rethinking the Ba'thist Period." In Jordi Tejel, Peter Sluglett, Riccardo Bocco, and Hamit Bozarslan (eds.), *Writing the Modern History of Iraq: Historiographical and Political Challenges*. Singapore: World Scientific Publishing, 2012, pp. 143–152.

Brynen, Rex, Pete W. Moore, Bassel F. Salloukh, and Marie-Joëlle Zahar. *Beyond the Arab Spring: Authoritarianism and Democratization in the Arab World*. Boulder: Lynne Rienner, 2012.

Cammett, Melani. *Compassionate Communalism: Welfare and Sectarianism in Lebanon*. Ithaca: Cornell University Press, 2014.

Cammett, Melani and Sukriti Issar. "Bricks and Mortar Clientelism: Sectarianism and the Logic of Welfare Allocation in Lebanon." *World Politics* 62:3 (2010): 381–421.

Cigar, Norman. *Iraq's Shia Warlords and their Militias: Political and Security Challenges and Options*. Carlisle, PA: US Army War College Press, 2015.

Clark, Janine and Bassel F. Salloukh. "Elite Strategies, Civil Society, and Sectarian Identities in Postwar Lebanon." *International Journal of Middle East Studies* 45:4 (2013): 731–749.

Cole, Juan. "A 'Shiite Crescent'? The Regional Impact of the Iraq War." *Current History* 105 (January 2006): 20–26.

Colgan, Jeff. "How Sectarianism Shapes Yemen's War" *The Monkey Cage* (*Washington Post* blog), April 13, 2015, https://www.washingtonpost.com/blogs/monkey-cage/wp/2015/04/13/how-sectarianism-shapes-yemens-war/.

Collins, John J. *Scriptures and Sectarianism: Essays on the Dead Sea Scrolls*. Tübingen: Mohr Siebeck, 2014.

Cook, Michael. "Weber and Islamic Sects." In Toby E. Huff and Wolfgang Schluchter (eds.), *Max Weber and Islam*. New Brunswick: Transaction, 1999, pp. 273–279.

Corboz, Elvire. *Guardians of Shi'ism: Sacred Authority and Transnational Family Networks*. Edinburgh: Edinburgh University Press, 2015.

Cox, Fletcher, Catherine Orsborn, and Timothy D. Sisk. "Religion, Peace-building, and Social Cohesion in Conflict-Affected Countries." Sié Chéou Kang Center for International Security and Diplomacy, Josef Korbel School of International Studies, University of Denver, 2015, http://www.du.edu/korbel/sie/media/documents/faculty_pubs/sisk/religion-and-social-cohesion-reports/rsc-researchreport.pdf.

Daoudy, Marwa. "Sectarianism in Syria: Myth and Reality." *openDemocracy*, July 22, 2013, https://www.opendemocracy.net/marwa-daoudy/sectarianism-in-syria-myth-and-reality.

Davis, Eric. "Introduction: The Question of Sectarian Identities in Iraq." *International Journal of Contemporary Iraqi Studies* 4:3 (2010): 229–242.

Day, Stephen. *Regionalism and Rebellion in Yemen: A Troubled National Union*. Cambridge: Cambridge University Press, 2012.

Denison, Benjamin and Jasmin Mujanovic. "Syria isn't Bosnia. And no, the Problem isn't 'Ancient Hatreds'." *The Monkey Cage* (*Washington Post* blog), November 17, 2015, https://www.washingtonpost.com/news/monkey-cage/wp/2015/11/17/syria-isnt-bosnia-and-no-the-problem-isnt-ancient-hatreds/.

Ehteshami, Anoushiravan and Raymond A. Hinnebusch. *Syria and Iran: Middle Powers in a Penetrated Regional System*. London and New York: Routledge, 1997.

Ehteshami, Anoushiravan, Raymond Hinnebusch, Heidi Huuhtanen, Paola Raunio, Maaike Warnaar, and Tina Zintl. "Authoritarian Resilience and International Linkages in Iran and Syria." In Steven Heydemann and Reinoud Leenders (eds.), *Middle East Authoritarianisms: Governance, Contestation, and Regime Resilience in Syria and Iran*. Stanford: Stanford University Press, 2013, pp. 222–244.

Fakhro, Elham. "Revolution and Counter-Revolution in Bahrain." In Adam Roberts, Michael J. Willis, Rory McCarthy, and Timothy Garton Ash (eds.), *Civil Resistance in the Arab Spring: Triumphs and Disasters*. Oxford: Oxford University Press, 2016, pp. 88–115.

Fakhro, Munira A. "The Uprising in Bahrain: An Assessment." In Gary Sick and Lawrence Potter (eds.), *The Persian Gulf at the Millennium: Essays in Politics, Economy, Security, and Religion*. Basingstoke: Macmillan, 1997, pp. 167–188.

Farouk-Sluglett, Marion and Peter Sluglett. "Some Reflections on the Sunni/Shi'i Question in Iraq." *Bulletin of the British Society for Middle Eastern Studies* 5:2 (1978): 79–83.

Filiu, Jean-Pierre. *From Deep State to Islamic State: The Arab Counter-Revolution and its Jihadi Legacy*. London: Hurst, 2015.

Fischer, Martina (ed.). *Peacebuilding and Civil Society in Bosnia-Herzegovina*. Berlin: Berghof Center for Conflict Transformation, 2006.

Gause, F. Gregory III. *Beyond Sectarianism: The New Middle East Cold War*. Brookings Doha Center Analysis Paper no. 11, July 2014, http://www.brookings.edu/~/media/research/files/papers/2014/07/22%20beyond%20sectarianism%20cold%20war%20gause/english%20pdf.pdf.

———. *The International Relations of the Persian Gulf*. Cambridge: Cambridge University Press, 2010.

———. "Is This the End of Sykes-Picot?" *The Monkey Cage* (*Washington Post* blog), May 20, 2014, https://www.washingtonpost.com/news/monkey-cage/wp/2014/05/20/is-this-the-end-of-sykes-picot/.

———. *Oil Monarchies: Domestic and Security Challenges in the Arab Gulf Monarchies*. New York: Council on Foreign Relations Press, 1994.

———. *Saudi Arabia in the New Middle East*. Council on Foreign Relations Special Report no. 63. New York: Council on Foreign Relations, December 2011.

Gengler, Justin. "Bahrain's Sunni Awakening." *Middle East Report* (Middle East Research and Information Project), January 17, 2012, http://www.merip.org/mero/mero011712.

———. *Group Conflict and Political Mobilization in Bahrain and the Arab Gulf: Rethinking the Rentier State*. Bloomington: Indiana University Press, 2015.

———. "Royal Factionalism, the Khawalid, and the Securitization of 'the Shī'a Problem' in Bahrain." *Journal of Arabian Studies: Arabia, the Gulf, and the Red Sea* 3:1 (2013): 53–79.

Gerges, Fawaz. *ISIS: A History*. Princeton: Princeton University Press, 2016.

——— (ed.). *The New Middle East: Protest and Revolution in the Arab World*. Cambridge: Cambridge University Press, 2013.

Goldsmith, Leon T. *Cycle of Fear: Syria's Alawites in War and Peace*. London: Hurst, 2015.

Goodarzi, Jubin M. *Syria and Iran: Diplomatic Alliance and Power Politics in the Middle East*. London: I.B. Tauris, 2009.

Haddad, Fanar. "Iraq: Atrocity as Political Capital." In Bridget Conley-Zilkic (ed.), *How Mass Atrocities End: Studies from Guatemala, Burundi, Indonesia, the Sudan, Bosnia-Herzegovina, and Iraq*. Cambridge: Cambridge University Press, 2016, pp. 181–210.

———. "The Language of Anti-Shiism." *Foreign Policy*, August 9, 2013, http://foreignpolicy.com/2013/08/09/the-language-of-anti-shiism/.

———. "A Sectarian Awakening: Reinventing Sunni Identity in Iraq after 2003." *Current Trends in Islamist Ideology* 17 (2014): 145–176, http://www.hudson.org/research/10544-a-sectarian-awakening-reinventing-sunni-identity-in-iraq-after-2003.

———. *Sectarianism in Iraq: Antagonist Visions of Unity*. London and Oxford: Hurst/Oxford University Press, 2011.

———. "Sectarian Relations and Sunni Identity in Post-Civil War Iraq." In Lawrence G. Potter (ed.), *Sectarian Politics in the Persian Gulf*. Oxford and New York: Oxford University Press, 2014, pp. 67–115.

———. "Secular Sectarians." *Middle East Institute*. June 17, 2014, http://www.mei.edu/content/map/secular-sectarians.

———. "Sunni–Shia Relations after the Iraq War." United States Institute of Peace (USIP). Peace Brief 160, November 15 2013, https://www.usip.org/sites/default/files/PB160.pdf.

Hamid, Shadi. "The End of Pluralism." *The Atlantic*, July 23, 2014, http://www.theatlantic.com/international/archive/2014/07/the-end-of-pluralism/374875/.

Hashemi, Nader. "Religious Leaders, Sectarianism and the Sunni–Shia Divide in Islam." In Timothy Sisk (ed.), *Between Terror and Tolerance: Religious Leaders, Conflict, and Peacemaking*. Washington DC: Georgetown University Press, 2011, pp. 29–48.

Herb, Michael. *The Wages of Oil: Parliaments and Economic Development in Kuwait and the UAE*. Ithaca: Cornell University Press, 2014.

Heydemann, Steven. "Syria's Uprising: Sectarianism, Regionalisation, and State Order in the Levant." Fundación para las Relaciones Internacionales y el Diálogo Exterior (FRIDE), Working Paper no. 119, May 2013, http://fride.org/download/WP_119_Syria_Uprising.pdf.

Hof, Ambassador Frederic C. and Alex Simon, "Sectarian Violence in Syria's Civil War: Causes, Consequences, and Recommendations for Mitigation." Center for the Prevention of Genocide, United States Holocaust Memorial Museum, March 25, 2013, https://www.ushmm.org/m/pdfs/20130325-syria-report.pdf.

Hubbard, Ben and Mayy El Sheikh. "Wikileaks Show a Saudi Obsession with Iran." *New York Times*, July 16, 2015, http://nytimes.com/2015/07/17/world/middleeast/wikileaks-saudi-arabia-iran.html.

International Crisis Group. *Lebanon's Hizbollah Turns Eastward to Syria*, Report No. 153, Middle East & North Africa, 27 May 2014, https://www.crisisgroup.org/middle-east-north-africa/eastern-mediterranean/lebanon/lebanon-s-hizbollah-turns-eastward-syria.

————. *Popular Protests in North Africa and the Middle East (III): The Bahrain Revolt*, Report no. 105, Middle East & North Africa, 6 April 2011, https://www.crisisgroup.org/middle-east-north-africa/gulf-and-arabian-peninsula/bahrain/popular-protests-north-africa-and-middle-east-iii-bahrain-revolt.

Ismael, Tareq and Jacqueline Ismael. *Iraq in the Twenty-First Century: Regime Change and the Making of a Failed State*. London: Routledge, 2015.

————. "The Sectarian State in Iraq and the New Political Class." *International Journal of Contemporary Iraqi Studies* 4:3 (2010): 339–356.

Jarstad, Anna K. and Timothy D. Sisk (eds.). *From War to Democracy: Dilemmas of Peacebuilding*. Cambridge: Cambridge University Press, 2008.

Jones, Toby. "Embattled in Arabia: Shi'is and the Politics of Confrontation in Saudi Arabia." Combating Terrorism Center at West Point, Occasional Paper Series, June 3, 2009, http://arabia2day.com/wp-content/uploads/2010/12/Embattled-in-Arabia-Shiis-and-the-Politics-of-Confrontation-in-Saudi-Arabia.pdf.

Kadhim, Abbas. "Efforts at Cross-Ethnic Cooperation: The 1920 Revolution and Sectarian Identities in Iraq." *International Journal of Contemporary Iraqi Studies*. 4:3 (2010): 275–294.

Kamrava, Mehran. *Qatar: Small State, Big Politics*. Ithaca: Cornell University Press, 2013.

———— (ed.). *Fragile Politics: Weak States in the Greater Middle East*. London and New York: Hurst/Oxford University Press, 2016.

Kepel, Gilles. *Jihad: The Trail of Political Islam*. Cambridge, MA: Harvard University Press, 2002.

Kerr, Malcolm. *The Arab Cold War: Gamal 'Abd al-Nasir and his Rivals, 1958–1970*, 3rd ed. New York: Oxford University Press, 1971.

Kerr, Michael and Craig Larkin (eds.). *The Alawis of Syria: War, Faith and Politics in the Levant*. London: Hurst, 2015.

Khalaf, Amal. "Squaring the Circle: Bahrain's Pearl Roundabout." *Middle East Critique 22:3* (2013): 265–280.

Khouri, Rami G. "The Saudi-Iranian Rivalry Threatens the Entire Middle East." *Al Jazeera America*. January 5, 2016, http://www.america.aljazeera.com/opinions/2016/1/the-saudi-iranian-rivalry-threatens-the-entire-middle-east.html.

Khuri, Fuad I. *Tribe and State in Bahrain: The Transformation of Social and Political Authority in an Arab State*. Chicago: University of Chicago Press, 1980.

Kingston, Paul W.T. *Reproducing Sectarianism: Advocacy Networks and the Politics of*

Civil Society in Post-Civil War Lebanon. New York: State University of New York Press, 2014.

Kirkpatrick, David D. "Saudis Expand Regional Power as Others Falter." *New York Times*, January 25, 2015, http://www.nytimes.com/2015/01/26/world/middleeast/saudis-expand-regional-power-as-others-falter.html.

Krohley, Nicholas. *The Death of the Mahdi Army: The Rise, Fall, and Revival of Iraq's Most Powerful Militia*. London: Hurst, 2015.

Lacroix, Stephane. *Awakening Islam: The Politics of Religious Dissent in Contemporary Saudi Arabia*. Translated by George Holoch. Cambridge, MA: Harvard University Press, 2011.

Lister, Charles R. *The Syrian Jihad: Al-Qaeda, the Islamic State and the Evolution of an Insurgency*. London and New York: Hurst/Oxford University Press, 2015.

Littell, Jonathan. *Syrian Notebooks: Inside the Homs Uprising*. Translated by Charlotte Mandell. London: Verso, 2015.

Little, David. "Religion, Nationalism and Intolerance." In Timothy D. Sisk (ed.), *Between Terror and Tolerance: Religious Leaders, Conflict, and Peacemaking*. Washington, DC: Georgetown University Press, 2011, pp. 9–28.

Louër, Laurence. "Activism in Bahrain: Between Sectarian and Issue Politics." In Lina Khatib and Ellen Lust (eds.), *Taking to the Streets: The Transformation of Arab Activism*. Baltimore: Johns Hopkins University Press, 2014, pp. 172–198.

———. *Transnational Shia Politics: Religious and Political Networks in the Gulf*. New York: Columbia University Press, 2008.

Luciani, Giacomo and Hazem Beblawi (eds.). *The Rentier State*. London: Croom Helm, 1987.

Lund, Aron. "Chasing Ghosts: The *Shabiha* Phenomenon." In Michael Kerr and Craig Larkin (eds), *The Alawis of Syria: War, Faith and Politics in the Levant*. London: Hurst, 2015, pp. 207–224.

Luomi, Mari. "Sectarian Identities or Geopolitics? The Regional Shia–Sunni Divide in the Middle East." Finnish Institute of International Affairs, Working Paper 56, 2008. http://www.fiia.fi/en/publication/4/sectarian_identities_or_geopolitics/.

Lynch, Marc. "The Entrepreneurs of Cynical Sectarianism." *Foreign Policy*, November 13, 2013, http://foreignpolicy.com/2013/11/13/the-entrepreneurs-of-cynical-sectarianism/.

———. *The New Arab Wars: Uprisings and Anarchy in the Middle East*. New York: Public Affairs, 2016.

———. "Why Saudi Arabia Escalated the Middle East's Sectarian Conflict." *The Monkey Cage* (*Washington Post* blog). January 8, 2016, https://www.washingtonpost.com/news/monkey-cage/wp/2016/01/04/why-saudi-arabia-escalated-the-middle-easts-sectarian-conflict/.

Mabon, Simon. *Saudi Arabia and Iran: Soft Power Rivalry in the Middle East*. London: I.B. Tauris, 2013.

Machlis, Elisheva. *Shi'i Sectarianism in the Middle East: Modernisation and the Quest for Islamic Universalism*. London: I.B. Tauris, 2014.

Madelung, Wilferd. *The Succession to Muhammad: A Study of the Early Caliphate*. Cambridge: Cambridge University Press, 1997.

Makdisi, Ussama. *The Culture of Sectarianism: Community, History, and Violence in Nineteenth-Century Ottoman Lebanon*. Berkeley: University of California Press, 2000.

Marechal, Brigitte and Sami Zemni (eds.), *The Dynamics of Sunni–Shia Relationships: Doctrine, Transnationalism, Intellectuals and the Media*. London: Hurst, 2012.

Matthiesen, Toby. "Migration, Minorities and Radical Networks: Labour Movements and Opposition Groups in Saudi Arabia, 1950–1975." *International Review of Social History* 59:3 (2014): 473–504.

———. "(No) Dialogue in Bahrain." *Middle East Report* (Middle East Research and Information Project), February 13, 2014, http://www.merip.org/mero/mero021314.

———. *The Other Saudis: Shiism, Dissent and Sectarianism*. Cambridge: Cambridge University Press, 2015.

———. *Sectarian Gulf: Bahrain, Saudi Arabia, and the Arab Spring That Wasn't*. Stanford: Stanford University Press, 2013.

———. "Syria: Inventing a Religious War." *New York Review of Books*, June 12, 2013, http://www.nybooks.com/blogs/nyrblog/2013/jun/12/syria-inventing-religious-war/.

———. "Wanted: An inclusive Bahraini social contract." *Middle East Eye*, November 21, 2014, http://www.middleeasteye.net/columns/wanted-inclusive-bahraini-social-contract-856097571.

Migdal, Joel. "The State in Society: An Approach to Struggles for Domination." In Joel Migdal, Atul Kohli, and Vivienne Shue (eds.), *State Power and Social Forces: Domination and Transformation in the Third World*. Cambridge: Cambridge University Press, 1994, pp. 7–34.

———. *Strong Societies and Weak States: State-Society Relations and State Capabilities in the Third World*. Princeton: Princeton University Press, 1988.

Mikaelian, Shoghig and Bassel F. Salloukh. "Strong Actor in a Weak State: The Geopolitics of Hezbollah." In Mehran Kamrava (ed.), *Fragile Politics: Weak States in the Greater Middle East*. New York: Oxford University Press, 2016, pp. 119–143.

Nagle, John. "Between Entrenchment, Reform and Transformation: Ethnicity and Lebanon's Consociational Democracy." *Democratization 22* (2015): 1–21.

Nasr, S.V.R. "Communalism and Fundamentalism: A Re-examination of the Origins of Islamic Fundamentalism." *Contention* 4:2 (1995): 121–139.

———. "Democracy and the Crisis of Governability in Pakistan." *Asian Survey* 32:6 (June 1992): 531–537.

———. "Pakistan: State, Agrarian Reform, and Islamization." *International Journal of Politics, Culture and Society* 10:2 (1996): 249–272.

———. "The Rise of Sunni Militancy in Pakistan: The Changing Role of Islamism and the Ulama in Society and Politics." *Modern Asian Studies* 34:1 (2000): 139–180.

Nasr, Vali. *The Shia Revival: How Conflicts within Islam Will Shape the Future.* New York: W.W. Norton, 2006.

———. "The War for Islam." *Foreign Policy*, January 22, 2016, http://foreign-policy.com/2016/01/22/the-war-for-islam-sunni-shiite-iraq-syria/.

Naylor, Hugh. "The Seven Most Important Moments of the Saudi-Iranian Rivalry." *Washington Post.* January 4, 2016, https://www.washingtonpost.com/news/worldviews/wp/2016/01/04/the-most-important-moments-of-the-saudi-iranian-rivalry/.

Nerguizian, Aram. "Assessing the Consequences of Hezbollah's Necessary War of Choice in Syria." Center for Strategic and International Studies, June 17, 2013, http://csis.org/publication/assessing-consequences-hezbollahs-necessary-war-choice-syria.

Norton, Augustus Richard. "The Shiite 'Threat' Revisited." *Current History* (December 2007): 434–439.

Osman, Khalil F. *Sectarianism in Iraq: The Making of State and Nation since 1920.* London: Routledge, 2015.

PBS, *The Rise of ISIS. Frontline* documentary, October 28, 2014, http://www.pbs.org/wgbh/pages/frontline/rise-of-isis/.

Pearlman, Wendy. "Understanding Fragmentation in the Syrian Revolt." Project on Middle East Political Science (POMEPS), February 12, 2014, http://pomeps.org/2014/02/12/understanding-fragmentation-in-the-syrian-revolt/

Pew Research Center. *Religious Hostilities Reach Six-Year High*, January 14, 2014, http://www.pewforum.org/2014/01/14/religious-hostilities-reach-six-year-high.

Pierret, Thomas. *Religion and State in Syria: The Sunni Ulama from Coup to Revolution.* Cambridge: Cambridge University Press, 2013.

———. "The Reluctant Sectarianism of Foreign States in the Syrian Conflict." United States Institute of Peace, Peace Brief 162, November 18, 2013, https://www.usip.org/sites/default/files/PB162.pdf.

Pinto, Paulo G. "'Oh Syria, God Protects You': Islam as a Cultural Idiom under Bashar al-Asad." *Middle East Critique* 20:2 (2011): 189–205.

———. "Syria." In Paul Amar and Vijay Prashad (eds.), *Dispatches from the Arab Spring: Understanding the New Middle East.* Minneapolis: University of Minnesota Press, 2013, pp. 204–242.

Potter, Lawrence G. (ed.). *Sectarian Politics in the Persian Gulf.* London and New York: Hurst/Oxford University Press, 2014.

al-Qarawee, Harith Hassan. "Heightened Sectarianism in the Middle East: Causes, Dynamics and Consequences." Italian Institute for International Political Studies, Analysis no. 205, November 2013, 1–10, http://www.ispionline.it/sites/default/files/pubblicazioni/analysis_205_2013_0.pdf.

Al-Rasheed, Madawi. *A History of Saudi Arabia*, 2nd ed. Cambridge: Cambridge University Press, 2010.

————. *Is it always good to be King? Saudi regime resilience after the 2011 Arab popular uprisings*. LSE Middle East Centre Paper Series, 12 (December 2015). http://eprints.lse.ac.uk/64749/1/Al_Rassheed%20Is%20It%20always%20to%20be%20a%20king%20SaudiResilience.pdf.

————. *Contesting the Saudi State: Islamic Voices from a New Generation*. Cambridge: Cambridge University Press, 2007.

————. *Is it Always Good to be King? Saudi Regime Resilience after the 2011 Arab Popular Uprisings*. London: LSE Middle East Centre Paper Series, 12 (December 2015).

————. "Sectarianism as Counter-Revolution: Saudi Responses to the Arab Spring." *Studies in Ethnicity and Nationalism* 11:3 (2011): 513–526.

————. "The Shi'a of Saudi Arabia: A Minority in Search of Cultural Authenticity." *British Journal of Middle Eastern Studies* 25:1 (1998): 121–138.

Reiche, Danyel. "War Minus the Shooting? The Politics of Sport in Lebanon as a Unique Case in Comparative Politics." *Third World Quarterly* 32:2 (2011): 261–277.

Ryan, Curtis. "Regional Responses to the Rise of ISIS." *Middle East Report* (Middle East Research and Information Project) 276 (Fall 2015), http://www.merip.org/mer/mer276/regional-responses-rise-isis.

Salloukh, Bassel F. "Democracy in Lebanon: The Primacy of the Sectarian System." In Nathan Brown and Emad El-Din Shahin (eds.), *The Struggle over Democracy in the Middle East*. London: Routledge, 2009, pp. 134–150.

————. "The Geopolitics of the Struggle for Syria." *E-International Relations*, September 23, 2013, http://www.e-ir.info/2013/09/23/the-geopolitics-of-the-struggle-for-syria/.

————. "Lebanese Protesters United against Garbage … and Sectarianism." *The Monkey Cage* (*Washington Post* blog), September 14, 2015, http://www.washingtonpost.com/blogs/monkey-cage/wp/2015/09/14/lebanese-protesters-united-against-garbage-and-sectarianism/.

————. "The Limits of Electoral Engineering in Divided Societies: Elections in Postwar Lebanon." *Canadian Journal of Political Science* 39:3 (September 2006): 635–655.

————. "Overlapping Contests and Middle East International Relations: The Return of the Weak Arab State." Project on Middle East Political Science (POMEPS), August 12, 2015, http://pomeps.org/2015/08/12/overlapping-contests-and-middle-east-international-relations-the-return-of-the-weak-arab-state/.

Salloukh, Bassel F., Rabie Barakat, Jinan S. al-Habbal, Lara W. Khattab, and Shoghig Mikaelian. *The Politics of Sectarianism in Postwar Lebanon*. London: Pluto Press, 2015.

Salloukh, Bassel and Rex Brynen (eds.). *Persistent Permeability: Regionalism, Localism, and Globalization in the Middle East*. London: Ashgate, 2004.

Salmoni, Barak A., Bryce Loidolt, and Madeleine Wells. *Regime and Periphery in Northern Yemen: The Huthi Phenomenon*. Santa Monica, CA: RAND Corporation, 2010, http://www.rand.org/content/dam/rand/pubs/monographs/2010/RAND_MG962.pdf.

Salti, Nisreen and Jad Chaaban. "The Role of Sectarianism in the Allocation of Public Expenditures in Postwar Lebanon." *International Journal of Middle East Studies* 42:4 (2010): 637–655.

Shaery-Eisenlohr, Roschanack. *Shi'ite Lebanon: Transnational Religion and the Making of National Identities*. New York: Columbia University Press, 2008.

Shehabi, Ala'a and Marc Owen Jones (eds.). *Bahrain's Uprising: Resistance and Repression in the Gulf*. London: Zed Books, 2015.

Siegel, Alexandra. "Does Twitter bridge the Sunni-Shiite divide or make it worse?" *The Monkey Cage* (*Washington Post* blog), January 7, 2016, https://www.washingtonpost.com/news/monkey-cage/wp/2016/01/07/does-twitter-bridge-the-sunni-shiite-divide-or-make-it-worse/.

Sisk, Timothy D. "Peacemaking in Civil Wars: Obstacles, Options and Opportunities." In Ulrich Schneckener and Stefan Wolff (eds.), *Managing and Settling Ethnic Conflicts: Perspectives on Successes and Failures in Europe, Africa, and Asia*. New York: Palgrave Macmillan, 2004, pp. 248–270.

———. *Power Sharing and International Mediation in Ethnic Conflicts*. Washington, DC: US Institute of Peace Press, 1996.

———. *Statebuilding: Consolidating Peace after Civil War*. Cambridge: Polity, 2013.

———. (ed.). *Between Terror and Tolerance: Religious Leaders, Conflict, and Peacemaking*. Washington, DC: Georgetown University Press, 2011.

Sluglett, Peter. "The British, the Sunnis and the Shi'is: Social Hierarchies of Identity under the British Mandate." *International Journal of Contemporary Iraqi Studies* 4:3 (2010): 257–273.

Smock, David (ed.). *Religious Contributions to Peacemaking: When Religion Brings Peace, Not War*. Washington, DC: United States Institute of Peace, 2006, http://www.usip.org/sites/default/files/PWJan2006.pdf.

Steinberg, Guido. "The Shiites in the Eastern Province of Saudi Arabia (al-Ahsa), 1913–1953." In Rainer Brunner and Werner Ende (eds.), *The Twelver Shia in Modern Times: Religious Culture and Political History*. Leiden: Brill, 2001, pp. 236–251.

Strobl, Staci. "From Colonial Policing to Community Policing in Bahrain: The Historical Persistence of Sectarianism." *International Journal of Comparative and Applied Criminal Justice* 35: 1 (2011): 19–37.

Swatos, William H., Jr. "Weber or Troeltsch? Methodology, Syndrome and the Development of Church–Sect Theory." *Journal for the Scientific Study of Religion* 15:2 (1976): 129–144.

Traboulsi, Fawwaz. *A History of Modern Lebanon*. London: Pluto Press, 2007.

Ulrichsen, Kristian Coates. "Bahrain." In Larbi Sadiki (ed.), *Routledge Handbook of the Arab Spring: Rethinking Democratization*. New York: Routledge, 2014, pp. 133–144.

Muggah, Robert, Timothy D. Sisk, Eugenia Piza-Lopez, Jago Salmon, and Patrick Keuleers. *Governance for Peace: Securing the Social Contract*. New York: UNDP, 2012, http://www.undp.org/content/dam/undp/library/crisis%20prevention/governance-for-peace_2011–12–15_web.pdf.pdf.

Van Dam, Nikolaos. *The Struggle for Power in Syria: Politics and Society under Asad and the Ba'th Party*. London: I.B. Tauris, 1996.

Varshney, Ashutosh. "Ethnic Conflict and Civil Society: India and Beyond." *World Politics* 53:3 (April 2001): 362–398.

———. "Ethnicity and Ethnic Conflict." In Carles Boix and Susan Stokes (eds.), *The Oxford Handbook of Comparative Politics*. New York: Oxford University Press, 2009, pp. 274–294.

Vitalis, Robert. *America's Kingdom: Mythmaking on the Saudi Oil Frontier*. Stanford: Stanford University Press, 2007.

von Maltzahn, Nadia. *The Syria–Iran Axis: Cultural Diplomacy and International Relations in the Middle East*. London: I.B. Tauris, 2013.

Wedeen, Lisa. *Peripheral Visions: Publics, Power, and Performance in Yemen*. Chicago: University of Chicago Press, 2008.

Wehrey, Frederic. *Sectarian Politics in the Gulf: From the Iraq War to the Arab Uprisings*. New York: Columbia University Press, 2014.

Weiss, Max. *In the Shadow of Sectarianism: Law, Shi'ism, and the Making of Modern Lebanon*. Cambridge, MA: Harvard University Press, 2010.

Weiss, Michael and Hassan Hassan. *ISIS: Inside the Army of Terror*. New York: Regan Arts, 2015.

Wells Goldburt, Madeleine. "The Danger to Kuwait is Authoritarianism." *Sada* (Carnegie Endowment for International Peace), July 21, 2015, http://carnegieendowment.org/sada/?fa=60802.

White, Benjamin Thomas. *The Emergence of Minorities in the Middle East: The Politics of Community in French Mandate Syria*. Edinburgh: Edinburgh University Press, 2011.

Worth, Robert F. "Yemen: The Houthi Enigma." *NYR Daily* (*New York Review of Books* blog), March 30, 2015, http://www.nybooks.com/blogs/nyrblog/2015/mar/30/yemen-houthi-enigma/.

SELECT BIBLIOGRAPHY

Yadav, Stacey Philbrick. *Islamists and the State: Legitimacy and Institutions in Yemen and Lebanon*. London: I.B. Tauris, 2013.

Yassin-Kassab, Robin and Leila Al-Shami. *Burning Country: Syrians in Revolution and War*. London: Pluto Press, 2016.

Younis, Nussaibah. "A Cross-Sectarian Vision for Defeating the Islamic State in Iraq." Carnegie Middle East Center, July 6, 2015, http://carnegie-mec.org/2015/07/06/cross-sectarian-vision-for-defeating-islamic-state-in-iraq/icvn.

Zahar, Marie-Joëlle. "Power Sharing in Lebanon: Foreign Protectors, Domestic Peace and Democratic Failure." In Philip G. Roeder and Donald Rothchild (eds.), *Sustainable Peace: Power and Democracy after Civil Wars*. Ithaca: Cornell University Press, 2005, pp. 219–240.

Ziadeh, Hanna. *Sectarian and Intercommunal Nation-Building in Lebanon*. London: Hurst, 2006.

Zubaida, Sami. "Reading History Backwards." *Middle East Report* (Middle East Research and Information Project) 160 (September/October 1989), http://www.merip.org/mer/mer160/reading-history-backwards.

INDEX

361